T0366206

THE HEDGEHOG

EFFECT

THE HEDGEHOG

EFFECT

Executive Coaching and The Secrets of Building High Performance Teams

Manfred F. R. Kets de Vries

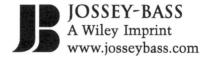

JOSSEY-BASS
A Wiley Imprint
www.josseybass.com

This edition first published 2011

Under the Jossey-Bass imprint, Jossey-Bass, 989 Market Street, San Francisco CA 94103-1741, USA
www.jossey-bass.com

Registered office
John Wiley & Sons Ltd, The Atrium, Southern Gate, Chichester, West Sussex, PO19 8SQ, United Kingdom

For details of our global editorial offices, for customer services and for information about how to apply for permission to reuse the copyright material in this book please see our website at www.wiley.com.

Library of Congress Cataloging-in-Publication Data

Kets de Vries, Manfred F. R.
  The hedgehog effect : executive coaching and the secrets of building high performance teams / Manfred F. R. Kets de Vries.
    p. cm.
  Summary: "The book is important as it is one of the very few that touches the topic of team coaching, and that deals with group coaching and change"—Provided by publisher.
  Includes bibliographical references and index.
  ISBN 978-1-119-97336-2 (hardback)—ISBN 978-1-119-96226-7 (ebk)—ISBN 978-1-119-96227-4 (ebk)—ISBN 978-1-119-96228-1 (ebk)
  1. Teams in the workplace–Management.   2. Employees–Coaching of.
  3. Leadership.   4. Organizational change.   I. Title.
  HD66.K48 2012
  658.4′022–dc23

                                                              2011036003

A catalogue record for this book is available from the British Library.

ISBN 978-1-119-97336-2 (hbk)   ISBN 978-1-119-96226-7 (ebk)
ISBN 978-1-119-96227-4 (ebk)   ISBN 978-1-119-96228-1 (ebk)

Set in 11.5/15pt Bembo by Toppan Best-set Premedia Limited
Printed in Great Britain by TJ International Ltd, Padstow, Cornwall, UK

To Sudhir Kakar

Life is made by the friends we choose. As my fellow traveler in the wilderness of this world, he helped to create a new world for me. During the years, we may have grown separately, but we have not grown apart.

TABLE OF CONTENTS

PREFACE

The well-run group is not a battlefield of egos.

—Lao Tzu

United we stand, divided we fall.

—Aesop

When spider webs unite, they can tie up a lion.

—Ethiopian proverb

A community is like a ship; everyone ought to be prepared to take the helm.

—Henrik Ibsen

The organizations we admire, and the places where most people would like to work, are known for having a special environment or corporate culture in which people feel, and perform, at their best. I call these authentizotic[1] organizations [1]. These companies have meta-values that give organizational participants a sense of

---

[1] From the Greek *authenteekos*, meaning authentic, and *zoteekos*, vital to life, and referring to best places to work.

purpose and self-determination. In addition, people feel competent, experience a sense of belonging, have voice and impact on
the organization, and they derive meaning and enjoyment from
their work. Employees are pleased and proud to work in such
exceptionally creative, dynamic, and productive environments.
They like working together, having understood that well-
functioning teams can be highly efficient, not to mention more
fun than working alone. Organizations with authentizotic cultures
are not only benchmarks for health and psychological well-being
in the workplace, but they are very often profitable, sustainable
enterprises as well.

A great place to work is one where people:

- **find meaning in their work**
- **trust the people they work for/with**
- **have pride in what they do**
- **enjoy the people they work for/with.**

  **The meta-values of authentizotic organizations are
fun, love (implying working with a close community of
people) and meaning (profit with purpose).**
  Are you working in one of these organizations?

I believe that one competitive advantage that comes from this
type of organizational culture is the ability to create effective work
teams. Competitive advantage now lies with organizations that
bring together their specialists in research, manufacturing, logistics,
talent management, marketing, customer service, and sales with
speed and efficiency to get their products and services to market.
Organizations in social services, education, health care, and government also operate in complex environments that face similar
issues and require a high degree of collaborative action. Across a

wide range of organizations, teamwork can provide the competitive edge that translates opportunities into successes.

So why is it that, although authentizotic organizations seem so desirable when seen from the exterior, and so pleasant when experienced as an employee, ultimately so few organizations can claim to have this culture? Why is it that teams are so often dysfunctional? Some answers may lie in our own human nature: our ability to trust one another just so far, and perhaps not far enough; and our inability to see past our own needs to understand that richer benefits, both psychological and material, may be easier to obtain through the collective efforts of a group rather than as individuals. But that is not so easy for us to accept, let alone change.

SCHOPENHAUER'S HEDGEHOGS

Arthur Schopenhauer, in his series of essays, *Parerga und Paralipomena* [2], included a tale about the dilemmas faced by hedgehogs during winter. The animals tried to get close to one another when it grew cold, to share their body heat. However, once they did so, they hurt each other with their spines. So they moved away from each other to be more comfortable. The cold, however, drove them together again, and the same thing happened. At last, after a great deal of uncomfortable huddling and chilly dispersing, the hedgehogs discovered they were best off remaining at a little distance from one another.

Schopenhauer's parable was quoted by Sigmund Freud in one of the footnotes to his 1921 essay *Group Psychology and the Analysis of the Ego* [3]. He related the hedgehogs' dilemma to the "sediment of feelings of aversion and hostility" in long-term relationships. In his essay, Freud asks a number of rhetorical questions about intimacy, the need for which is one of our most common, natural, human needs. How much intimacy can we really endure? And how much intimacy do we need to survive in this world? The hedgehogs' quandary is also our own.

Almost every long-term emotional relationship between two people or more contains this "sediment" of negative feelings, which escapes perception because of the mechanism of repression. As the hedgehogs' dilemma suggests, human relationships have a substantial degree of ambivalence, requiring us to contain contradictory feelings for the other person. We can see Schopenhauer's parable as a metaphor for the challenges of human intimacy. Are we destined to behave like these fabled hedgehogs—forever jostling for a balance between painful entanglement and loveless isolation? Will we always struggle with the fear of engulfment and the fear of loneliness?

Societal needs drive human hedgehogs together, but we are often mutually repelled by the many prickly and disagreeable qualities of others. We all have a simultaneous need for and fear of intimacy, creating a dilemma for commonsense living. The distance that Schopenhauer's hedgehogs at last discovered to be the only tolerable condition of mutual interface represents our common code of conduct. A certain amount of distance is part of the human condition. Although our mutual need for warmth is only moderately satisfied by this arrangement, we re less likely to get hurt. We will not prick others—and others will not prick us.

"How much closeness is too much? How much can we open up to others?"

We also see the hedgehogs' dilemma in group settings. How much closeness is too much? How much can we open up to others? What can we disclose about ourselves? What degree of intimacy is enough? And when is it necessary to set boundaries? Opening up too much can lead to an exposure of our weaknesses and make us vulnerable to shame and guilt reactions. This conundrum—our simultaneous need for closeness and distance—is a fundamental reason why people often find it so difficult to work successfully in groups and teams.

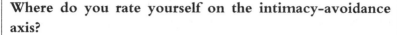

Where do you rate yourself on the intimacy-avoidance axis?

What kind of "hedgehog" are you?

1   2   3   4   5   6   7   8   9   10

I like to be
very close
to people

I prefer to be
very distant
from people

How does your position on this axis affect your relationships with others?

Reflect on your various relationships. Where would you place each of them on this axis?

THE PARADOX OF TEAMWORK

If we look closely at the organizational context, we can see how this dilemma plays out subtly, yet forcefully, in daily interactions. Teamwork is a crucial element of the effectiveness of organizations, not the least **"Teamwork is a crucial element of the effectiveness of organizations."** because well-aligned team thinking and goal orientation facilitates dealing with current crises and designing long-term strategies. The ability to work well in teams—to accept a certain degree of closeness—is undeniably essential in present-day organizations. Yet we too easily overlook the reality that for most teams, it can be very difficult to find the right balance between loose, inefficient connections at one extreme, and stifling interconnections at the other.

In addition, it is equally clear that many organizational leaders are ambivalent about teams. Too many of them have no idea how to put together well functioning teams. Their fear of delegating—losing control—reinforces the stereotype of the heroic leader who will do it all. For many, teams represent a hassle, a burden, or a necessary evil. This often becomes, not surprisingly, a self-fulfiling prophecy. Although many teams do generate remarkable synergy and excellent outcomes, some become mired in endlessly unproductive sessions, and are rife with conflict. As many of us have discovered to our despair, the price tag of dysfunctional teams can be staggering.

Team success

Think about effective and ineffective teams you have been a member of. What has made one type of team a success and the other a failure? Write a description of both teams.

Working in an effective team was like:

Working in an ineffective team was like:

Compare the two descriptions and figure out the differences between these two teams.

Paradoxically, the use of teams in the workplace is both a response to complexity and a further element of complexity. Ineffective teamwork can mean very high coordination costs and little gain in productivity. In some corporations and governments, the formation of teams, task forces, and committees is a defensive act that gives the illusion of real work while disguising unproductive attempts to preserve the status quo. At best, this does little harm because fundamentally it does nothing; at worst, team building becomes a ritualistic technique blocking important actions that might enhance constructive change. Dismantling a dysfunctional team might even require a kind of Gordian knot solution, which could lead to damaging outcomes both in economic and human terms.

MORE THAN MEETS THE EYE

Why do so many teams fail to live up to their promise? The answer lies in the obstinate belief that human beings are rational entities. Many team designers forget to take into account the subtle, out-of-awareness behavior patterns that are part and parcel of the human condition. Although teams are created as a forum for achieving specific goals, the personality quirks and emotional life of the various team members can cause deviations from the specified task. Indeed, there is often a degree of naivety among an organization's leadership, who fail to realize that a group dynamic can derail a scheduled direction, so that the team's real goals can deviate widely from its stated goals. Many people in positions of leadership fail to appreciate the real complexity of teamwork. They don't pay heed to the hedgehogs' dilemma.

Organizational designers need to accept that below the surface of human rationality lie many subtle psychological forces that can sabotage the way teams operate. But irrational as these behavioral patterns may be, there is a rationale to them, if we know how to disentangle the patterns. Meaningful teamwork entails numerous real risks for individuals, because of fear, anxiety, and uncertainty about the exercise of influence and power. If these concerns are not addressed, the anxiety generated by the risks involved in team working becomes too great and cannot be contained through leadership actions or facilitating structures: individuals will mobilize social defenses to protect themselves. These defenses, expressed through rituals, processes, or basic assumptions, displace, mitigate, or even neutralize anxiety but also prevent real work from being done. The result is preoccupation with dysfunctional processes and inhibiting structures that reinforce vicious circles preserving the status quo.

"Executives need to realize that, when they create teams, there is more going on than meets the eye."

Executives need to realize that, when they create teams, there is more going on than meets the eye. Teams are forums in which sensitive organizational and interpersonal issues are dealt with discretely (and often indiscreetly). If people are to function non-defensively in the face of performance pressures in the workplace, they need leadership and supporting conditions that convert risk and anxiety into productive work. Unfortunately, team designers are largely unaware of concepts from psychodynamic psychology and systems theory, and the rational-structural point of view usually dominates.

I argue that a purely cognitive, rational-structural perspective on teamwork will be incomplete if it fails to acknowledge the unconscious dynamics that affect human behavior. In too many instances, organizations are treated as rational, rule-governed systems, perpetuating the illusion of the economic man as an optimizing machine of pleasures and pains, and ignoring the multifarious peculiarities that come with being human. Like it or not, there is no such thing as a Holy Grail of rational management. The rational-structural view of organizations has not delivered the promised goods. It has only created economic chaos and grief. Organizational designers need to pay attention to the conscious and unconscious dynamics that are inherent in organizational life. They need to become familiar with the language of psychodynamics—although I realize that this could be uncomfortable and disturbing for those who come from a background in management or economics.

Creating and maintaining effective team-based work environments necessitates a dedicated focus on both the structural and the human aspects of organizational life. Innovative work arrangements provide a structure and platform for team organizations, but these are not enough. The leaders of the organization must also instill, through their own example and through well-communicated codes of conduct, an internal, interactive coaching culture in which participants can engage in candid, respectful conversations, unrestricted by reporting relationships, or fear of retribution. It means establishing, and perhaps even enforcing, core values of trust, commitment, enthusiasm, and enjoyment. This can be a daunting challenge. It takes openness throughout an organization, and a willingness to change from a mindset of "me first" to "what's best for the team?" But given the complexity of the new world of organizations, where those that master the multiplicity of lateral relationships will lead the pack, there is not much of a choice.

LEADERSHIP GROUP COACHING AND THE CREATION OF AUTHENTIZOTIC ORGANIZATIONS

The question is, how can organizations and their leaders initiate and perpetuate the kind of change in thinking and environment that supports an authentizotic culture based on thinking about the common good? One answer may be leadership coaching. This type of intervention, which most commonly takes the form of one-on-one interactions between an executive and a coach, has changed the way many progressive organizations view professional and personal growth and development. One-on-one leadership coaching is an investment in future service potential, through building the talent pool in the organization, and helping people adapt to change [4].

One-on-one coaching certainly has its benefits, but personal experience has taught me that leadership group (or team) coaching—in essence, an experiential training ground for learning to function as a high performing team—is a great antidote to organizational silo formation and thinking, and a very effective way to help leaders become more adept at sensing the hidden psychodynamic undercurrents that influence team behavior. In leadership group coaching sessions, people from already existing working groups, or participating in mixed-function groups, can test degrees of closeness, metaphorically speaking, under the guidance of a trained facilitator. They experience openness and trust in a safe setting, and see the advantages of better understanding the strengths and weaknesses of each individual. Knowledge transfer among group members becomes a natural activity, rather than something to be controlled. Essentially, people come to see the importance of effective group cohesion by experiencing it in the group coaching session.

Group coaching interventions are more likely to induce alignment between the goals of individual group members and those of the organization, creating greater commitment, accountability, and higher rates of constructive conflict resolution. Effective group coaching not only helps develop the coaching skills of each group member (through the process of peer coaching); it also accelerates an organization's progress by providing a greater appreciation of organizational strengths and weaknesses, which will lead to better decision making. It fosters teamwork based on trust; in turn, the culture itself is nurtured as people become used to creating teams in which people feel comfortable and productive. When they work well, team-oriented coaching cultures are like networked webs in the organization, connecting people laterally in the same departments, across departments, between teams, and up and down the hierarchy.

ABOUT THIS BOOK

In this book, I examine both the conscious and unconscious aspects of behavior in group situations. I include systemic factors and highlight what organizational designers or change agents must do to make teams effective. I look at organizational and individual phenomena above and below the surface.

Many of the concepts I introduce are not easy to grasp, let alone put into practice. To help the reader, I have divided this book into three parts. In Part One, I move from the surface to a more in-depth analysis to obtain a better understanding of what teams and groups are all about. I also discuss how a group becomes a team and give an elaborate example of a team intervention. In addition, I discuss the intricacies of leadership coaching. In Part Two, I take a psychodynamic lens to better understand the dynamics of teams and groups, presenting the clinical paradigm. I also take a closer look at relationship patterns and discuss how groups evolve, exploring the phenomenon of the group-as-a-whole. In Part Three, I move to a more systemic view, addressing the fundamental challenges change processes pose for people in organizations. I deal with the question of how to create authentizotic organizations—best places to work. In the final chapter, I recount the story of an organizational change initiative that was accomplished through group coaching.

The real reward is to see participants who have been through a group coaching intervention process put into place coaching cultures that sustain not only development and performance, but also a more fundamental sense that the people in the organization are human, not machines. In the end, challenges are much easier to face when we combine our strengths through honest and open communication and create effective teams. Such interventions contribute to the creation of more humane, sustainable organizations.

ACKNOWLEDGMENTS

This book is the outcome of many years of work with a host of top executive teams. My original "laboratory" has been a CEO program that I have run for over 20 years at INSEAD, "The Challenge of Leadership: Creating Effective Leaders." I owe huge thanks to its participants for the many insights they have provided me with over the years. I must also pay special tribute to my friend of so many years and collaborator in this program, Sudhir Kakar, who in his inimical way provided a path through the many group muddles that most others would fail to negotiate.

A second program for which I am partly responsible as Scientific Director is "Consulting and Coaching for Change." I am especially grateful to my two principal collaborators, Roger Lehman and Erik van der Loo, who have been instrumental in making this executive master's degree seminar such a success, year after year.

In addition, I am also very obliged to the many CEOs and other senior executives who had the courage to offer me the opportunity to work with their teams by engaging the KDVI consulting firm. Embarking on a group coaching intervention process is not for the fainthearted—whether you are a participant or a coach. I have learned a lot from their wisdom.

I should like to thank my team at INSEAD's Global Leadership Center (IGLC) who have always been supportive of my work. I am grateful not only to the administrative staff but also to my program directors and coaches, who had the vision to recognize the value of this form of intervention—and have taken it to new heights.

Finally, I would like to thank Elizabeth Florent-Treacy, Alicia Cheak-Baillargeon, and Murray Palevsky for their willingness to have a serious look at this manuscript in its early form. Elizabeth in particular has been a great help in restructuring the manuscript as it appears today. And, as always, I acknowledge my debt to Sally Simmons, my imperturbable editor, who keeps her good cheer while solving what often look to me like labyrinthine problems.

In my work with teams, I never learned much by just talking—most of my learning came about by asking questions, listening, and reflection. This book is an effort to help people to experience fully what happens in teams, in particular to better understand the out-of-awareness processes that are endemic to team dynamics, and to demystify what may appear mysterious. My hope is that this book will help the reader realize the full potential of teams, and contribute to the creation of better places to work.

I view the readers of this book first and foremost as people in the coaching profession who want to deepen their insights into the conundrum of group coaching. This book will also be very helpful to human resource professionals interested in the question of how to create an effective coaching culture in their organization. Last (but certainly not least), this book is aimed at the informed executive who realizes the importance of running effective teams, and wants to know how to go about it. Managing talent well has become the name of the game. As the famous American basketball player Michael Jordan once said, "Talent wins games, but teamwork and intelligence win championships."

REFERENCES

1 Kets de Vries, M. F. R. (2001a) "Creating Authentizotic Organizations: Well-functioning Individuals in Vibrant Companies." *Human Relations*, 54 (1), 101–111.
2. Schopenhauer, A. (1851). *Parerga und Paralipomena: kleine philosophische Schriften*, Vol. 1–2. Berlin: Julius Frauenstädt.
3. Freud, S. (1921). "Group Psychology and the Analysis of the Ego." In J. Strachey (Ed.) (1950), *Collected Papers of Sigmund Freud*, Vol. V. London: Hogarth Press and the Institute of Psychoanalysis.
4. Crane, T. J. and Patrick, L. N. (Eds) (2002). *The Heart of Coaching: Using Transformational Coaching to Create a High-Performance Coaching Culture.* San Diego, CA: FTA Press.

ABOUT THE AUTHOR

Manfred F. R. Kets de Vries brings a different view to the much-studied subjects of leadership and the dynamics of individual and organizational change. Bringing to bear his knowledge and experience of economics (Econ. Drs., University of Amsterdam), management (ITP, MBA, and DBA, Harvard Business School), and psychoanalysis (Canadian Psychoanalytic Society and the International Psychoanalytic Association), Kets de Vries scrutinizes the interface between international management, psychoanalysis, psychotherapy, and dynamic psychiatry. His specific areas of interest are leadership, career dynamics, team building, coaching, executive stress, entrepreneurship, family business, succession planning, cross-cultural management, and the dynamics of corporate transformation and change.

A clinical professor of leadership development, he holds the Raoul de Vitry d'Avaucourt Chair of Leadership Development at INSEAD, France, Singapore & Abu Dhabi. He is the founder of INSEAD's Global Leadership Center. In addition, he is program director of INSEAD's top management program, "The Challenge of Leadership: Creating Reflective Leaders," and "Consulting and Coaching for Change" (and has five times received INSEAD's distinguished teacher award). He is also the Distinguished Visiting Professor of Leadership Development Research at the European School of Management and Technology (ESMT) in Berlin. He has held professorships at McGill University, the Ecole des Hautes Etudes Commerciales, Montreal, and the Harvard Business School, and he has lectured at management institutions around the world.

The Financial Times, *Le Capital*, *Wirtschaftswoche*, and *The Economist* have rated Manfred Kets de Vries one of world's leading leadership theoreticians. Kets de Vries is listed among the world's top 50 leading management thinkers and among the most influential contributors to human resource management. He has been the recipient the "Harry and Miriam Levinson Award" from the American Psychological Association and the "Freud Memorial Award" from the Dutch Psychoanalytic Institute. He has also been given the "Lifetime Achievement Award" (the Leadership Legacy Project of the International Leadership Association), being viewed as one of the world's founding professionals in the development of leadership as a field and discipline. Presently, Kets de Vries is seen as the leading figure in the clinical study of organizational leadership.

Kets de Vries is the author, co-author, or editor of more than 35 books, including *Unstable at the Top*; *The Neurotic Organization*; *Organizational Paradoxes*; *Leaders, Fools, and Impostors*; *Life and Death in the Executive Fast Lane*; *The Leadership Mystique*; *The Happiness Equation*; *Lessons on Leadership by Terror*; *The New Global Leaders*; *The Leader on the Couch*; *Coach and Couch*; *Family Business: Human Dilemmas in the Family Firm*; *Sex, Money, Happiness, and Death*; *Reflections on Character and Leadership*; *Reflections on Leadership and Career Development*; *Reflections on Groups and Organizations*; *The Coaching Kaleidoscope*; *Leadership Development*; and *Tricky Coaching*.

Further titles are in preparation. His books and articles have been translated into over 31 languages.

In addition, Kets de Vries has published over 350 scientific papers as chapters in books and as articles. He has also written approximately a hundred case studies, including seven that received the Best Case of the Year award. He is a regular writer for a number of magazines. His work has been featured in such publications as *The New York Times*, *The Wall Street Journal*, *The Los Angeles Times*, *Fortune*, *Business Week*, *The Economist*, *The Financial Times*, and *The International Herald Tribune*. He is a member of 17 editorial boards and has been elected a Fellow of the Academy of Management. He is a founding member of the International Society for the Psychoanalytic Study of Organizations of which he became a lifetime distinguished member.

Kets de Vries is a consultant on organizational design/ transformation and strategic human resource management to leading US, Canadian, European, African, and Asian companies. He is the Chairman and principal owner of the Kets de Vries Institute (KDVI), a global leadership development consultancy firm. As an educator and consultant he has worked in more than 40 countries.

The Dutch government has made him an Officer in the Order of Oranje Nassau. He was the first fly fisherman in Outer Mongolia and is a member of New York's Explorers Club. In his spare time he can be found in the rainforests or savannas of Central Africa, the Siberian taiga, the Pamir and Altai Mountains, Arnhemland, or within the Arctic Circle.

www.ketsdevries.com
www.kdvi.com

PART ONE

AN INTRODUCTION TO THE LIFE OF GROUPS AND TEAMS

CHAPTER 1

HOW A GROUP BECOMES A TEAM

Individually, we are one drop. Together, we are an ocean.

—Ryunosuke Satoro

Sticks in a bundle are unbreakable.

—Kenyan Proverb

Never doubt that a small group of thoughtful, committed citizens can change the world; indeed, it's the only thing that ever has.

—Margaret Mead

"One for all, and all for one"—the famous oath from Alexandre Dumas's *The Three Musketeers*—symbolizes the quintessence of teamwork. It is through cooperation, rather than conflict, that we attain our greatest successes. If we are prepared to support each other, the greater part of our problems will already be solved. As d'Artagnan and the three musketeers understood, their fate as individuals was tied to their fate as a group.

As novels on camaraderie go, it would be hard to find one as famous, or that has so completely captured the popular imagination, as *The Three Musketeers*. It is a confounding narrative: joyful, maddening, eccentric, full of convoluted twists and turns. It dramatizes significant events in the history of France—the action begins in 1625 and ends three years later—and entertains the reader with spectacular displays of bravery, loyalty, and wit on the part of the three musketeers and their young comrade-in-arms, d'Artagnan. The four heroes of the tale are involved in labyrinthine intrigues concerning the weak King Louis XIII of France, his powerful and cunning advisor Cardinal Richelieu, the beautiful Queen Anne of Austria, her English lover, George Villiers, Duke of Buckingham, and the siege of the rebellious Huguenot city of La Rochelle.

With great ambitions, d'Artagnan, the main protagonist of the story, sets out for Paris with three gifts from his father: the modest sum of 15 crowns, a horse, and a letter of introduction to the captain of the King's Musketeers, a military unit serving as the protectors of the Royal Household. D'Artagnan wants to become a musketeer himself, and must prove himself worthy of such a position; however, he doesn't have much going for him except his wits and his skill as a swordsman. But with the help of his fellow musketeers—the legendary and noble Athos, the devoted Porthos, and the cunning Aramis—d'Artagnan succeeds in gaining glory, and fulfills his destiny.

Teamwork saves the day in *The Three Musketeers*. Loyal to each other to the death, the musketeers have no compunction at pulling a fast one on their enemies. The strength they have in working as a team, their devotion to excellence, their willingness to sacrifice, their great trust in each other, their generosity of heart and spirit, and—the most powerful virtue of all—their unshakable dedication to a cause greater than themselves, inspire the reader's imagination. It is a tale that can be viewed as a moral lesson, highlighting the importance of cooperation, unity, and perseverance.

A team like the three (or, even better, four) musketeers is timeless. The characters in this book are so life-like and the dialogues so real that we can easily transplant this 19th-century novel about 17th-century events to our day and age, laugh at the comedic elements in the tale, and cry at the tragic ones. In many ways, the adventures of d'Artagnan and the three musketeers are universal— teams are an inspiring feature of human life. To quote a Japanese proverb, "None of us is as smart as all of us."

This story touches on many of the themes we will explore in the various chapters of this book. The best team is one where members are ready to take personal risks, prepared to tackle conflict, and willing to have courageous conversations. These developments, however, are contingent upon an underlying team culture of trust, reciprocity in self-disclosure to improve interpersonal dialogue, and constructive conflict resolution.

The story of Dumas's heroes also helps to make a connection from the wide-ranging exploration of the group-as-a-whole, to a more specific description of well-functioning teams. Just as individuals have moods, emotions and other peculiarities, groups (or teams) have similar characteristics, which influence aspects such as cohesiveness, performance and the emotional state of other group members.

The musketeers' battle cry—"All for one, and one for all"— reveals some of the signifiers that make teams work. The musketeers believed that when one of them was in trouble, they were all in trouble. If one of them needed help, they all provided it. If one succeeded, they all succeeded. For them, reciprocity and interpersonal trust were indisputable. At both a conscious and at an unconscious level, their behavior was in sync. Due to their team spirit and friendship, the musketeers discovered they could accomplish anything as a team, if they just put their mind to it.

Alexandre Dumas's fictional 17th-century adventure remains an effective prescription for our third millennium workplace; the underlying, out-of-awareness psychodynamic individual and team processes of his musketeers were aligned with the task at hand. Helping to create this kind of team is one of the over-arching objectives of executive and leadership group coaching.

TEAMS: WHAT, WHY, AND HOW

Before discussing teams, let's first specify the difference between a group and a team. A group is any number of individuals who form a recognizable unit, cluster, or aggregation.

Teams are specific groups of people with (it is hoped) complementary skills and abilities who join together to collaborate. People in a team possess a high degree of interdependence geared toward the achievement of a common goal or completion of a task for which they hold one another mutually accountable. In contrast to most groups, teams often identify and reach an agreement on their common goals and approaches, rather than looking to a leader to define them. What's more, the outcome of a team's activities will affect team members as a whole, not just each member individually. In the organizational context, team members are empowered to share responsibility for specific performance outcomes, and work together for a limited period of time. The most effective size for teams is between five and 12 people. Larger teams require more structure and support, while smaller teams often have difficulty engaging in robust discussions when members are absent [1–7]. (As groups and teams essentially differ depending on the degree and intensity of interdependence, throughout this book these two terms will be used interchangeably).

As a caveat here, I should point out that although well-functioning teams are essential to the world of work, there are occasions when putting together a team to get a project off the ground may not really be the best option. Some jobs or projects can be completed much more effectively if assigned to one person. But when jobs are very interdependent and the task is highly complex, teams can replace individual executives to carry out what used to be traditional, single-executive functions.

Having asserted how important well-functioning teams will be in this new world of work, we need to ask ourselves how truly effective most teams really are. We know (frequently from per-

Are you a part of a team or do you merely belong to a group of people?

Study the following questions and answer them either YES or NO

	YES	NO
1. Do the people you work with have a high degree of interdependence, geared toward the achievement of a common goal or completion of a task for which they hold themselves mutually accountable?		
2. Do you belong to a group of people with complementary skills and abilities who come together to collaborate?		
3. Does the outcome of your activities affect not merely you, but all the other people you work with?		

If you answered YES to all these questions, you are most likely part of a team.

sonal experience) that many teams do not live up to their billing. A substantial body of research shows that many claims about the benefits of teamwork appear to be more fantasy than reality [8, 9]. There are numerous damning signifiers of people's negative experiences of teamwork, for example: "A committee is a group of people who can do nothing individually but who, as a group, can meet and decide that nothing can be done"; "A team is a group of the unwilling, picked from the unfit, to do the unnecessary"; "A team is an animal with four back legs." Far too often, teams soak up too much time and too many resources, flounder, and become quicksands of tension and antagonism.

Creating a winning team implies taking a collection of individuals with different personalities (perceptions, needs, attitudes, motivations, backgrounds, expertise, and expectations), and trans-forming them into an integrated, effective, holistic work unit. This can be quite a challenge. Some personality types just do not click. For many different reasons, some people's character and behavior are like the proverbial red rag to a bull [10].

Teams and need systems

One way to approach the challenge of creating well-functioning teams is to focus not on what makes people different, but on what they have in common. For example, teams can satisfy our sense of belonging. In other words, while teams may initially be formed to fulfill a task, they may also meet other needs at an individual level. Many people like working in teams because they desire a sense of social interaction, affiliation with a community, and pride of accomplishment or greater purpose. In fact these intrinsic rewards may be even more important to individual members than financial or other tangible means of compensation. Therefore, addressing individual needs may well contribute to motivating team membership and performance.

"Most people have a powerful desire to be part of a group in which they feel recognized and understood."

Most people have a powerful desire to be part of a group in which they feel recognized and understood. Belonging—being part of a social context—is essential for the development of self-esteem and self-confidence. Social outcasts may end up feeling empty and depressed. Social connection (and fear of losing it) is crucial to the quality (in some cases, even the duration) of our lives. Applying this lens to teams, it is clear that individuals in teams are less anxious about the work they need to accomplish when they are part of a team that takes the time to build a sense of community and belonging for all members.

Is altruism important to you?

Study the following questions and answer them YES or NO

	YES	NO

- Are you the type of person who will do anything for others?
- Are you able to give and share or are you quite self-centered?
- Are you willing to help someone even if helping doesn't benefit you immediately?
- Are you the kind of person who freely offers help when someone else is in need?
- Do you enjoy helping people?
- Do you feel bad when you see people who are less fortunate than you?
- Are you always prepared to help strangers?

If you answered YES to most of these questions, your score on the altruism test is high. You often go out of your way to help others, and in some cases do so without even being asked.

Altruism—the desire to make a difference—also draws people to work in teams.

Many aspects of human social relations exist within a complex web of kin and reciprocal altruism [11]. Working in teams that have a meaningful purpose may help people feel that their own ability to make a difference is magnified by the power of the group. The musketeers were not only a band of brothers, in a sense, but together they were serving a great cause.

Fundamentals

The experience of the individual is the first layer at which it is possible to assess a team. Does the team have a shared sense of purpose? Do its members all pull in the same direction at the same time? Is there complementarity in skills and competencies? Is each member of the team pursuing the same thing? Have the team's goals and objectives been discussed and agreed openly? Does the team stick together through highs and lows, taking both the blame and the rewards as something to be shared by all? Do team members seem to be enjoying working together most of the time? Ensuring that these fundamental criteria are present will help to lay the groundwork for trust and a willingness to put the team's goals first.

The interpersonal relationships that arise from team dynamics need to be managed in a strategic rather than opportunistic manner. And that's easier said than done. Many things can go wrong. For example, which team member is going to take charge? Who sets the boundaries? Who is going to be the main action driver? And how will all these decisions be made?

One of the most dangerous ways to manage the dynamics of a team is to allow the most forceful individuals to drive decisions about resources, thus creating a profound sense of unfairness and helplessness among the other members of the team. And group dynamics can become even more dysfunctional when the organization is in the throes of a succession process. In such instances, a zero-sum-game mentality—"I win, you lose"—may dominate team dynamics, with each member of the team trying to position him- or herself for the top job.

For all the reasons given above, a critical moment in team building comes as each member is integrated into the team; it should made be clear what skills he or she has, and what contribution can be expected. Newcomers quickly, albeit instinctively, figure out how they fit within the team and the complementary roles they can play. At some level, their own individual hopes and wishes will also come into play as they enter the team. The integration process, however, is far more difficult than it would seem.

THE DARK SIDE OF DYSFUNCTIONAL TEAMS

A powerful lion, a donkey, and a fox decided to go out hunting together. That way, they thought, they would get much more than if they each hunted alone—and they were right. At the end of the day they had amassed a huge heap of food. "Right," said the donkey, "let's divide it all up between us." And he shared it out in three equal piles. When the lion saw what the donkey had done, he roared, "What's this?" jumped on the donkey, killed him, and ate him. Then he turned to the fox, saying, "Now it's your turn to divide the food." The fox had more emotional intelligence than the donkey. He made two piles—a very big one, and a very small one. "Hmm," said the lion, pulling the big pile toward him. "Who taught you to share things out so well?" "That would be the donkey," replied the fox.

It's easy to see dysfunctional dynamics at work. They dominate teams whose stated goal is not the real one, or teams with fuzzy goals, or rapidly changing priorities. We can see them in teams rife with role conflict and ambiguity, unresolved overt and covert conflicts, poor timekeeping and absenteeism; teams that cannot reach closure, that have rigid, ritualistic meetings, uneven member participation, tunnel vision, indifference to the interests of the organization as a whole, and a lack of resources, skills, knowledge, and accountability. There is no genuine collegiality, collaboration, or coordination in these teams. These are the teams that give teamwork a bad reputation.

Highly dysfunctional teams are like a contagious disease; they have an insidious influence and create a toxic environment. Competitive feelings among team members can result in sabotage

---

Is your organization beset by team killers?

Study the following questions and answer them either YES or NO

                                                                    YES   NO

- Does your team suffer from fuzzy goals/changing priorities?
- Do you think there is a false consensus among the members of your team?
- Does your team have unresolved overt conflicts?
- Does your team find it difficult to reach closure?
- Are calcified meetings characteristic of your team (i.e., people coming late or arriving not at all)?
- Does your team suffer from uneven participation?
- Do the members of your team not feel accountable to one another?

If most of your answers are YES, your team is in a lot of trouble.

It may not even be a team.

---

of each other's work, unjustified criticism, and withholding information and resources, contributing to the breakdown of the team's proper functioning and the creation of neurotic organizations [12, 13]. All these activities can be very subtle.

The situation is aggravated by the fact that some people who act this way may feel justified in doing so, from a sense of being personally wronged. This is fair process or equity theory taken to the absurd. Yet insidious and irrational as these acts may be, they will be very damaging to the organization and its members.

In many dysfunctional teams, blaming and scapegoating will become major dynamics, doing very little for the organization's productivity and the creative process. In these teams, members avoid dealing with conflict, preferring to resort to veiled discussions and guarded comments. Discussions are likely to consist of generalities and platitudes. Unsurprisingly, many such teams morph into highly constipated, slow decision-making bodies, underperforming and floundering despite all the resources made available to them. Predictably, their decision outcomes will be sub-optimal [14–18].

Despite the strong forces of cohesiveness and groupthink within teams, members (like the hedgehogs) have constantly to cope with forces of attraction and separation. Although there will be strong forces aiming at harmony and cooperation, forces of polarization and regression will always be present, as will a regressive tendency toward "splitting," the unconscious failure to integrate aspects of self or others into a unified whole. As human beings, we have a tendency to regress and separate or "split" people into different categories, labeling the aspects of them that we find acceptable "good" and the things we find painful or unacceptable "bad." As a result, and because this is an interactive process, we may alternate between over-idealizing and devaluing individuals, teams, and organizations [19–22]. Groupthink may raise its ugly head [23].

While personality conflicts are very troublesome, structural organizational design errors can bring additional misery. Essentially, if good people are put into bad systems, we should not be surprised by their poor results. If teams are created merely as a gesture that some form of action has been taken, without giving the members of the team a clear mandate for what needs to be done, form will take precedence over substance, and empty rhetoric over doing real work. For example, teams may have been created without a clear goal and measures of success, with fuzzy boundaries, and with very poorly defined tasks. Teams may be composed

What are the signs of groupthink?
Study the following questions and answer them YES or NO

YES   NO

Have you ever been a member of team where

- there was an illusion of invulnerability, creating a false consensus?
- there was an unquestioned belief in the morality of the group?
- there was, in each instance, a collective rationalization of the team's decisions?
- opponents were stereotyped?
- you engaged in self-censorship—where no criticism was tolerated?
- illusions of unanimity prevailed, creating a false consensus?
- there was strong pressure on dissenters to conform?
- there were self-appointed "mind guards" protecting the group from negative information?

If you answered YES to most of these questions, you may have been part of a groupthink process, making hasty, irrational decisions. In this situation, individual doubts are set aside, for fear of upsetting the team's balance. In an attempt to reduce conflict and reach consensus, you may not have analyzed an important issue critically.

of people with the wrong talents—individuals who would do better staying where they are. And so on and so on.

Senior executives can also play a highly dysfunctional role by putting people into teams for purely political reasons—creating teams in name only. The members of these teams end up engaging in social rituals, merely playing roles in each other's presence. This behavior prevents team members knowing each other on a deeper level. Recognizing the futility of their activities, they may resent the time they spend with the team. They may feel—rightly so—that they have better things to do. So they go through the motions, feeling increasingly alienated from the organization's overall mission. In fact, the permutations of team dysfunctionality are endless.

> **"If good people are put into bad systems, we should not be surprised by their poor results."**

What role do you play in a team?
Review the following questions.
> Which role fits you best?
> In teams, is your role more task oriented?
> Do you take on a more social role?
> Is your role more divergent?

- Are you the deviant?
- Are you the rebel?
- Are you the martyr/scapegoat?
- Do you play the clown?
- Are you the aggressive one?

> Do you play a more marginal role?

- Are you the silent type?
- Are you the private one?
- Are you the cautious one?

THE VIRTUES OF TEAMS

Having dwelt on the dark side of team working, I want to reiterate at this point that in spite of all the shortcomings teams may have, the advantages of working as a team greatly outweigh the disadvantages.

Two of the most valued outcomes of teamwork are efficiency and effectiveness. If the team shares involvement, ownership, and a sense of urgency, successful implementation is highly probable. If team members feel committed to carry out whatever needs to be done to make the project a success, they can accomplish more than a similar number of individuals working alone. By dividing responsibilities, different activities can proceed in parallel and the ultimate goal will be achieved much faster.

Complementarity

However talented a person may be, no one has all the skills needed to do everything—although we may be able to hold a tune, we cannot whistle a whole symphony by ourselves. Working as a team reduces the burden placed on any single individual; large tasks can be broken up into smaller assignments and assigned to the people best suited to the job. For example, some people excel at generating ideas. Some love detail, while some prefer to focus on the big picture. Some can be counted on for implementation and follow-up of a project. While an individual tends to look at a problem or issue from only one perspective, teams present a variety of working hypotheses. Team building should be seen as an opportunity creatively and constructively to maximize each individual's strengths and compensate for weaknesses, enabling the team to produce top quality results. It is important that team designers recognize complementarity of talent to be able to create effective executive role constellations [24–26].

Dysfunctional team work, as I said earlier, can be contagious. By the same token, the attitude and mood state of a successful team can energize an entire organ-

"We cannot whistle a whole symphony by ourselves."

ization, creating a greater sense of satisfaction, establishing a learning, collaborative culture, and contributing to a high degree of creativity and innovation. In organizations with an effective team culture, information flows freely—up, down, and laterally; people who are prepared to share their knowledge are more effective and more productive.

What kind of contribution do you make to the team?
Study the following statements and label them either TRUE or FALSE, as you think they apply to you.
Select more than one if appropriate.

	TRUE	FALSE
1. I have great strategic sense.		
2. I take on the role of deal maker, always prepared to make propositions about new business deals.		
3. I am highly experienced at turning around difficult situations.		
4. I suggest entrepreneurial ways of developing the business.		
5. I come up with a number of new product or process innovations.		
6. I promote and monitor structures, systems, and tasks.		
7. I am very interested in devising creative ways to develop people.		
8. I take on the role of communicator.		

What is your leadership style? (The numbers in the box above each refer to a specific leadership style.)

1. Strategist
   - the leader as chess player
2. Change-Catalyst
   - the leader as implementation/turnaround specialist
3. Transactor
   - the leader as deal maker/negotiator
4. Builder
   - the leader as entrepreneur
5. Innovator
   - the leader as creative idea generator
6. Processor
   - the leader as efficiency expert
7. Coach
   - the leader as people developer
8. Communicator
   - the leader as the great stage manager

The emotional dimension

All of us, at one time or another, have been members of a team; all of us have had the opportunity to observe that teams can evoke strong and often conflicting reactions. Many of us have learned from personal experience that being part of a team can be highly attractive and repellent, extremely satisfying and deeply disappointing, depending on how well the team is functioning. Many of us know first hand that a great deal of the energy generated and dispensed within a team revolves around frustration, tension, and ambivalence. We might reflect on how we habitually deal with such problems: Do we try to find a solution? Do we step back and wait for someone else in the team to take the lead? Do we withdraw into a state of suspended animation?

Given the importance of the emotional dimension of team-work, people prepared to be team players have to focus not only on the tasks that need to be done but also on the processes. They need to be prepared to deal with the elephants in the room and the snakes under the carpet.[1] I recall a very task-driven logistics team that, having dealt with their concerns during their weekly meeting, would always have a short follow-up discussion, exploring their experience of the meeting, and what could be done to improve future meetings. These post-meeting sessions would lead to passionate dialogues, as they discussed what every member of the team could have done better to make their exchanges more effective.

A word about vulnerability

In organizational life, our willingness to be vulnerable before team members will always be an issue. Opening up and talking about personal issues—how we look at and interpret things—carries the risk of looking foolish. Publicly revealing our own vulnerability or others' weaknesses within a team contains a potential threat to our self-worth and sense of dignity. Self-disclosure may be associated with painful, deep-seated memories of childhood situations where we may have been exposed to public ridicule and humiliation. Furthermore, there will always be a limit to self-disclosure. Teams in organizations are not like therapy groups, which have their own boundaries. Too much self-disclosure may leave team members with highly ambivalent feelings, creating an increasing sense of vulnerability.

"Talking about personal issues always carries the risk of looking foolish."

[1] There is a Sufi tale about a man who noticed a disturbing bump under a rug. He tried everything to flatten the rug, smoothing, rubbing, and squashing the bump, but it kept reappearing. Finally, frustrated and furious, the man lifted up the rug, and to his great surprise, out slid a very angry snake. This tale is a highly illustrative metaphor of the need to deal with the real issues. Staying at a surface level will only give limited results.

Do you have the mindset to build a real team?

Study the following questions and answer them either YES or NO

YES   NO

- Are you prepared to reveal your thoughts, feelings, aspirations, goals, failures, successes, fears, and dreams as well as your likes, dislikes, and favoritisms to other people?
- Are you willing to share with others information that helps them understand you better?
- Are you willing to put yourself at risk through intimate disclosure?
- Are you the kind of person who believes in the integrity, ability, character, and truth of other people?
- Do you have confidence in the capability of other people to make good on their promises?
- Are you always prepared to position yourself as vulnerable to others?
- Are you convinced that others will not abuse your confidence due to your trusting behavior?

If most of your answers are YES, it will be relatively easy for you to build intimate relationships with the members of your team.

Allowing a tolerable amount of vulnerability is necessary, however. As members of a team get to know their colleagues better, they will come to understand the things that will and will not work for different people. For example, if the members of the executive team know that one of their colleagues has problems with closeness, they will understand why that person prefers to work independently, rather than assuming he or she is simply not interested in working with others.

I remember a group where at one point, one of the members of the executive committee said to another, "John, we've worked with you for 20 years. But I know more about you in these last three days than I knew in all that time. I know more about your likes and dislikes. I have a better sense of what drives you—and what drives you crazy. I wish I had known these things years ago."

I felt a bit sad when I heard this comment. Obviously, these two men had communicated with each other, but never really talked. But even though it was very late in the game, having a better understanding of what made each other tick would benefit them in the future. This sort of incident clarifies why a clear set of behavior and communications expectations is such an important aspect of creating high performance teams. These expectations help to build empathy and understanding, and ensure that individual preferences are not given more importance than team objectives.

As we can see, the degree to which a team works well together is dependent on a multi-factorial process. From a factual point of view, it depends on the team's members, environment, and tasks. Superficially, team cohesion depends on the extent to which the individuals in the group want to accomplish its primary task. Less obvious contributing factors include the members' attraction to the group, the developmental phase the team is in, normative and informational influences, and external sources—all adding to a team's complexity. Given the influence of all these variables, team dynamics can take on a life of their own, influencing participants in significant ways. So leadership group coaches not only need to focus on the team's primary task, they also need to make the nature of specific team-as-a-whole dynamics more overt so that tasks will not be derailed by unconscious acting out.

WHAT HAVE WE LEARNED SO FAR?

To sum up, I have argued that well-functioning teams are a critical element of global organizations, particularly those dependent on virtual, highly diverse teams who must assemble, produce, and disband rapidly. Such entities, if not handled properly, will be rife with paranoid and depressive anxiety. The likelihood of this happening needs to be minimized. We need a better understanding of individual relationship processes, group dynamics, and the vicissitudes of teams to see the warning signs of inner rot. At the same time, it leaves us with a number of important questions. How can people in organizations build corporate cultures that foster teamwork? And how can leadership group coaching help? And above all, what is group coaching all about?

REFERENCES

1. Fisher, B. A. and Ellis, D. G. (1974). *Small Group Decision Making*. New York: McGraw-Hill.
2. Dyer, W. G. (1977). *Team Building*. Reading, MA: Addison-Wesley.
3. Cummings, T. G. (1981). "Designing Effective Work Groups." In P. C. Nystrom and W. H. Starbuck (Eds), *Handbook of Organizational Design*. New York: Oxford University Press, pp. 250–271.
4. Hackman, J. R. (1990). "Creating more Effective Work Groups in Organizations." In J. R. Hackman (Ed.), *Groups that Work (and Those that Don't)*. San Francisco, CA: Jossey-Bass, pp. 479–504.

5. Parker, G. M. (1990). *Team Players and Teamwork: The New Competitive Business Strategy.* San Francisco, CA: Jossey-Bass.

6. Katzenbach, J. R. and Smith, D. K. (1993). *The Wisdom of Teams.* Boston, MA: Harvard Business School Press.

7. Levi, D. (2007). *Group Dynamics for Teams.* Los Angeles, CA: Sage.

8. Hackman, J. R. (2002). *Leading Teams: Setting the Stage for Great Performances.* Boston, MA: Harvard Business School Press.

9. Levi, D. (2007). *Group Dynamics for Teams.* Los Angeles, CA: Sage.

10. Kets de Vries, M. F. R. (2001). "Creating Authentizotic Organizations: Well-functioning Individuals in Vibrant Companies." *Human Relations,* 54 (1), 101–111.

11. Gintis, H., Bowles, S., Boyd, R., and Fehr, E. (2003). "Explaining Altruistic Behavior in Humans." *Evolution and Human Behavior,* 24, 153–172.

12. Kets de Vries, M. F. R. and Miller, D. (1984). *The Neurotic Organization.* San Francisco, CA: Jossey-Bass.

13. Kets de Vries, M. F. R. and Miller, D. (1987). *Unstable at the Top.* New York: New American Library.

14. Fisher, B. A. and Ellis, D. G. (1974). *Small Group Decision Making.* New York: McGraw-Hill.

15. Porter, T. W. and Lilly, B. S. (1996). "The Effects of Conflict, Trust, and Task Commitment on Project Team Performance." *International Journal of Conflict Management,* 7, 361–376.

16. De Dreu, C. K. W. and Van Vianen, A. E. M. (2001). "Responses to Relationship Conflict and Team Effectiveness." *Journal of Organizational Behavior,* 22, 309–328.

17. Hackman, J. R. (2002). *Leading Teams: Setting the Stage for Great Performances.* Boston, MA: Harvard Business School Press.

18. Hackman, J. R. and Wageman, R. (2005). "When and How Team Leaders Matter." *Research in Organizational Behavior,* 26, 39–76.

19. Kets de Vries, M. F. R. and Miller, D. (1984). *The Neurotic Organization.* San Francisco, CA: Jossey-Bass.

20. Hirschhorn, L. (1988). *The Workplace Within: Psychodynamics of Organizational Life.* Cambridge, MA: MIT Press.

21. Hirschhorn, L. (1991). *Managing in the New Team Environment: Skills, Tools, and Methods.* Reading, MA: Addison-Wesley.

22. Smith, K. K. and Berg, D. N. (1987). *Paradoxes of Group Life: Understanding Conflict, Paralysis, and Movement in Group Dynamics.* San Francisco, CA: Jossey-Bass.

23. Janis, I. L. (1972). *Victims of Groupthink*. Boston, MA: Houghton Mifflin Company.
24. Kets de Vries, M. F. R. (2006b). *Leadership Archetype Questionnaire: Participant Guide*. Fontainebleau, France: INSEAD Global Leadership Centre.
25. Kets de Vries, M. F. R. (2006c). *Leadership Archetype Questionnaire: Facilitator Guide*. Fontainebleau, France: INSEAD Global Leadership Centre.
26. Kets de Vries, M. F. R. (2007). "Decoding the Team Conundrum: The Eight Roles Executives Play." *Organizational Dynamics*, 36 (1), 28–44.

CHAPTER 2

SWIMMING IN THE RELATIONAL "SOUP"

A good coach will make his players see what they can be rather than what they are.

—Ara Parasheghian

A committee is a group that keeps minutes and loses hours.

—Milton Berle

An unconscious consciousness is no more a contradiction in terms than an unseen case of seeing.

—Franz Clemens Brentano

The nice thing about teamwork is that you always have others on your side.

—Margaret Carty

In every human interaction, there are visible, intentional behaviors that are fairly easy to understand, and there are also sub-texts, or unconscious motivators, that influence those actions. We often think of the message provided by the sub-texts (for example, body language, tone of voice, facial expressions) as impeding communication and understanding. In the case of teams and groups, the negative associations can be even stronger. Who hasn't complained about committee indecision, political gridlock, or the idiots in a specific department or division of an organization? This is what I call the relational soup. Such situations can turn into a sloppy, unappetizing mess. And while we are swimming in this soup, we tend to overlook the fact that team or group dynamics, when properly facilitated, can fuel efficient and effective individual and group actions and behavioral change.

I have taught or advised thousands of business people at all levels—MBA students, board members, senior executives, entrepreneurs—over the years in my career as a psychoanalyst, leadership coach, and business school professor of leadership. Earlier in my career, I believed that if I made the effort to interact with people individually, I could help them change and reach their professional and personal goals. I did, and still do, a great deal of one-to-one leadership coaching, a type of intervention that can be very effective.

About 20 years ago, however, I realized that my potential to influence change in people's lives was limited, both in time and in scope. There was only so much I could do. But I wanted more: I wanted to help people go back into their organizations and create profitable and sustainable places that in addition would be great places to work for, where employees felt their labor had some purpose. I believed that it was possible for most employees to get up most mornings and feel good about going to work, to create more effective, healthier, or what I described earlier as authentizotic organizations, places where people feel at their best. But to have this kind of effect, I needed to intervene on a larger scale, by giving the responsibility for creating this kind of organization to the employees themselves.

I realized that the kind of corporate culture I was looking for could be fostered and supported through the presence of a systemic coaching structure, in which people could build trusting and transparent relationships with one another that would facilitate innovation and adaptability. In this kind of culture, leadership would be distributed, rather than concentrated at the top. People would work effectively in teams to act quickly and proactively on challenges, and understanding that knowledge sharing and focusing on team goals are keys to success not only for the team, but also ultimately for the organization and even the individuals themselves.

But still I wondered how to instill this kind of corporate culture in a world where organizations are rife with paranoid thinking. In spite of the danger of negativity, the idea that the future of organizations lay in harnessing the power of groups (or teams) was not an exciting proposition. To get there would be quite a challenge. I could see that there was still work to be done to help people create effective work teams.

It is not enough to throw people together and expect them to work efficiently, even if the team has a clear, engaging goal and sufficient resources. As any student of human nature knows—and I am one—there is much more to group interactions than meets the eye. In fact, although most people do not realize it, the invisible undercurrent of group dynamics can either create a group effect that is more powerful than the sum of its parts, or dash the group against the rocks.

"The invisible undercurrent of group dynamics can either create a group effect that is more powerful than the sum of its parts, or dash the group against the rocks."

Thinking about how to harness the potential force of group dynamics, I began experimenting with leadership group coaching in a multi-module program for top executives. There, whether I liked it or not, I realized that I had no choice but to dive into the relational soup—the often confusing and unsettling interrelationships that exist among members of groups—and take my students with me. I believed that by helping senior executives to see below the surface, they would be better prepared to instill a corporate culture of team-based distributive leadership in their own organizations.

In a fairly revolutionary move for the time, I decided to abandon the standard Harvard Business School case study model, and replace it with the live case study instead. It was quite a challenge to make the live case study effective. Generally, it only worked after a modicum of trust had been established in the group. In the case of my CEO seminar, each of the participants was given the opportunity to stand in front of the small group of 20 participants to share their thoughts, concerns, challenges, fears, and desires related both to their career and life in general. To such presentations, the members of the group would respond with respect, support, associations, and recommendations. Not only did the participants learn by making their own presentations, but they also learned a great deal by listening to the presentations of others. In addition, an important part of the learning experience for the participants was to identify and evaluate their own options in the time between modules—and take constructive action.

I was fascinated and delighted to see how group members took on the task of "coaching" each other (it wasn't yet called coaching in those days). In addition, over the course of the one-year, four-module program, the participants experimented with creating effective teams and coaching cultures in their organizations, reporting back to the other seminar participants in subsequent modules. It made me appreciate the luxury of working with individuals who had the power to make changes in their organizations, and from their reports, I could see that change was happening.

My co-director, Sudhir Kakar, and I retained the role of guiding figures and facilitators for the group, but it was the group itself, in a business school classroom, that played the most important role. Given what they had learned in the classroom—having engaged in cognitive and emotional reframing of their life situation (what used to be a negative outlook)—the participants realized that they could now hope for a better future. But they also knew that their good intentions for change had to go beyond the typical New Year's resolutions that never materialize. It was the design of the seminar, however, that made a difference. Encouraged by their peers, participants had the feeling that change was indeed possible and attainable.

Over the years of running this program, it became obvious that a small group, when initiated and guided by clinically informed faculty members, could be far more effective in fostering change and development than one-to-one coaching. In 2000 (based on my experiences from the CEO program), I started a second, comparable program with two other faculty co-directors; this program was aimed at HR and leadership development directors, as well as others who were directly responsible for the human capital in organizations, such as coaches, consultants, senior executives, or entrepreneurs. This was a longer program, seven (now eight) modules over a period of 15 months. Here, as in the other program, an important pedagogical tool was small group peer coaching. Once again, I saw that group dynamics and the life case study could be brought into the classroom in an experiential learning method that had a parallel benefit. Not only did it help participants understand the systemic influences within their own organizations, they also experienced the way in which small, trusting groups of peers can identify and support change and personal development. They took these insights back into their organizations and applied them to the creation of working teams. A new approach to supporting leadership development, and a process for creating effective teams had taken form: leadership group coaching.

A group coaching session

- How would you go about creating a memorable team experience?
- What would you do to get the process on its way?
- What would you be trying to accomplish?
- How would you like the session to end?
- What would you like to see as next steps?

To provide individuals with concrete material for reflection in executive group coaching sessions and programs, I developed (helped by my team members) a number of 360-degree leadership behavior questionnaires, as they help jump start the coaching intervention by providing a snapshot of how participants saw themselves compared to their colleagues' perceptions. Such feedback, particularly when there are large gaps between the perception of self and others, can have a great emotional impact—a key facilitator of change (see Appendix for a description of the instruments). Apart from the two lengthy seminars mentioned earlier, I also created a group coaching process that could be included in short interventions in other executive development programs. These shorter interventions became the backbone of INSEAD's Global Leadership Center (IGLC) and my consulting firm, the Kets de Vries Institute (KDVI).

I founded IGLC in 2003 to coordinate our leadership group coaching activities and leadership research; many top coaches from other institutions, and selected graduates of INSEAD's own program joined our pool of dynamically oriented group coaches. Since then, over 10,000 executives have been through one of these short leadership group coaching days (over 80,000 people have filled in our 360-degree leadership survey instruments, including the participants' observers). The two top leadership development programs described above (which to this day still focus on live case studies, peer group coaching, and experiential learning), are oversubscribed year after year.

To my great satisfaction, 20 years after my first experiments with my CEO participants, the leadership group coaching method has taken root far beyond our doorstep. Students and professors, who have worked with me at IGLC, are using it in companies and executive programs in other universities. A large virtual community has been established. Some of my former students have set up consulting firms in places like Canada, Brazil, Malaysia, India, Australia, and South Korea. Others, who returned to their roles as HR or leadership development directors, are weaving this philosophy into the daily lives of many of the world's leading organizations. The group effect is powerful indeed—and as I dreamed, it is making a difference to human lives. The benefits of becoming more effective as a group or a team can be remarkable.

What do you view as the virtues of teamwork?

Answer the following questions YES or NO, depending how closely each reflects your own situation

YES   NO

- Do you believe that teamwork fosters greater efficiency and effectiveness?
- Do you think that the quality of output is higher due to teamwork?
- In your opinion, are decisions made more quickly when working as a team?
- Do you think teamwork builds greater commitment among team members?
- In your opinion, does teamwork foster the maximum use of each individual's capabilities?
- Do you think teamwork helps the cross-fertilization of ideas?
- Do you believe that teamwork creates a greater sense of belonging?

If you have answered YES to most of these questions, you have the mindset to benefit greatly from teamwork.

LEADERSHIP GROUP COACHING: AN ART AND A SCIENCE

When I look at the world of leadership coaching (not to mention all the other types of coaching) with a more critical eye, I come across many people who are attracted to the considerable amounts of money that can be made. I see self-anointed coaches, who have some familiarity with the training of athletes, pop psychology, or an elementary knowledge of group dynamics. Given their ignorance, these people are like the sorcerer's apprentice. They don't seem to be aware of the fundamental forces they are unleashing, or the potential harm they may cause. Frankly, there are times when I become quite concerned about the proliferation of "snake oil salesmen" in the coaching profession.

When I started INSEAD's Global Leadership Center, I told the coaches who joined me that—unlike what takes place at other centers—I was not a believer in a cookie cutter approach to group coaching. I suggested to them that they should use the approach that felt most natural to them. The only requirement I had—and it is an important one—is that they have a modicum of psycho-dynamic awareness. I want them to realize when they are out of their depth in coaching, and when they should ask for help from someone more steeped in psychotherapy, psychoanalysis, or psychiatry.

Initially, I was somewhat surprised that short group coaching interventions work so well for most people, judging by the appre-ciation (reflected in the ratings and commentary) the coaches at IGLC receive. Quite often, participants hail the leadership coach-ing intervention session as the best thing that has happened to them during an executive program. The coaches themselves, after each coaching session, often talk with each other about the excit-ing day they had, and the tipping point moments they witnessed. Many executives contact their coach months or years later, telling them about the major career and life decisions that they have made, and thanking the coach for their part in making it happen. Coaches often mention to me that they feel privileged their intervention had made this possible. Of course, these statements are valid not only for short group coaching interventions but also in building high performance, top executive teams.

Best and worse experiences

- What has been your best experience running a group coaching session?
- What has been your worst experience running a group coaching session?
- What has been your best experience being a participant in a group coaching session?
- What has been your worst experience being a participant in a group coaching session?
- While being in a group coaching session, have you seen people (including yourself) reach a tipping point—an experience of quantum change?

In 2010, as we celebrated 10 years of INSEAD's "Consulting and Coaching for Change" program, I reflected on what has been accomplished over the years. I realized that I had contributed to the development of an intervention technique that proved to be extremely useful for executives, and often created an inflection point in their lives. But despite this success, there was something that concerned me. Over the years, most of the coaches did not seem, as a group, to be analyzing how and why the group coaching process worked. The catchphrase (not without reason) was "trust the process." Also, executives, although excited about the coaching interventions they experienced, did not understand why this kind of intervention was so effective. No one seemed to be thinking about the underlying rationale of the process. This worried me. Intuition—an element of using "self as an instrument"—is very important in coaching, but I also feel it is necessary to understand the reasons for success, as well as the derailing factors linked to any process. If such understanding is lacking, group interventions risk becoming yet another management fad. We've been very successful at developing executive group coaching, but resting on our laurels is a dangerous pastime.

I am always pleased to see how often coaches come out of the short, day-long interventions on a high: drained, yet euphoric, with the feeling that they have made a difference in people's lives. When it goes well, it's like magic. And over time, many coaches take this magic for granted. But coaches who do not understand the forces that make the "magic" happen, that is, the group dynamics at play, may be at a loss if the process begins to derail. In addition, they may not be fully aware of how their own actions affect the group dynamics. They may bring up elements of a participant's life that cannot be fully dealt with in one session, leaving the person feeling unsettled. They may cause implosions in a person's life. What I'm saying is that the magic occurs when the coach not only trusts the process, but also understands the elements of group dynamics that will lead the coaching session to success or failure.

"When coaching goes well, it's like magic."

A LEADERSHIP GROUP COACHING STORY

Before going on to discuss salient elements of group processes in subsequent chapters, I want to put you (the reader) inside the skin of a leadership coach who is leading a group coaching session. Leadership coaching assignments, I always say, are like detective work. You go in not really knowing what the problem is, let alone the solution. The only thing you can do is look for patterns and themes, and try to create a picture that will be the sum of not only the visible, but also the invisible parts that are presented to you. As that picture slowly comes into focus—as the group works to put the puzzle together—the individual can begin to evaluate options. The following "detective" story can be viewed as a composite based on what a leadership coach will experience.

Are you with me Dr Watson?

You are asked to run a group coaching session for the top executive team of a medium-sized global bank. You wake up in the morning in your hotel room and a jolt of adrenalin hits you. You glance at the clock by your bed—damn, it's only 4:00 a.m., and you've only slept for four hours. It always happens when you are in strange hotel rooms. You don't have to get started until early midday, but now you're awake and the scared feeling in the pit of your stomach reminds you that you'll be leading a high performance team building session for these bankers for the coming days. You get up and eat a light breakfast. For the next two hours, you go over the 360-degree leadership behavior feedback reports and biographical information about the six people of the executive team. You look at the notes you made when you interviewed them—as you have made it a habit (when it concerns a top team) not to go in cold. The risks are too high. You want to know some of the issues that are important to them. You want to be aware of the dynamics between them. You want to know whether there are some "undiscussables" between them. You look at the PowerPoint presentation you made about your observations of the organization.

You already spent the evening looking at the reports, making interpretations, highlighting points to cover, but you feel that you need to go over them one last time. You have three reports that you can already tell are harbingers of a tough day to come. The CEO, Patrick, is an over-estimator, giving himself ratings much higher than his observers: Is this an indicator of his narcissism?

Maria, the CFO, on the other hand, gave herself ratings that bump along the bottom of the chart: Does she suffer from low self-esteem? A third report shows that Robert (head of retail banking) not only has a low rating on visioning and empowering, but also scores poorly on emotional intelligence. The written comments suggest that other people see him as a pain in the neck, not giving them enough freedom to do their work. He could be a tough case. Then you remind yourself of the importance of positive reframing. To make the group process work, many positive observations are needed to neutralize a negative comment.

You know from your experience that some of these bankers probably had a sleepless night too; in fact, your difficulty sleeping is probably related to the stress level that you know you will have to face when the group meets—and you're the one responsible for creating a safe, relaxed environment in which they can explore their results, and figure out how to become more effective.

Of course, you have a considerable amount of training and experience as a leadership coach. You recall how years ago, you were a participant yourself in a program during which you had a group coaching experience (similar to the one you plan to organize for the banking team), complete with your own feedback reports. It was a powerful experience; the group helped you reach some new insights about your career, and this indirectly led to your decision to become a coach yourself. After further training, you spent some time shadowing experienced coaches in many leadership group coaching sessions. The various coaches you observed were excellent, handling the different groups smoothly, making it a great learning experience.

The time has come. You enter the meeting room in the hotel. You recognize the faces from having interviewed them before. After some pleasantries, you tell them how you have planned the day. You want to start by making a short presentation about effective leadership, high performance teams, and vanguard organizations, then talk about their own organization, and finally discuss the feedback instruments.

The discussion that your presentation invites is very animated. Subsequently, you tell the participants that your interviews with them and some other key players in the company have led you to make a number of observations about the organization. You emphasize that these are merely initial impressions—and that some of them could be completely wrong. Whatever impressions they may be, when you present your findings, a very lively discussion follows, including comments about a number of otherwise "undiscussables." You realize that, in this company, one of the "elephants in the room" has been the state of the IT platform. The various geographical regions of the company are reluctant to create a centralized one, given the costs and the risks. You address this but don't belabor the point. Without saying too much, everyone in the room knows that it is a problem.

It is close to 6:00 p.m. The time has come to deal with the final part of the afternoon. You try to enlighten them about the two questionnaires completed by the participants. You explain some of the basic properties of the Global Executive Leadership Inventory and the Personality Audit (see Appendix). You hope that this short presentation will help them to make sense of the findings. You explain to them that they should not consider the findings as written in stone—people are far too complex to be captured by a simple questionnaire. They should look at the results as only the beginning of a discussion. You also tell them that tomorrow, during the discussion, they will all become experts in deciphering the questionnaires.

As the final part of the day, you ask them to do their self-portrait. When you say this, they don't look very happy but you are used to that reaction. With some cajoling, telling them that their children can draw—and they were children once too—you get them to do it. You send the group off with colored felt pens and large sheets of paper to spend 20 minutes drawing images (no words allowed) to illustrate what is in their head, heart, stomach, in the past and future, and in their work and leisure. And in fact, after finishing the self-portrait exercise, most look rather proud of their productions.

After putting all these "masterpieces" on the wall, it is time to give them an envelope containing the two reports. You suggest having drinks at the bar. As they make themselves comfortable, some cannot wait to open the envelope, anxious to know how others see them. Others are more relaxed about it. You tell them that you look forward to the start of the group coaching intervention the next day.

The next morning you ask the members of the team if they have slept well. Did they have any interesting dreams or nightmares? What do they expect from the day? To your disappointment, nobody volunteers a dream. Instead what you get is a not very subtle reaction from Mark (head of investment banking): "I hope this activity is not going to be a waste of time. I've done so many of these 360-degree things before, and I'm just not into it. You know from our interview, that these groupie things are not really my kind of thing." Fortunately, Maria comes to your defense, telling Mark that she feels a team intervention can be very helpful. She adds, "Mark, do you really think that we work so well together? Our grade on teamwork wouldn't be that high. But can't we do better?" After Maria is finished, you add: "Mark, I understand that having to go through yet another 360-degree feedback exercise can be tiring. I do value your perspective. I think your comments will be very valuable for the team." At that point, Patrick chimes in: "Come on Mark, chill out, go with the flow!"

Quietly, you congratulate yourself on getting over the first hurdle of the day. Before moving on to the first activity, you remind the group of the ground rules: you refer to the Hippocratic oath, "Do no harm." It is important when going through such an exercise that nobody should get hurt. You also tell them that whatever happens in this room is confidential. In addition, slightly jokingly, you mention that another good rule to live by is "to strike when the iron is cold." You explain to them that during the process, you may have a very good insight, but that sometimes the time is not right to say it out loud. At times, it is much better to keep your mouth shut.

You remind the group that their task, with you as a facilitator, is to listen to the story that each person tells related to the six drawings hanging on the wall, the results of the feedback—and some of the questions you will ask to get a better sense of their life history. You tell them that you are managing the time. In general, each participant gets about 90 minutes to two hours in the "hot seat."

You ask Robert (retail banker) to "volunteer." He starts by explaining his self-portrait. His commentary is quite perfunctory and shallow. There is not much to be learned from his presentation. Most of his comments about his life refer to his quick rise in the bank—and a tedious description of the various functions he has occupied. But tedious or not, his career history is quite impressive. He rose quickly through the ranks in the company, and is presently operating as head of retail banking. After a little time, Maria stops him, and asks him a question about the image in his drawing related to his past. She mentions that it seems quite dark, small, and detached from the other images. Robert pauses, takes a deep breath, and then talks about how his father died when he (the oldest child of five) was only nine years old. After his father's death, Robert became the "man" of the family, which he says was only natural, as his mother had enough on her hands trying to keep the children together and a roof over their heads.

The group seems to sense that Robert needs to explore this story further. Looking at the comments section of his feedback report, they see that many people have written that Robert can be an annoying micro-manager. In contrast, other comments suggest that Robert has the potential to be more effective, but he seems to be over-extended, unable to devote the time necessary to the big picture thinking that is important in his position in the bank. Looking at the data, his visioning part on the Global Executive Leadership Inventory leaves something to be desired, although he rates himself quite high. Maria also points out that Robert's observers seem to think that he is not very emotionally intelligent and, from his own self-rating, it looked as though he agreed with them. "Do you think the results are accurate?" Maria asks.

Robert responds, "I know people think I am not a good listener, and I am often impatient. I have a tendency to finish other people's sentences. Also, I just don't have the time to be a social butterfly. I've got to control significant accounts and movement of funds. Bankers are under a lot of scrutiny right now. I also agree that I should take more time to think strategically. But I can't do that without shutting my door. Somehow, I never come to it."

At this point, you tell Robert that it is time for him to just listen. He should not react to whatever the others say. To get the discussion going, you tell the others that they should imagine that Robert is an animal. As they now know quite a bit about him, what animal do they imagine he would be? This idea of creating an animal farm creates an amount of playfulness in the room. One of the participants sees Robert as a beaver—he always seems so busy. Someone else sees him as an ant, referring to his over-organization. Maria says she sees him as a dog—the kind that guides the blind. She says his need to control everything sometimes gets to her and that some people in the company describe him as a bit of a control freak. She reminds him of the number of times they have argued and how often she has been irritated by his behavior, his need to meddle in everything. Thinking about the various animals in the "animal farm," Maria gently wonders whether there was a pattern here: Robert was able to take on the role of man of the house at an early age. He was the one responsible. But is this role still applicable? Does he still think of himself, at some level, as the one who has "to keep the family together"—not only the family at home but also at work? Mark adds, "You know, Robert, as I listen to you in this session, I realize how capable you are, but at the same time, you are not someone I would like to work for. It is my impression that your 'mother hen' behavior can be quite stifling. I also realize, however, listening to what you have to say, that you are a person who deeply cares about the company and the people who work for you. It's too bad that people can't see that other side of you."

Seeing the opportunity for closure, you ask the group to help Robert identify two or three action points related to this behavior that he can work on over the next few months, and which you and the group will discuss in your follow-up conference call in six weeks. The question you present to the group is: "As a friend what would you tell Robert?" Everyone obliges, and gives Robert a number of insightful suggestions. The group also helps Robert understand that working on his emotional intelligence is not a waste of time. On the contrary, spending more time listening to his people, as opposed to telling them what to do, could pay off handsomely.

It is now time for Robert to open his mouth. He first smiles at Mark, and says, "Thanks, Mark and Maria for your comments. No one has ever given me this kind of honest feedback. My mother still counts on me to be the family patriarch, even though all of her children are grown up. But I guess I'm so used to that role that I act that way at work too. I realize that sometimes I can be a pain in the neck."

Robert continues by saying that he has decided to take the time to have a real conversation with each of his subordinates, asking for their help in becoming better in running his team. He adds that he plans to schedule lunches with his peers, to get to know them better. In addition, he plans to share with them some of the findings of the questionnaires, and ask them to help him to be less of a micro manager. Obviously, his lateral relationships with his peers also leave something to be desired. In addition, he notes that he will schedule a twice-yearly, off-site meeting with his whole team to discuss some of the strategic issues faced by retail banking.

Systematically, one after the other, members of the team have their place in the "hot seat." At the end of the day, you suggest that it is the turn of Patrick, the CEO (you usually save the CEO for last or last-but-one). When you ask him how he experienced his ratings, Patrick does not beat about the bush. He responds immediately that he is not very happy with the results. The information made it clear to him that he has been living in "la-la" land, going his own way. After a further explanation of his self-portrait and the information in the questionnaires, it is time for Patrick to be quiet and listen.

After a discussion of his "animal farm," the interchange really gets going. Jorgen (head of risk at the bank) starts, saying, "Patrick, I love working for you but you often behave like a racehorse. It would be nice if sometimes you would look back and see if the other horses are still with you. Too often, at least I think so, you leave us far behind and I feel lost. Usually, I am afraid to say so. I don't think you would appreciate it. What's more, I often don't know what you are trying to accomplish by racing along like this. At times, your behavior makes me feel really inferior. Don't take this negatively. I view you as a great visionary, but without really explaining what you are trying to accomplish, it is hard for us to come along. It is not easy to understand you."

At this point, Maria chimes in. "Even when we try to slow you down, you ignore it, and you make it sound like we are wrong to do so. Frequently, you ask my opinion about certain things but I get the feeling that you don't really care about my answer. Your body language tells me that whatever I say, it doesn't matter very much. I am with Jorgen in that I often feel inferior when dealing with you. And I am also not sure if you really care about the feedback we are giving you. I find it very hard to read you. I never really know what you think."

The others seem to be on the same wavelength as Jorgen and Maria. The theme of the racehorse that doesn't look back and the difficulty in reading him play out for a while. "As a friend," the team members make a number of suggestions about how Patrick can be more effective in his role as CEO.

You feel that the time has come to let Patrick talk. Looking at him, he seems less self-assured, rather shrunken. His opening comment is, "You may not think so, but I am very much affected by your frank comments. I'd like to thank you for what you have said. The information from the questionnaires and your comments have made me realize that it is high time I did something about the way I interact with you. It is a pattern that needs to be broken.

"To explain where I come from, I should probably say a few more things about myself. Let me start by saying that I have always been highly competitive. I've been doing some self-searching and I have come to realize that the main reason for this behavior has been my father. He was a man who never appreciated anything I did to get his attention. I think—and my wife has often said this— that it resulted in an attitude on my part of 'I don't care,' a cover-up for caring too much. I learned that if I showed I really cared, my father would make fun of me, cut me down. From what my wife tells me, I have become a master at presenting a poker face. I now realize how much this kind of behavior is affecting all of you. The ghosts of the past are still present but I realize the time has come to be a ghostbuster and experiment with different ways of relating to people."

At this point, Patrick becomes silent, but not in a pregnant, oppressive way. You realize that he needs some time for himself. You also note that Maria looks uncomfortable. You look at her, which encourages her to say to Patrick, "You may think our comments were somewhat harsh but I'd like to thank you for all the things you have taught me to be more effective as one of the leaders in the company."

There is a silence. Now, you are trying to understand where, emotionally, the group is. To deal with your own anxiety, you ask Maria how she is feeling at that moment. Maria responds: "I can't answer your question exactly. But I would like to tell you about a dream I had last night that's still bothering me. It somehow keeps on coming back. Let me tell you: I was driving a car but had great difficulty doing so because I got caught in a tornado. The wind made the car uncontrollable. I tried everything to hold on to the steering wheel but I was powerless. Suddenly, out of nowhere, a man appeared on the road. He saw me, but he refused to move out of my way. To avoid him, I managed to swerve, but lost control and crashed into a tree. At that moment I woke up. I didn't feel very good. What do you make of that?"

You aren't quite sure how to respond. Fortunately, Jorgen jumps in, saying that a few days previously he had been watching *The Wizard of Oz* with his children. You have an inkling of the connection, but you let Jorgen continue his train of thought. Mark asks what the film is about. Jorgen tells him about Dorothy, a lonely orphan living on a dusty Kansas farm with her aunt and uncle. According to the story, she daydreams about traveling "over the rainbow" to a different world, a world in Technicolor. Her wish is granted when a tornado whisks her and her little dog, Toto, to the magical, beautiful, but dangerous Land of Oz. There, Dorothy meets a number of magical characters: a Scarecrow whose dearest wish is to have a brain, a Tin Man who longs for a heart, and a Cowardly Lion who wishes for courage. They join Dorothy, who is herself desperate to find her way home, in a quest to find the famous Wizard of Oz in the hope that he will give them all what they are looking for.

Maria interrupts at this point and says, "Aren't we also on a quest? Isn't the story line a little bit about what we are doing here today? From what I can remember, *The Wizard of Oz* is set in a magical but frightening land. Like us, Dorothy is an ordinary person, but she faces real challenges. And although she seems to be a simple and harmless little girl, she is the one who kills the wicked witches of East and West."

Jorgen goes on, "That's right, Maria, in the case of Dorothy and her companions, there is more than meets the eye. The Scarecrow thinks he needs brains but whenever the four companions find themselves at an impasse, it is the Scarecrow who comes up with the clever plan to help them. The Tin Man thinks he lacks a heart, but he is so full of sentiment that he is always weeping. The Cowardly Lion seems to be a coward but he is the one who acts bravely to save the team whenever they are threatened by danger. The Wizard seems to be great and powerful, but turns out to be a fraud.

"Dorothy is successful in her quest because she is helped by these extraordinary and magical friends. Her companions, like Dorothy herself, already have within themselves the qualities they say they are looking for. They just need to find out for themselves. To be more specific, what makes Dorothy such a highly effective leader is that she takes someone with no brains, someone with no heart and someone with no courage and develops them into a highly effective team that successfully accomplishes its mission."

Maria carries on: "We've already seen today that someone like Robert, who comes across at first as rather difficult, is really someone who wants to be sure that the people who work for him are safe and have what they need. This team intervention session, like travelling to the Land of Oz, is a chance to get the best out of each other. Going to Oz is like an allegory of initiation and growth, where we all discover what we are really good at."

But Maria doesn't stop here. She goes on: "I didn't see what you were getting at, Jorgen, with the Oz story, but it seems to have triggered something for me. I think you are right about helping each other discover what we are good at. I may have come across somewhat strongly when I gave feedback to you

Robert, and I regret that. I could have been subtler, although I think my comments do contain some seeds of truth. But as I listened to Jorgen, I had a sudden insight. I put two and two together, thinking about patterns in Robert's family, and the way that can affect how we see, or don't see, individuals' true qualities. I just realized that the reason I am often so irritated by Robert's behavior is because he reminds me of my younger brother. When we were growing up, my brother frustrated the hell out of me. He never listened to anything I had to say. He always knew better. As a matter of fact, the man who suddenly appeared on the road in my dream was blocking my path, just like my brother. Somehow, with Robert, I went on automatic pilot—and returned to the kind of behavior I learned earlier in life."

At that point, Robert responds, "It's OK. You did piss me off Maria, but you had a point. As a matter of fact, your comments are in sync with the written feedback I got from my observers, both peers and subordinates. I am very good at sabotaging situations I don't agree with. But I don't really express what I think. I realize that it can irritate the hell out of people. "

And gradually the day comes to an end. Everyone has taken his or her turn in the hot seat, using their self-portrait as an ice breaker to start to point out highlights and lowlights in their life story, and taking in the group's reflections on the feedback report. As time goes by the participants are more comfortable with each other, and the process, and the atmosphere in the room, become quite playful. Even Mark has made a very insightful presentation, using a number of problems from the past to explain some of his present behavior. Furthermore, as the discussion evolves, some more systemic organizational skeletons come out of the closet, including the problems with IT. Constructive suggestions are made about how to deal with it.

In the summing up session the next morning, everyone in the room has a much clearer idea of what issues they need to work on, and how. They were aware of some of these points already (at least subliminally), but have never really done anything about them. There are also some obvious team issues that need their attention. You emphasize to them that there will be a follow-up session two and a half months from now to discuss their progress vis-à-vis their various action points. You also mention that this session will give an opportunity to discuss further the various challenges the bank is facing. You also set a date with them for a group conference telephone call in six weeks' time to discuss the progress of their action plans. And, on a more individual basis, each of the team members commits to being the learning partner, or "peer coach" of another team member—they will contact each other regularly to encourage, challenge, and support the change process.

As you all leave the room, everyone shakes your hand warmly. They thank you for the meaningful days, and tell you that they are really looking forward to seeing you again. You feel it is time for some fresh air and a walk. You need to let the events of the past days clear your mind: but once again, the magic has worked.

GROUP COACHING: A SOCIAL LEARNING EXPERIENCE

What I have tried to illustrate in this coaching vignette is the concept that in group coaching, participants engage in a social learning process. They learn through identification with each other and the coaches. There is an enormous emphasis on mutual self-help. Through participation, observation, and interaction with others, members of the team start to change habitual thought processes, feelings, and behavior patterns. Peer and coach pressure, and the provision of continual feedback, influence behavior modification. Gradually, particularly if there is more than one team building session, the members of the team gain greater self-confidence in engaging in courageous conversations, develop new leadership skills, and become better at solving their own problems and coaching others.

These social learning processes take place as multiple dynamics occur simultaneously. One dynamic is individual-to-group, that is, the group's focus on and reaction to the issues raised by the person in the hot seat. A second dynamic is what I call the "cloud dynamic." Like cloud computing, which uses a network as a means to connect the user to resources that are based in the "cloud," as opposed to actually possessing them, cloud dynamics refers to themes in the mind of the group-as-a-whole that are brought out as the group creates a collective consciousness during discussions. These themes could be, for example, anxiety, irritation, envy, competitive feelings, boredom, awe, or a collective sense of release as one member gets a burst of helpful insight. Often these "clouds" are left untouched by the group, even though the themes are affecting everyone in the room.

Some of the more sensitive (and more effective) coaches, however, will point to the issues in these clouds when appropriate. "Cloud" observations can be helpful when the group discussion seemed to have come to a halt. For example, Jorgen and Maria made a cloud observation to Robert by using the story *The Wizard of Oz*, as they voiced the group's unspoken annoyance with his irritable behavior patterns. Also, as we can see in this vignette, dreams can play an important role as catalysts.

Another dynamic has to do with the relationship of the group to the coach. One of the most important roles of the coach is to construct a safe space for participants, a place where they can talk about difficult issues, possibly for the first time. Group coaches— using themselves as instruments—need to monitor the mood states of the team constantly. For example, heightened feelings of anxiety among team members can be a sign of the active co-creation of the collective cloud. This is often the moment when thematic patterning of interactions within the team comes to the fore—as we saw when the interaction between Maria and Patrick led to an

What are your dreams trying to tell you?
Reflect on a recent dream and ask yourself what it represents.

- My dream represents a conflict that has been bothering me for some time.
- My dream represents an impending crisis.
- My dream represents an important insight about my life.
- My dream represents a specific mood state.
- My dream represents another way of looking at myself.
- My dream represents relational transference patterns concerning a person I know.
- My dream is defensive, covering up an issue I don't really want to deal with.
- My dream represents the solution to a difficult problem.

Can you find one of these themes in your dream? If so, pay attention—these dreams can help you to better understand yourself.

apparently unrelated comment from Jorgen about a movie. This interlude triggered new thinking in both Maria and Patrick.

A very important element of the group dynamic is the cathartic experience. It can be very liberating to tell one's life story and to be listened to respectfully by others. What's more, while listening to other people's life stories, the participants come to realize that they are not alone in their confusion. The realization of the universality of some problems—seeing that others struggle with the same problems—can bring a great sense of relief. This "just join the human race" effect has great benefits. Mutual identification—a

> "It can be very liberating to tell one's life story and to be listened to respectfully by others."

sense that you share a commonality with someone else—offers many opportunities to discuss other ways of doing things. It also makes for mutual support and guidance.

People interested in creating high performance teams soon discover that each team they work with has specific moods and identities of its own—states of mind that can (and will) be expressed by members of a team. Frequently, without conscious awareness, some members of a group will take the initiative to articulate things that have been left unspoken by others. Fantasies, dreams, screen memories, erotic expressions, transference reactions,[1] somatic conditions, or mood states may be externalized and resonate within the group-as-a-whole. These revelations can lead to insights, and open the door to change.

In my team coaching vignette, we also saw the importance of the interpretation of patterns and themes in our lives. Although we don't describe it in so many words to group members, group coaching draws on a psychodynamic paradigm that says that much of our behavioral repertoire is formed early in life (we'll come back to this in detail in Chapter 4). As adults, we may discover that some of our behavior patterns (extremely useful as they may have been at an early age), may be completely inappropriate in adulthood, as was hinted at in Robert's and Patrick's tales. The group coaching process can encourage individuals to experiment, trying to do a few things differently.

As the term group coaching implies, I also draw on the dynamic of affiliation (or sense of community). For example, particularly for coaching groups who have to work as a team in their organization, being a kind of "tribe" that has gone through a coaching experience helps to create a sense of mutual support for whatever action steps need to be taken. This feeling of social

---

[1] See Chapter 4 for an explanation of transference.

belonging can be a very helpful catalyst for change—and remains strong long after the coaching day is just a memory.

All of these fundamental elements of group dynamics should be within the conscious awareness of the coach, if he or she is to make the most of the group session. It has been said that the most important person in an orchestra is the conductor, because the conductor decides how a piece is to be interpreted. Conductors need extensive knowledge of all the instruments, music history, music theory, the composer's life, and the players' ability to make the piece a success. While individual musicians learn their own part, the conductor of an orchestra must learn the entire score.

Helping to create a high performance team is very much like conducting an orchestra. Effective change agents like group coaches need to be able constantly to shift focus and emphasis. They need to pay close attention to the ups and downs of each member of the team. At the same time, they need to be able to appreciate and encourage the dynamics of the group-as-a-whole, to contain the blurring of individual separateness, and be ready to appreciate the actions generated by the "cloud," the collective conscious and unconscious of the members of the team.

> **"Effective change agents need to be able constantly to shift focus and emphasis."**

People wanting to create high performance teams also need to know how to make sense of attachment behavior, transference processes, mirroring, and emotional and social contagion; how to recognize the forces of regression and progression; be aware of the nature of paranoid and depressive processes; and understand, from a linear, mono-mythical, and helical point of view, the ways teams develop or evolve (these themes will be discussed in later chapters). In addition, they need to be highly skilled in using themselves as an instrument [1]. They need to be aware what makes them feel mad, sad, bad, or glad.

What makes you feel sad, mad, bad, or glad? How do you manage your emotions?

What makes you sad? Think about some occasions when you felt sad.

How did you express your feelings? Could some of those emotional experiences have been avoided?

What makes you mad? How do you express your anger? Can you think of different ways of handling your anger in the future?

What makes you feel bad? What kind of situations arouse these feelings? How do you handle these feelings? How do you get over them?

What makes you glad? Think about the kinds of situations that make you happy. Are there ways to increase your happiness? What options can you think of?

Write down your responses and reflect on them. This will provide you with greater insight about the way you handle your emotions.

During a team intervention, individuals' habitual modes of relating will unfold within the microcosm of the group. They will recreate the social hemisphere in which they live. They will also repeat potentially maladaptive behavior within the here-and-now of the team, making for very illuminating interplay between individuals and the dynamics of the group-as-a-whole—if the coach is skilled enough to facilitate this delicate situation.

Thus a team intervention becomes a kind of laboratory where the interpersonal dynamics of the various individuals are displayed—not only manifest behavior but also more latent patterns. These dynamics offer excellent opportunities for the members of the group to witness and comment on these behaviors, and their consequences. Encouraged by other members of the group, each individual may explore new ways of dealing with previously rigid, ritualistic behavior. The insights provided in the group are often carried over into the individual's larger social environment. The objective for a team building session is that individuals will have "Aha!" moments of greater understanding of their own behavior, and thus will be better prepared to shape and meet the demands of their organization.

> "The insights provided in the group are often carried over into the individual's larger social environment."

In team building sessions, leadership coaches (or any change catalysts) and participants should be prepared to "use themselves as instrument" to better understand their own inner theater, but also (at appropriate times) use their fantasy life to make cloud observations. There are strong parallels between a team building session that is in the zone (with everyone achieving their true performance level) and the observations of Zen masters, who tend to be extremely adept at cloud observations.

For example, there is the story of the great Taoist master Chuang Tzu who once dreamt that he was a butterfly fluttering around. In his dream, the idea that he was a person was alien to him: he was only a butterfly. Suddenly, he awoke and found himself lying there, a person once again. But then Chuang Tzu thought to himself, "Was I before a man who dreamt about being a butterfly, or am I now a butterfly who dreams about being a man?" Or, to shift focus while being in a team building session, "Is the fantasy that haunts me my fantasy, or is it the fantasy of the group-as-a-whole?"

REFERENCES

1. Kets de Vries, M. F. R., Guillen, L., Korotov, K., and Florent-Treacy, E. (2010). *The Coaching Kaleidoscope: Insights from the Inside*. New York: Palgrave/Macmillan.

CHAPTER 3

LEADERSHIP COACHING AND HIGH PERFORMANCE TEAMS

Great things are done by a series of small things brought together.

—Vincent van Gogh

If you deliberately plan on being less than you are capable of being, then I warn you that you'll be unhappy for the rest of your life.

—Abraham Maslow

People will exceed targets they set themselves.

—Gordon Dryden

It is a paradoxical but profoundly true and important principle of life that the most likely way to reach a goal is to be aiming not at that goal itself but at some more ambitious goal beyond it.

—Arnold Toynbee

A group of frogs was hopping contentedly through a swamp, doing whatever it is frogs do, when two of them fell into a deep hole. The other frogs gathered around to see what they could do to help their friends. When they saw how deep the hole was, they gave up. They told the two poor frogs in the hole that they should abandon hope and prepare themselves for death.

Unwilling to accept their fate, the two frogs tried with all their might to jump out of the hole. The frogs in the marsh kept calling down to them, insisting that their situation was hopeless, and that the best they could do was to save their energy and wait patiently for death. They did not hesitate to add that the frogs would not be in this unfortunate situation if they had been more careful, and listened to their elders.

But the two frogs continued jumping as high as they could. Gradually, they grew tired. Finally, one of the frogs took heed of his friends' words. Spent and disheartened, he quietly accepted his fate, lay down at the bottom of the hole, and died as the others looked on in grief.

But the other frog was more persistent. He continued to jump with every ounce of energy he had, although his body was wracked with pain. Once again, the crowds of frogs, hanging over the hole, yelled at him to stop this nonsense, accept his fate, and just die. Undaunted, the weary frog jumped harder and harder and— wonder of wonders—finally leapt so high that he got out of the hole. Amazed, the other frogs celebrated his miraculous return to freedom and then, gathering around him asked, "Why did you carry on jumping when we told you to give up?"

The poor frog stared at them in astonishment. "But, my friends," he said, "I am deaf. At that distance I could not read your lips. When I saw you waving and shouting, I thought you were encouraging me *not* to give up. That's why I kept on trying." As this paradoxical tale illustrates, having your team-mates on your side can be very powerful. Their support may stimulate you to perform beyond expectations.

THE VICISSITUDES OF TEAMS

In our global, highly complex world, the heroic leadership figure has increasingly become a relic. Frankly, in spite of their popular positioning as heroic figures, leaders cannot do it all. The 21st century will be the age of teams. The network organizations of tomorrow have very little choice but to accept the demise of the heroic leader. What counts in today's organizational world are lateral communication and a much higher degree of interdependency between the various roles and tasks in organizations. This makes it increasingly difficult for the heroic executive to be the sole gatekeeper of quality decisions.

> "The network organizations of tomorrow have very little choice but to concur in the demise of the heroic leader."

Operating in today's organizations requires leaders with collaborative, problem-solving and influencing skills— executives with emotional intelligence, who have an astute understanding of how to analyze complex processes and grasp the intricacies of the company's value chain; who know how to deal with inefficiencies and recognize interdependencies among other stakeholders in the organization; and who are prepared to acquire the emotional know-how to motivate and empower employees to perform at peak capacity [1–3]. The organizations of tomorrow will need executives who can deal with both the advantages and disadvantages of teamwork, and know how to be effective as a member of a team. As I have said before, today's world of work requires the kind of executive who moves beyond the more cognitive, rational-structural point of view of organizations and pays attention to both the overt and covert forces underlying organizational life.

Over the last ten years, organizations have removed management layers, built networks, increased spans of control, and increasingly relied on cross-functional and virtual teams to improve their decision-making capacity. However, working with highly diversified, virtual teams has created its own challenges. Although diversity has a positive effect on creativity, it also comes at a price. Enabling collaboration in these complex constellations of very diverse people (gender, culture, nationality, age, and functional background) necessitates serious emotional and cognitive investment up front to prevent paranoid processes (and other forms of dysfunctional behavior patterns) from getting the upper hand. When this kind of behavior comes to the fore, regressive team dynamics will take over, contributing to toxic organizational cultures and neurotic organizations. Sadly enough, when such dysfunctional patterns prevail, they will eventually destroy organizations [4, 5].

The extensive changes that are taking place in the world of work put executives under enormous pressure. And although these changes, whether large- or small-scale, can be regarded negatively (because they can bring negative reactions to stress, such as distress, trepidation, apprehensiveness, fear, anxiety), they can also open up new opportunities for growth, development, and creativity. Macro changes can lead to organizational rejuvenation; meso changes will affect the performance of teams; while changes on an individual, micro level can be starting points to help people reinvent themselves.

	Traditional Teams	**Virtual Teams**
Proximity	proximal	spatially separated
Communication	face-to-face	cyberspace
Task	more general	more specialized
Roles	focused	multiple
Structures & Routines	simple	more complex
Tenure	longer	shorter
Cross-cultural	simple	more complex
Time	discontinuous	continuous
Team development	gradually	greater investment needed up front
Leadership	more directive	self-managing teams

Are you working in a traditional or virtual team? Check the items and find out where you belong.

WHERE LEADERSHIP GROUP COACHING COMES IN

When dysfunctional group dynamics prevail, and executives perform below their capacity, the price can be considerable. This is one of the reasons why leadership coaching has become such a growth industry. Organizations with powerful leadership development practices—that take talent management seriously—consistently produce more desirable long-term results. For these organizations, the statement that "people are our greatest assets" is not merely an empty slogan but an expression of a commitment that is taken seriously. Top management uses leadership coaching as a vehicle to make their executives more effective and to build up strong interactive networks in the organization. With the support of the senior team, leadership coaching can help employees develop the qualities associated with success; coaching interventions can make good people even better.

Leadership coaching is based on the concept that individuals learn most by trying things out in practice—a central theme is learning from experience. (It may also be called executive coaching; both terms refer to the goal of helping individuals improve their performance in their organizational role.) As a catalyst for change, leadership coaching (whether individual or in a group setting) can help organizational participants cope with our changing world.

Leadership coaching is a specific form of intervention that can be carried out strategically with individuals, teams, or an entire organization [6–10]. Its aim is to direct a person or group of people toward a specific, mutually determined goal, accelerating organizational progress by providing focus and awareness. It is about helping the people who are being coached to reach their full

"Leadership coaching is all about helping executives to identify and define their specific goals, then organize themselves to find a way to attain them."

potential, assisting them in actualizing their strengths and minimizing their weaknesses.

Leadership coaching is all about helping executives to define their specific goals, and then organize themselves to find a way to attain them. Such coaching draws on the clients' inner knowledge, resources and ingenuity to help them become more effective. It creates impact by building executives' personal skills, finding better ways to communicate, and sculpting leadership style, decision-making skills, and problem solving. Effective leadership coaches also help executives develop cognitive agility, emotional intelligence capacities, motivation, skills, knowledge, and expertise. They assist executives in refining their goals and strategies, challenging and reassessing their assumptions, and refining and improving their leadership style. Furthermore, effective leadership coaches also encourage executives to be more effective team managers. They learn to become better at constructive conflict resolution, and at creating commitments and accountability for their people, thus contributing to better results [11].

Notwithstanding its increasing popularity, there is considerable confusion about what leadership coaching really is. Under the leadership coaching umbrella, we hear about performance or skills coaching, career coaching, behavioral, life, and strategic coaching, and there are distinctions to be drawn between all of them. Performance coaching includes how-to techniques, skill development, and attaining stretch goals [12]. Career coaching, unsurprisingly, is oriented toward an individual's career concerns, with the coach eliciting and using feedback as part of a discussion of career options. On a higher plane, behavioral coaching is concerned with emotional intelligence and developing a more effective leadership style. Life coaching concentrates on personal growth and career development, and the focus of strategic coaching is introducing new change initiatives. The transition from one form of coaching to another can be relatively fluid, however, and for a major organizational change effort, all these various forms of coaching can be used at once. These distinctions are not merely notional; however, I should point out that I am not even taking into consideration the (often subtle) differences between what is meant by coaching, mentoring, process consultation, counseling, and short-term psychotherapy.

What kind of coaching should you choose?
Study the following statements and label them TRUE or FALSE

                                                              TRUE   FALSE

1. I need to enhance my performance at
   work and to increase my effectiveness
   and productivity.
2. I need greater clarity about my future
   career prospects.
3. I need to develop my emotional
   intelligence and a more effective
   leadership style.
4. I need to make some significant
   changes in my life.
5. I need to be more effective strategically
   to introduce new change initiatives in
   the organization.
   1 Performance/skills coaching
   2 Career coaching
   3 Behavioral coaching
   4 Life coaching
   5 Strategic change coaching

Delivery of coaching presents further variations. Organizations may employ internal or external coaches, or a combination of both. Internal coaches are regular employees of the organization, while external coaches are contracted in from outside. Although internal coaches will be more familiar with the ins-and-outs of the organization, the notion of confidentiality frequently becomes troubling for their clients. To what extent will the information provided to the coach remain confidential? Will it be passed on to other people in the organization? Will the HR department keep a dossier? Clearly, for coaching to be most effective, there must be absolute trust between the parties involved. Effective coaching needs a safe space—that is, clients must feel certain that their exchanges with the coach will remain confidential and will not affect their employment or status within the organization. A permanent preoccupation with internal coaches is whether they will be able to set and maintain "Chinese walls." Of course, this issue is less critical when external coaches are used.

"For coaching to be most effective, there must be absolute trust between the parties involved."

Leadership coaches question and challenge their clients in order to help them modify their behavior; they encourage executives to be more open to change; they help executives gain confidence and validation; they foster entrepreneurship, team behavior, accountability, and commitment; they help executives deal with the everyday dilemmas and paradoxes of their work; and they help them become more responsible corporate citizens. Given all these developmental factors, coaching can make a serious contribution to the bottom line.

Most important, however, is helping executives tune in to their emotional intelligence, have a better understanding of their own strengths and weaknesses, and be more aware of the impact they have on others. This self-knowledge will help them monitor their own performance, give feedback, improve their ability to resolve conflicts, become better communicators, and be more effective decision makers. Coaching is about helping their clients fulfill their full potential, truly know themselves and, within this knowledge, feel comfortable with who and what they are, thus being more authentic.

A further function of leadership coaches is to help executives understand (in the age of the broken psychological contract between employer and employee) that career development is an individual responsibility and that lifelong learning is a central theme. Organizations may provide opportunities to grow and learn, but career management is an increasingly personal responsibility. Executives have to own their own life, not wait for their organization to take responsibility for them. People who do not continue to learn will lose ground.

Unfortunately, in far too many organizations, leaders expend a lot of time, energy, and frustration on common resource drains and organizational inefficiencies—high staff turnover, troublesome employees, low productivity, lack of innovativeness, poor or mediocre customer service, failed change efforts, conflict between teams, turf fights, lack of cooperation among employees, job overload, role conflict, high stress, low morale, and numerous other dysfunctional factors [13]. However, change agents like leadership coaches can help leaders to stay focused on what is essential to the success of the organization.

Leadership coaching also provides a sort of non-intrusive guidance for long-term developmental needs. Astute interventions made at the right time may prevent executives or new leaders derailing from their career and minimize the difficulties involved in "on-boarding"—taking on a new executive position. Although coaching will not necessarily eliminate failure, it may speed up the time to success. The reduction of development time may contribute added value, especially if it prevents an organization taking the wrong course.

However, there are situations where coaching is an uphill struggle. In organizations characterized by mistrust, fear, and a culture of blame; in companies with extremely short-term reward structures; and in organizations where people are viewed as disposable goods, coaching efforts yield poor returns. Neurotic organizations are not the most fertile terrains in which to operate [14].

Attempting to change such organizations is an enormous challenge; in most cases the chances of failure are high. On the other hand, when leadership coaching is a well-functioning element of an organization's leadership development portfolio, the visible business outcomes are long-term improvements, measured by profit or cost-containment, or both. At its best, leadership coaching can be an ongoing professional relationship that helps people produce extraordinary results in their lives, careers, and organizations. When executives improve their performance by finding more creative ways to deal with their work environment, social network contagion processes act as catalysts to spread the benefits throughout the organization. Exposing senior executives to coaching (as I do in my executive programs or consulting assignments described earlier) helps disseminate a coaching culture within the workplace. Other people in the organization in turn will follow their example [15–18].

It should also be emphasized that leadership coaching is not about identifying "what's wrong"; it is about how to make effective executives even better. Instead of zooming in on dysfunctionality, a more constructive approach is to focus on creative solutions and moving forward—assessing where people are now and where they want to be. Effective coaches go to great lengths to emphasize and develop the unique potential of the people they work with, maximizing their performance. The challenge for leadership coaches is to arrive at a systematic approach to bring about real change by providing structures for goal setting, standards of accountability, and a big-picture focus while giving honest feedback.

"Leadership coaching is not about identifying "what's wrong"; it is about how to make effective executives even better."

While we consider exactly what leadership coaching is, it is important to understand what it is not. In a growing field, offering diverse options, this can be confusing. At times, coaching can look like career counseling, consulting, mentoring, or training—but it is none of these things. Coaches do not necessarily provide answers, although they may make (rare) suggestions. Essentially, coaches ask questions—their skill lies in asking the right ones, open-ended and intriguing, that will help people think and encourage them to come up with their own ideas and answers.

Leadership coaching is more an art of discovery than a technology of delivery. Coaching, by its nature, has a Socratic quality—that is, it involves asking a series of questions about a central issue, and trying to find satisfactory answers through these exchanges. The use of questions and conversation implies that a leadership coach begins from a position of humility and curiosity, not one of authority and knowledge. Leadership coaches need to remind themselves that they are guides, not drill sergeants, and catalysts in the client's journey of self-discovery. Applying this Socratic method, clients set better goals, take more effective action, make better decisions, run better teams, have a more holistic view of their organization, and use their natural gifts and talents more fully.

"Leadership coaches are guides, not drill sergeants, catalysts in the client's journey of self-discovery."

If this process of inquiry is going to be effective, it is important for the coach to take the expertise of the client for granted. The inquiry model is built on a belief that real growth comes from within the other. Using this method, leadership coaches as change agents need to act like mirrors; they help people work out what they want, what they are good at, what they are not so good at, and where and how they can improve. Effective leadership coaches are masters in the art of cognitive and emotional reframing. Furthermore, they provide their clients with a safe transitional space, where they can experiment with fresh perspectives and action plans [19]. They know how to effect transformational change by creating this transitional space for participants, creating enough interpersonal trust to enable them to deal with "undiscussables," the elephants in the room. Facing "undiscussables" usually opens the way for new, highly productive discussions, and unblocks the change and decision-making process.

TEAM COACHING: MULTIPLYING THE POWER OF INDIVIDUALS

As I suggested in the previous chapters, I (like many others) have experienced team or group coaching as a great way to create high performance teams and better organizations. This intervention technique has proven to be a highly effective way of obtaining more systemic insights into the functionality and dysfunctionality of a team and an organization.

But this change technology has a number of additional advantages. One obvious benefit of the group coaching intervention technique is the economies of scale, leveraging time and resources, of bringing a group of people together. This is more efficient than a one-on-one approach. What's more, team coaching can contribute to a deepened understanding of different areas of the business through the sharing of experiences. Discussing different areas of the company is conducive to greater awareness of how to resolve shared problems; when held among the members of the top executive group, such discussions will make buy-in more likely. It breaks the silos that can create so much dysfunctionality in organizations. In addition, team coaching fosters synergy—an elusive entity in many organizations. Real knowledge management is another beneficiary of this intervention technique. People will not share knowledge when they do not trust each other. As trust is a critical dimension in the group coaching intervention technique, it will be more likely that such exchanges will occur.

As we saw in the vignette presented in Chapter 2, team coaching also helps the participants in the process to acquire a sense of belonging, or community, which provides a diverse and stimulating environment in which to grow and learn. It builds supportiveness and interdependence; sharpens empathic skills; provides affirmations of individuality; develops an appreciation that everyone has unique and special characteristics and abilities; provides peer models; provides opportunities to put themselves in other people's shoes; develops respect and sensitivity for others' quirks and limitations; teaches collaborative problem-solving skills; and provides teamwork skills. Team coaching is a prescription for social network contagion and other processes to induce change.

As I will describe in the following chapters, teams also exist as entities beyond the individuals who comprise them. Together, members of a team feel, think, and act differently than they would as individuals. This group-as-a-whole dynamic—this "cloud" experience—can be extremely powerful. At times, the reassurance of belonging to a group produces dramatic behavior. The intense uniformity of feelings can be overwhelming; people may be emotionally swept away by the intensity of the process, creating a synergy of energy, commitment, and excitement. Encouraged by the group coach, team members learn from both their own and others' experiences—vicarious learning is a great way to obtain insight into our own behavior.

The group coaching intervention technique also creates an opportunity to be coached while benefiting from the successes and challenges of other team members. It provides opportunities to discover similarities and differences, as individual team members see themselves reflected in others. The team becomes like a hall of mirrors in which members see how others engage in self-defeating behavior, and begin to explore the extent to which they are similarly engaged. This leads to an increased sense of self-mastery and the development of more effective leadership skills, as each team member supports and coaches the others. Moreover, although individual members of the team often know what they need to work on, discussion provides greater clarity and may create the kind of momentum that makes change inevitable. However, the scalability of the process is its most important characteristic, making transformational change in organizations more likely.

There are other advantages to group coaching. Frequently, the members of senior leadership teams do not have a forum to talk about the challenges they face, and how they feel about them. A difficulty common to most teams (given the usual competitiveness of team members) is establishing a climate that encourages enough transparency and security to enable joint work. The group coaching intervention technique diminishes this kind of anxiety.

Group coaching expedites the process of getting a working team to the stage of productivity. On the other hand, group coaching a team can, exceptionally, reveal that some people cannot work together, help the group to accept the consequences and reconsider who should be included in their team, instead of letting a difficult and counter-productive situation fester on interminably. As people become used to group coaching, they become "experts" themselves, able to discuss overt and covert conflicts openly, in a manner requiring implicit and explicit mutual responsibility. They are able to put together effective teams on their own without the further intervention of a group coach.

The capacity to build effective teams rapidly gives an organization an enormous competitive advantage. When a team operates at full capacity, all members pull their weight and are accountable for their contribution to the team performance. Team coaching is also highly recommended for teams going through the kind of significant change effort that usually creates conflict—the on-boarding of a new CEO for example. It is also ideal for newly created teams that want to get off to a flying start.

THE HOLISTIC PICTURE: MICRO, MESO, AND MACRO

Coaching can be a powerful way to shift change behavior, increase engagement, enhance thinking and generally make a difference to the way people do business. At a micro level, leadership coaching can contribute to greater satisfaction at work and at home; it may even result in lower stress levels, less frustration, and increased self-esteem [20–22]. Congruence between public and private life can help executives acquire a greater sense of authenticity when dealing with their constituency, contributing to the creation of better places to work. From this perspective, effective leadership coaching can be viewed as an ongoing partnership that helps clients produce fulfiling results in both their personal and professional lives.

At the meso (or team) and macro (or organizational) levels, however, leadership coaching may help transform an organization's culture, preferred leadership styles, and patterns of decision making. At a meso level, special attention will be paid to team dynamics. From a systemic point of view, if leadership coaching is to work, attention must be paid to an organization's team development and corporate culture [23, 24]. At the macro level, leadership coaches working in organizations can have significant impact if they learn how to use salient aspects of organizational culture to nurture creativity, productivity, innovation, and human motivation. A company culture that welcomes communication and rewards creativity, builds long-term client relationships, and fosters sound leadership practices, knows how to differentiate itself from its competitors and conveys a unique identity to its various constituencies.

CREATING A COACHING CULTURE IN ORGANIZATIONS

Understanding the role that culture plays in defining the opportunities available to an organization is like receiving the proverbial keys to the kingdom. Effective leadership coaching can shift organizational culture and influence behaviors, so that it reflects an inclusive environment that respects a diversity of thought, personalities, lifestyle, and ethnicity. People who are familiar with the vicissitudes of cultural change, and who conduct cultural audits through surveys, interviews, and/or focus group methods, will know how to establish a base for cultural transformation. Drawing on the data they acquire, they can ask questions that will encourage the organization's leadership to identify and articulate the salient elements of an organization's culture to engage in appropriate change programs.

A coaching culture provides the stability and protocol for all interactions within the group. It serves as a mechanism that defines the acceptable parameters of behavior (what we do or say) and the desired activities that reinforce the espoused values of the organization. Such a culture will have the type of environment in which continuous learning, the exchange of explicit and tacit knowledge, peer coaching, and self-development are actively encouraged and facilitated. These organizations will have a strong corporate identity; their employees are committed to and proud of the organization. They have a strong sense of ownership. All organizational participants understand the goals of the organization, and the personal contributions needed to achieve them. They have all learned to value feedback and to use it effectively; they build high performance teams with strong motivation and a love of learning. They know the value of courageous conversations; they do not let difficult issues fester.

From my own research experience and that of others, organizations that have developed a coaching culture report significantly reduced staff turnover, increased productivity, and greater happiness and satisfaction at work. In such companies, the organizational participants benefit from more open communication, a more compassionate attitude, less stress, more interest in their talent development, and a greater sense of well-being. Listening, inquiry, and exploration skills are ingrained in the organization's culture. A coaching culture also contributes to a sense of mutual ownership, better networking, more effective leadership practices, and higher commitment, creating better results across the organization. In organizations with a coaching culture people are continually discovering how they create their own reality—and how they can change it [25–27].

Implementing a coaching culture requires a multitude of interventions. The challenge is to retain the organization's competitive advantage. Many questions need to be answered, however. If we create a coaching culture, how different can we be from our competitors? If we make these changes, will we continue to serve the needs of our clients? Do members of the organization have what it takes to see these changes through? Are they resilient enough to hang in there during the change process? The answers to these questions will depend on the organization's leadership, the kind of people the organization attracts, and the context within which it operates.

> "In organizations with a coaching culture people are continually discovering how they create their own reality—and how they can change it."

What is a coaching culture?

Do people in your organization have:

- relationships of interpersonal trust, self-disclosure, and openness?
- a focus on self-awareness and personal development (prepared to assess their strengths and weaknesses)?
- a preparedness to have courageous conversations?
- a willingness to give clear and constructive feedback?

If you answer YES to these four questions, your organization is well on the way to having a coaching culture.

A multi-pronged approach, using a number of different change interventions simultaneously, will be needed to effect real and sustainable change. The organization's leadership must be committed to the long haul, and not get cold feet when there are setbacks. The support of a leadership coach who knows how to operate at micro, meso, and macro levels (particularly one experienced in organizational change and transformation) can contribute dramatically to the success of a cultural change and transition effort.

I should add, as a caveat, that a coaching culture alone will not be enough to drive change, improve performance, increase job satisfaction, and lift the level of commitment of an organization. It should be used in conjunction with a viable business strategy. A mere focus on a "coaching culture" as a means of change runs the risk of losing sight of the end. Commitment and engagement with coaching work best in a dual context. Enhancing leadership coaching skills should always be done in the context of the business. Coaching should always be part of the process of making work more effective. In other words, coaching should not be yet another item to add to the to-do list; it should be seen as a way of reducing each individual's workload, of becoming more effective. Context allows executives to perceive coaching both as a support and a solution—not just the latest human resources fad.

Change agents, like coaches, at times need to take on the role of the wise fool [28, 29]. Fools have existed in all world cultures throughout history. Leaders in all organizations need someone like the wise fool who is willing to speak out and tell them how things really stand. All too frequently, the emperors of the organizational world (like the one in Hans Christian Andersen's fairy tale) are walking around naked. Top executives rarely receive the unvarnished truth and most organizational cultures don't encourage telling it how it is. Blind spots in leaders' thinking keep them from receiving critical information. This lack of truth-telling may create a cycle of arrogance that feeds on itself. Narcissism may flourish.

The "sage-fool," however, can be a countervailing power against the regressive forces inherent in leadership, challenging the status quo, illuminating blind spots, and reinforcing a senior executive's capacity for reality testing. They can take on the role of "insultant." A change agent like a coach will be an important asset if an organization is seeking continuous improvement.

"All too frequently, the emperors of the organizational world are walking around naked."

Having made these comments, let me end this chapter with a short story told to me once by one of my student coaches, who had been concerned about one of her clients, a hard-working, creative man whom she had helped in his career. When she met him the first time during a team coaching session, she had been impressed by his selflessness, and his willingness to help the other members of the team. His talents had taken him to the top of the organization and it had been a long time since they last met. As she was one of the presenters at a conference in the town where her former client's company had its head office, she had contacted him, telling him that it would be nice to meet once more. He had been very pleased for them to meet—but for her, the meeting was a disappointment.

Her former client had picked her up from her hotel. The conversation had stumbled along as he showed her some of the sights of the city. He had asked her opinion of his sports car; during the conversation he had done a fair amount of name-dropping, mentioning all the important people he knew; he also wanted to show her his private airplane. She remembered that even before his success as an executive, he used to be very socially attuned—status had been important to him—but now he seemed to care only about the luxuries the world was offering him. Upon returning to the hotel, she invited her ex-client for a drink in the lounge.

As he got up to leave, she asked him to look out the window: "What do you see?" "I see lots of people minding their own business," was his answer. "Now, please look in this mirror," said the coach, showing him the mirror hanging over the fireplace in the lounge. "What do you see now?" His ex-client looked, and smiled at what he saw. "I see myself."

"You know," the coach said, "the difference between plain glass and a mirror is the reflective layer of silver on the back. Sometimes when we add a little silver, all we can see is ourselves." She hoped by her comment to remind him of his more altruistic side, which seemed to have been lost over the years, but also, more importantly, of the humility and emotion he had felt, and expressed gratitude for, when his peers had given him honest feedback about his leadership style in their earlier group coaching session. She hoped to remind him that the opinion of others is often less warped, and can therefore be more valuable, than one's own self-image.

REFERENCES

1. Kets de Vries, M. F. R. (2001b). *The Leadership Mystique*. London: FT Prentice-Hall.
2. Kets de Vries, M. F. R. (2006a). *The Leader on the Couch: A Clinical Approach to Changing People and Organizations*. New York: Wiley.
3. Kets de Vries, M. F. R. and Korotov, K. (2007). "Creating Transformational Executive Education Programs." *Academy of Management Learning & Education*, 6 (3), 375–387.
4. Kets de Vries, M. F. R. and Miller, D. (1984). *The Neurotic Organization*. San Francisco, CA: Jossey-Bass.
5. Kets de Vries, M. F. R. and Miller, D. (1987). *Unstable at the Top*. New York: New American Library.
6. Flaherty, J. (2005). *Coaching: Evoking Excellence in Others*. Burlington, MA: Elsevier Butterworth-Heinemann.
7. Kets de Vries, M. F. R. (2005a). "Leadership Group Coaching in Action: The Zen of Creating High Performance Teams." *The Academy of Management Executive*, 19 (1), 61–76.
8. Kets de Vries, M. F. R., Korotov, K., and Florent-Treacy, E. (2007). *Coach and Couch: The Psychology of Making Better Leaders*. New York: Palgrave/Macmillan.

9. Kilberg, R. R. (2000). *Executive Coaching.* Washington, DC: American Psychological Association.
10. Palmer, S. and Whybrow, A. (2007). *Handbook of Coaching Psychology: A Guide for Practitioners.* London: Routledge.
11. Ibid.
12. Kilberg, R. R. (2000). *Executive Coaching.* Washington, DC: American Psychological Association.
13. Kets de Vries, M. F. R. and Miller, D. (1984). *The Neurotic Organization.* San Francisco, CA: Jossey-Bass.
14. Ibid.
15. Grant, A. M. and Stober, D. R. (2006). *Evidence-Based Coaching Handbook.* London: John Wiley & Sons Ltd.
16. Hunt, J. M. and Weintraub, J. R. (2002). *The Coaching Manager.* London: Sage Publications.
17. Pederson, D. B. and Hicks, M. D. (1995). *The Leader as Coach: Strategies for Coaching and Developing Others.* Minneapolis, MN: Personnel Decisions.
18. Whitmore, J. (2002). *Coaching for Performance: Growing People, Performance and Purpose.* London: Nicholas Brealey Publishing.
19. Winnicott, D. W. (1951). *Transitional Objects and Transitional Phenomena. Collected Papers: Through Paediatrics to Psycho-analysis.* London: Tavistock Publications.
20. Flaherty, J. (2005). *Coaching: Evoking Excellence in Others.* Burlington, MA: Elsevier Butterworth-Heinemann.
21. Hudson, F. M. (1999). *The Handbook of Coaching: A Comprehensive Resource Guide for Managers, Executives, Consultants, and Human Resource Professionals.* San Francisco, CA: Jossey-Bass.
22. Hunt, J. M. and Weintraub, J. R. (2002). *The Coaching Manager.* London: Sage Publications.
23. Schein, E. H. (1985). *Organizational Culture and Leadership.* San Francisco, CA: Jossey-Bass.
24. Schein, E. H. (1992). *Organizational Culture and Leadership.* San Francisco, CA: Jossey-Bass.
25. Hudson, F. M. (1999). *The Handbook of Coaching: A Comprehensive Resource Guide for Managers, Executives, Consultants, and Human Resource Professionals.* San Francisco, CA: Jossey-Bass.
26. The Executive Coaching Forum. (2004). *The Executive Coaching Handbook: Principles and Guidelines for a Successful Coaching Partnership.* Available online as at 17 May 2011: www.executivecoachingforum.com.

27. Hunt, J. M. and Weintraub, J. R. (2006). *The Coaching Organization: A Strategy for Developing Leaders*. New York: Sage.

28. Kets De Vries, M. F. R. (1990). "The Organizational Fool: Balancing a Leader's Hubris," *Human Relations*, 43 (8), 751–770.

29. Kets de Vries, M. F. R. (1993). *Leaders, Fools and Impostors: Essays on the Psychology of Leadership*. San Francisco: Jossey-Bass.

PART TWO

A PSYCHODYNAMIC PERSPECTIVE ON INDIVIDUALS AND GROUPS

CHAPTER 4

UNDERSTANDING INDIVIDUALS IN GROUPS

Every extension of knowledge arises from making the conscious the unconscious.

—Friedrich Nietzsche

Analysis does not set out to make pathological reactions impossible, but to give the patient's ego freedom to decide one way or another.

—Sigmund Freud

Everything that irritates us about others can lead us to an understanding of ourselves.

—Carl Jung

Man lives consciously for himself, but is an unconscious instrument in the attainment of the historic, universal, aims of humanity.

—Leo Tolstoy

There was once a small boy who banged a drum all day and loved every moment of it. He refused to stop banging, no matter what anyone said or did. His distracted neighbors consulted a series of so-called wise women and asked them to do something about the child. The first wise woman told the boy that if he continued to make so much noise he would perforate his eardrums; but her reasoning was too advanced for the child, who was neither a scientist nor very bright. The second wise woman told him that drum beating was a sacred act and should be carried out only on special occasions. The child continued to drum happily. The third found a simple solution, and offered the neighbors plugs for their ears. The fourth gave the boy a book so he could focus his energy on other things. But obviously, books were of little interest to him. The fifth gave the neighbors books on anger management. The sixth gave the boy meditation exercises to make him placid and explained that all reality was imagination. Like all placebos, some of these remedies worked for a short while, but none worked for very long.

Eventually, a truly wise woman came along. Handing the boy a hammer and chisel, she asked, "I wonder what is *inside* that drum?"

This story strikes me as highly appropriate to executive coaches: I have always maintained that, as coaches, we should work not only from the outside in, but also from the inside out. Coaching can be generalized as a method of helping a person or group of people, with the aim of achieving some specific goal or developing specific skills. But all coaches need to go beyond quick-fix approaches, and deal with the real underlying issues that can hamper organizational processes.

"Coaches should work not only from the outside in, but also from the inside out."

The call for more lasting, durable change as an outcome of coaching is the reason why much of my work in organizations is grounded in the clinical paradigm. I view the clinical paradigm as a very effective toolkit for an organizational coach. The term *clinical* technically means "by the bedside." In the context of the work I do, I use the term *clinical* to show that I (and people of a similar orientation to organizational change) work very closely with clients, taking their own lives and experiences as important sources of learning and development, rather than simply applying one-size-fits-all, ivory tower theorizing. I try to get the best out of different schools of psychology (and fortunately, many schools of psychotherapy seem to be converging) and I must admit, given my psychoanalytic training, that I am somewhat biased toward a psychodynamic point of view. Currently, most schools of psychotherapy, whatever their persuasion, increasingly pay attention to their clients' emotional life; they recognize that much of our behavior is beyond our conscious awareness. They also realize that the working alliance between therapist and client is what makes all the difference [1]. Therefore, I emphasize that an in-depth exploration of the self in relationship to the other can help people better understand their conscious and unconscious mental life. As the philosopher Kierkegaard observed, "Life can only be understood backwards; but it must be lived forwards." In my work, I try to encourage people to loosen their bonds with the past and help them see new possibilities in the future.

The clinical paradigm greatly increases effectiveness in individual and organizational analysis. Whether the coach is working with an individual or with groups, coaching that takes a psychodynamic approach brings a more holistic, systemic orientation—paying attention to the micro, meso, and macro processes I described in the previous chapter—which we can visualize as interwoven individual, group, and organizational interactions.

THE CLINICAL PARADIGM EXPLAINED

Applying the clinical paradigm can be described metaphorically as a way of exploring an individual's inner theater. Behind the curtain of

"Behind the curtain of our inner theater, a rich tragi-comedy plays out on our inner stage, with key actors representing the people we have loved, hated, feared, and admired throughout our lives."

our inner theater, a rich tragi-comedy plays itself out on the stage, with key actors representing the people we have loved, hated, feared, and admired throughout our lives. Some evoke painful memories; others fill us with a sense of well-being. These internal figures had a strong influence on the development of our values, beliefs, and attitudes, which lay the foundation of our personality, patterns of behavior, preferred leadership styles, and courses of action. Of course, what we see most prominently are the actions that result from these underlying influences.

If we want a better understanding of ourselves (and this advice goes for change agents such as coaches as well as their clients), we need to explore these themes in our inner theater and pay attention to our wishes, desires, and fantasies. We need to identify recurring themes, patterns, or schemata and explore repetitive attempts to avoid distressing thoughts and feelings. Specifically, we need to pay attention to our interpersonal bonds as our early life experiences may be re-enacted over and over again in our current relationships, in the form of transference or counter-transference reactions—inappropriate (but interesting) repetitions of relationships that were once important in our past (with a parent or sibling, for example), but are now unconsciously redirected and acted out in the present [2, 3].

These unconscious forces affect not only the way we love, choose our friends, or express ourselves, but also influence patterns of relationships with bosses, colleagues, and subordinates. Transference reactions permeate all our life experiences. Like a movie projectionist screening a film, we project these early experiences on others and these projections affect the way we make decisions, our preferred leadership style, the way we communicate, and the degree to which we (like Schopenhauer's hedgehogs) are able to work together closely in teams. In the context of leadership development, if we want to help people change their actions or behaviors—and not just engage in patchwork—we need to take these deeper layers into consideration.

The premises of the clinical paradigm

The clinical paradigm, therefore, is an orientation that helps us examine and reflect on our own behavior and enables us to change some elements of it. It consists of a number of premises:

- *Rationality is an illusion*
  Irrationality is grounded in rationality. Irrational behavior is a common pattern in our lives, although in fact it will always have a rationale, or meaning, to it. Nothing that we do is random. Elements of psychic determinism are a fact of life. Understanding this rationale is critical to making sense of our own and other people's inner theater—the core themes that affect personality, behavior, and leadership style.
- *What we see isn't necessarily what we get*
  Much of what happens to us is beyond our conscious awareness. Most of our behavior is driven by unconscious forces. To have a better understanding of these unconscious patterns we need to explore our own and other people's inner desires, wishes, and fantasies; we need to pay attention to the repetitive themes and patterns in our lives, and in the lives of others.
- *The past is the lens through which we can understand the present and shape the future*
  All of us are the product of our past. Like it or not, there's a continuity between past and present. We are inclined to view the present through the microscope of past experiences. Our personality structure is due to our genetic endowment and the developmental outcome of our early environment. To make

sense of our behavior, we must explore our interpersonal history, including our original attachment relationships.

- *The significance of transference and counter-transference relationships*
  Because of the heavy imprinting that takes place in the earlier stages of life, we tend to repeat certain behavior patterns. To make sense of what makes us behave the way we do, we need to explore our interpersonal relationships. Adaptive and non-adaptive aspects of our operational mode will be affected by how our original attachment relationships—the relationships with our first caregivers—have evolved. As there will be repetitive themes in the lives of ourselves and others, these themes will be re-activated in the relationships we have with the people we deal with in the present. To understand our and others' behavior we need to identify these recurrent themes and patterns. These problematic relationship patterns (transference and counter-transference reactions) provide a great opportunity to explore and work through difficult issues in the here-and-now. Exploring the relationships between past and present enables us to be liberated from ingrained, automatic behavior.

- *Nothing is more central to who we are than the way we express and regulate our emotions*
  Intellectual insight is not the same as emotional insight, which touches us at a much deeper level. Emotions play a vital role in shaping who we are and what we do. Nothing is more central to who we are than the way we express and regulate emotions.

- *We all have blind spots*
  There are many things we don't want to know about ourselves. We all have our shadow side. We use defensive processes and resistances to avoid problematic aspects of our experiences. Many people derail due to the blind spots in their personality. Exploring the avoidance of distressing thoughts and feelings gives us another snapshot of our own personality and that of

others. These resistances come to the fore because of conflicts within ourselves; we need to accept that inner dissonance is part of the human condition.

• *Motivational need systems determine our personality*
The motivational need systems that represent the interface of nature and nurture create the tightly interlocked triangle of our mental life (the three points of which are cognition, affect, and behavior). There are five basic motivational need systems, three of which impact the workplace only peripherally. The first encompasses our physiological requirements, such as food, drink, elimination of waste, sleep, and breathing; the second our need for sensual enjoyment and (later) sexual excitement; the third our need to respond aversively to certain situations through antagonism and withdrawal. In addition to these, there are two systems that impact the workplace directly and powerfully: the need for attachment/affiliation and the need for exploration/ assertion. Our essential humanness is found in our need for attachment/affiliation—in seeking relationships with other people, and in striving to be part of something larger. The need for attachment drives the process of engagement with another human being; it's the universal experience of wanting to be close to another, to have the pleasures of sharing and affirmation. When this need for intimate engagement is extrapolated to groups, the desire to be associated with others can be described as a need for affiliation. Both attachment and affiliation play an emotional balancing role by confirming our self-worth and contributing to our sense of self-esteem. The other motivational need system that is crucial for the workplace—the need for exploration/assertion—involves the ability to play, think, learn, and work. Like the need for attachment/affiliation, these needs begin early in life. Playful exploration and manipulation of the environment in response to exploratory-assertive motivation produces a sense of effectiveness, competency, autonomy, initiative, and industry.

What now seem to be psychological difficulties (inappropriate behavior in the workplace, for example) can be more easily understood, and possibly modified, if we see them as being residual effects of adaptive solutions to the problem of living. To illustrate, a story told by an executive from Lebanon is quite illuminating. Comments on his 360-degree feedback report were related to his aggressiveness toward his boss, and his overprotective stance toward his team of employees. He mentioned during his self-portrait presentation that he had grown up in, and later fled, the civil war in his country. Without digging too far into what was clearly a painful topic, the group helped him see the connection between behavior that was necessary for survival as a child in a war-torn city, and appropriate behavior as a leader in a stable organization. The goal of applying the clinical paradigm is to help people to revisit past experiences and to become more aware of their choices and how they behave in the here-and-now. It is essential for healthy functioning that we do not remain strangers to ourselves. We need to free ourselves from the bonds of past experience to be able to explore new challenges in life.

"It is essential for healthy functioning that we do not remain strangers to ourselves."

When using a clinical lens to study the life of people in organizations, remember that:

1. Rationality is an illusion.
2. Much of what happens to us is beyond conscious awareness.
3. The past is the lens through which we can understand the present and shape the future.
4. Nothing is more central to who we are than the way we express and regulate emotions.
5. We all have blind spots.
6. Basic motivational need systems determine our personality.

Applying the clinical paradigm in coaching situations helps to tease out the central interpersonal role in which our clients consciously and unconsciously cast themselves. It also helps us to explore the roles in which other people are positioned in an executive role constellation. This term describes the way the strengths and weaknesses of members of a team can actually be complementary, creating a group that is much more balanced than the sum of its parts would suggest. For example, although a group of techies or creative types might feel more comfortable at first working in teams with people who think the way they do, the goal of the team will probably be better served if there is a mix of personality types and backgrounds [4, 5].

The clinical paradigm also helps us identify self-defeating expectations and negative self-appraisals, as well as outdated perceptions of ourselves. This approach also helps coaches to identify and address attempts at avoidance of distressing thoughts or feelings. What is left out, at times, can be as important as what is left in. In the group coaching story in Chapter 2, it was Jorgen and Maria who pointed out that Robert did not seem to be engaging in the process—he seemed to be avoiding something. Their approaches may have been somewhat maladroit—and too forceful, at times—but the group coach allowed the moment to play out, and all participants gained new insights through the interaction.

When possible, the group coach should try to scrutinize the here-and-now relationship among the group members, and between the group and the coach as the nature of the transference-counter-transference interface is a very important source of information [6]. Coaches are not austere observers positioned on the boundary of the group. They are very much part of the process. Like the projectionist and the screen, the members of the group will project many fantasies onto the coach. Coaches should heed their clients' reactions to them and constantly ask themselves what these reactions mean. For example, it is a telltale sign if a client is hostile, suspicious, feels rejected, or is ingratiating toward the coach. All of these reactions can be taken as signifiers of more generalized behavior patterns that are worth greater exploration.

A CLOSER LOOK AT RELATIONSHIP PATTERNS

Many therapists [7, 8] have stressed the importance of examining the relationships between people and their communication patterns, rather than merely focusing on the private wishes and fantasies of the individual. To the anthropologist Gregory Bateson, communication meant forms and rules of interaction, meaningful words and gestures that involved a sender and a receiver. Communication was to be understood not just from the point of view of the individual but specifically in the context of a relationship between people.

The double bind

Applying these ideas about communication to mental disorders (for example, people with schizophrenia), Bateson and other communication specialists suggested that the problem of psychological disturbances did not merely originate from within the individual patient but also had something to do with the nature of the interaction patterns in the patient's family network. Bateson demonstrated how certain communications patterns embody logical errors that prevent a message from being received correctly—creating what he described as "double binds."

"A double bind is a communicative situation where someone receives conflicting messages, one at a verbal level, one at a more covert level."

A double bind is a communicative situation where someone receives conflicting messages, one at a verbal level, one at a more covert level. The tension created by the simultaneously contradictory demands of this kind of message creates a psychological impasse for the individual. No matter which message is accepted, the response will be construed as incorrect as a choice has to be made between equally unsatisfactory alternatives. The classic example given of a negative double bind is of a mother telling her child that she loves him or her, while at the same time turning away in disgust (there is a contradiction between the words and behavior). Naturally, for any relationship where people are dependent on one another for physical and emotional survival (for example, in families), the effect of paradoxical communications can be devastating. And unfortunately, as I have learned from experience, double-bind communication is all too common in groups.

I was presented with one example during a team coaching session with the executive committee of an IT services company. The group coach had observed repeated situations where the CEO simultaneously praised members of his team while cutting them down. In one incident the CEO complimented the financial officer for successfully avoiding a financial quagmire—his conservative view of the economy had paid off—but at the same time berated him for his lack of creativity in providing the other members of the team with more financial resources to play with. Although the financial officer had not been as commercial as he might have been, his actions had saved the company. While he initially seemed grateful for the compliment from his boss—and started to thank him for it—the second comment made him stiffen up; he no longer knew how to respond or what to do. Seeing his confusion, the CEO asked him if he felt his observation was correct. The financial officer hesitated, and the CEO responded that he should not be so easily discouraged and afraid to express himself; he should loosen up more. This was only one of many instances of double-bind communication by this CEO. It was little wonder that the financial officer remained silent, while the other members of the team behaved as though they were walking on glass.

Let's take a closer look at what was happening here. If the financial officer interprets his CEO's messages correctly, he can only conclude that to remain in his boss's good graces, he must not show gratitude for compliments; yet if he fails to show gratitude (stiffening up and becoming silent) he will lose his boss's affirmation. Whatever he does, he will end up a loser. The great talent of this particular CEO was his apparent ability to drive his subordinates crazy. Later on in the day, when the group had learned more about the CEO's background, I realized that the CEO was repeating patterns he had learned in childhood, from his mother's disturbing habit of expressing her love for him while simultaneously pushing him away.

As this example illustrates, individuals who use disturbing communication patterns cannot be understood without examining the matrix of their earliest relationships. Just as there is no baby without a mother, and no child without a family, there is little in the way of miscommunication that cannot be understood by using a psychodynamic lens.

The double bind describes how families create dysfunctional communication feedback loops, where family members get stuck in vicious circles—themes that are very likely to be repeated in a group setting. Many of these deeply engrained patterns will be re-enacted and dramatized, albeit unconsciously. Instead of family members, team members in organizations become the ones to be victimized. These patterns of interaction may reinforce the ties between team members, albeit in a destructive way. The double bind is a pattern to watch for when coaching groups of natural working teams from the same organization.

As biological evolution is the crucible of social relationships, we need to understand the psychological, evolutionary, and ethological processes that determine the kind of relationships that exist between human beings, how these can be acted out within groups, and how these antecedents affect an individual's ability to manage emotional containment. These early relationships also form the basis of how a person will relate to others. It will color their interactions in group situations.

Attachment behavior

To start at the beginning, it is a biological imperative that, for reasons of survival, the human animal likes to maintain close proximity to its principal attachment figure. The fundamental organizing principle driving and structuring human existence is the need for affiliation.

"The fundamental organizing principle driving and structuring human existence is the need for affiliation."

These attachment needs will continue to manifest themselves throughout our life. The breaking of these bonds may lead to feelings of annihilation, persecution, and loss. However, we need to remember that, like Schopenhauer's hedgehogs, human beings require both attachment to, and separation from, other human bodies, not only to survive but also to regulate the intensity of our interactions. We need to find a satisfactory balance between these two forces to arrive at a psychological equilibrium. Because human infants, like other mammalian babies, cannot feed or protect themselves, they depend on the lengthy care and protection of adults. We are born with instinctive behaviors that help us to survive. Crying, smiling, vocalizing, grasping, and clinging keep us close to our primary caretakers, who protect us from predators, feed and comfort us, and teach us the good and bad things about the environment we live in. Nature equips attachment figures with their own innate and complementary behaviors: soothing, calling, and restraining, for example. They keep infants safe and cement the bond between mother and child. But according to psychiatrist John Bowlby [9], there are individual differences in the way children appraise the accessibility of the attachment figure and how they regulate their own attachment behavior.

The most important tenet of attachment behavior theory propositions is that a young child needs to develop a relationship with at least one primary caregiver to enable normal social and emotional development. Without such a relationship, the child will face permanent psychological and social damage. Depending on these early experiences with caregivers, a system of thoughts, memories, beliefs, expectations, emotions, and behaviors about the self and others gradually emerges, making social behavior possible [10, 11, 12].

Discover your attachment style

Study the following statements and label them TRUE or FALSE

TRUE   FALSE

1. It is relatively easy for me to become emotionally close to others. I am comfortable depending on others and having others depend on me.
2. I want to be emotionally intimate with others, but I often find that others are reluctant to get as close as I would like.
3. I am comfortable without close emotional relationships. It is very important to me to feel independent and self-sufficient, and I prefer not to depend on others or have others depend on me

If you select 1, you may be securely attached. If your answer is 2, you may fall into the anxious attachment group. If your answer is 3, you may be avoidant attached.

The developmental psychologist Mary Ainsworth (building on the concepts developed by Bowlby) introduced the concept of the "secure base" and developed a theory of a number of attachment patterns in infants [13, 14, 15]. These attachment patterns become internalized, and can be observed as the child matures. In the case of separation or the threat of separation from principal attachment figures, different forms of "attachment behavior" will be acted out, indicating which pattern has become internalized. (In adulthood, these attachment patterns will mainly be acted out in partner relationships. Organizational "partnerships", however, will also be affected.) The nature of an individual's attachment relationships will determine whether the outcomes lead to feelings of security or insecurity [16].

For example, consistent, good-enough caregiver responsiveness will be associated with a secure attachment style. Over time, secure children mature into adults who expect their partners to be trustworthy and responsive, reactions that help them perceive themselves as worthy of love. Secure adults find it relatively easy to get close to others and are comfortable depending on others and having others depend on them. They don't often worry about abandonment or others' proximity to them. They tend to have a positive view of life, know how to manage and express their feelings, and have good social skills. Secure adults have a relatively high sense of self-esteem, feel well liked by others, and build relationships relatively easily [17, 18]. They are the hedgehogs that feel the desire to come closer together.

In contrast, the anxious-ambivalent style attachment pattern is a result of inconsistent caregiver responsiveness. People who are anxious or preoccupied with attachment issues tend to have a less positive view of themselves. They often doubt their worth as a partner and blame themselves for their partner's lack of responsiveness. What may have begun as an attempt to hold on to an unreliable caregiver leads to attempts to hold on to others by using strategies that frequently backfire. Anxious/ambivalent adults find that others are reluctant to get as close to them as they would like. Predictably, they often worry that their partner doesn't really love them or won't want to stay with them. Given their level of anxiety, they may want to "merge" completely with another person. Ironically, this desire may scare others away. Furthermore, they may create conflict with people in positions of authority in order to get their attention. They are the hedgehogs that struggle to find the appropriate distance.

Finally, an avoidant style is associated with consistent caregiver unavailability and non-responsiveness. Avoidant people are uncomfortable being close to others; although they may want emotionally close relationships, they find it difficult to trust others completely, or to allow themselves to depend on others. They become nervous at proximity. They are more likely to lack empathy, may even take pleasure in the misery of others, and can be perceived as highly infuriating. These are the hedgehogs that keep their distance, fearful that they may get hurt.

Beyond the dyadic mother-infant or caregiver-infant relationship, the situation becomes more complex as other family members and significant figures enter the frame. The family becomes a matrix that provides the child with crucial meanings for constituting a stable image of the self. The child in turn transforms these meanings into personal interpretations of the world. These interpretations will play a specific role in the development and configuration of the child's (and the later adult's) attachment and relational skills [19].

Our family script, our model of how we relate to each other (shared in family myths, legends, stories, and romances), becomes the script that we use in other inter-relational contexts—like teams. In group or team settings, attachment relationships will be played out in various ways. And because all the scripts in the actors' internal worlds vary, the way they interact and are integrated will determine the dynamics of the group-as-a-whole. The "underworld" where the attachment patterns of the various members interface gives the team interaction its special

"Our family script becomes the script that we use in other inter-relational contexts—like teams."

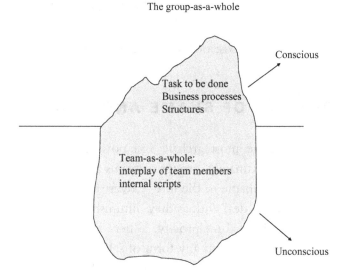

Figure 4.1   The group-as-a-whole

character. This explains why specific themes pop up and are acted out when a group or team is together, and why the sum of the group's collective consciousness is greater than its parts (Figure 4.1).

Attachment behavior counts. This is the crux of Schopenhauer's dramatization of the hedgehogs' dilemma. It's all about our position on the attachment–avoidance axis. Our attachment script affects our emotional management and will determine the roles we play in a group setting.

As this discussion of the psychodynamic approach to group coaching shows, the variety and intensity of group coaching interactions depend greatly on the personal histories of the participants. In a group intervention, it is possible that many key themes in personal scripts may come to the surface for discussion: fantasies of death, illness, and loss of loved ones; intense love and dark aggression; feelings of envy, jealousy, persecution, shame, and guilt. These strong, underlying emotions have a major impact on our inner life, and consequently on our behavior. The emotional nature of these scripts is played out in the degree of closeness a person can tolerate. This is the crux of Schopenhauer's dramatization of the hedgehogs' dilemma. It's all about our position on the attachment-avoidance axis; our attachment script affects our emotional management.

THE DEMONS OF SHAME AND GUILT

Shame is one of the most archaic and powerful of our human emotions and, unfortunately, groups or teams are ideal contexts for bringing feelings of shame to the fore. Covert feelings of shame are a formidable force to deal with as they diminish interpersonal trust, self-disclosure, and social reciprocity. Where there is shame, there is fear and reluctance toward any form of self-exposure. However, it is not necessarily easy to recognize these feelings when they surface: shame comes in many disguises.

Are you haunted by feelings of shame or guilt?
Label the following statements TRUE or FALSE

TRUE   FALSE

- I constantly think about past failures or experiences of rejection.
- I have always had a sense of inferiority.
- I am generally disgusted with myself.
- I have never liked the way I look.
- I am extremely sensitive to criticism.
- When criticized, I tend to blame others.
- I am very anxious in public situations.
- I am considered shy.
- I have always doubted myself.

If most of these statements are TRUE, you are prone to strong feelings of SHAME. You are very critical of yourself. You have a constant fear of rejection.

Shame is the dread of being condemned or thought badly of by other people. It is about feeling like an outsider, about rejection, not belonging, and exclusion. Shame evokes feelings of self-loathing, self-exposure, embarrassment, and extreme vulnerability. Shame makes us feel flawed and unworthy of acceptance.

Shame-prone people are preoccupied with negative aspects of the "self," the total, essential being of what we are. For them, shame becomes an automatic and insidious reaction in all situations ("I'm a horrible person for doing these things"; "It's clear that everybody dislikes me; I know everyone hates me.") This inner voice keeps on condemning, saying, "Something must be wrong with me," "I am inferior to others," "I'm undeserving" [20, 21, 22, 23]. Shame is an attack on ourselves, a personal feeling that can cause embarrassment even when things happen that are beyond our control, such as feeling ashamed of the color of our hair, of not driving the "right" car, or of not being able to afford the most fashionable clothes.

"Shame is an attack on ourselves."

Shame weighs on anyone who is self-conscious about the real or imagined negative judgments of others. Any public situation enhances such feelings—speaking up in a group is a typical example. In fact, anyone who has the attention of others, by definition, will be subject to criticism and judgment, but being in the public eye can make some people even more critical of themselves. As Konrad Adenauer, the German Chancellor, once said, "A thick skin is a gift of God." Working in a team is quite a challenge for shame-prone people.

Shame and a low sense of self-esteem are intimately related, as both are associated with negative perceptions of the self. Such self-conscious feelings can be extremely painful and ugly to deal with so it is little wonder that shame-prone people will do anything in their power to protect themselves by hiding these feelings from others. A common tactic is withdrawal from public settings. Another is lashing out, or making fun of others, as a way of denying similar feelings inside themselves, behavior that can be quite disruptive, particularly in a team context.

This emotional muddle is complicated by other uncomfortable, related feelings, such as fear, anger, vulnerability, neediness, dependency, and sadness. Shame has also been associated with outbursts of anger, aggression (including family violence), depression, substance abuse, eating disorders, and even suicide. Unfortunately, instead of attempting to deal constructively with any one of these other reactions, shame-prone individuals prefer to wallow in self-deprecatory thoughts [24].

As these negative associations indicate, suffering caused by shame will affect our personal well-being. Mounting evidence has demonstrated that this kind of mental stress can even exacerbate cardiac problems and weaken the immune system, suggesting shame can have extremely undesirable effects.

Shame is an inner-directed emotion, whereas guilt is a more outer-directed emotion. Both can have an effect on group dynamics. Although shame is closely related to guilt, there are key qualitative differences. We feel shame about *who we are*, but we feel guilt about *what we have done*. Guilt says, "What I *did* was not good"; shame says, "I *am* no good." Guilt says, "I've *done* something wrong"; shame says, "There is something wrong with *me*." Shame involves the desire to hide something about the self, perceived as "bad," from others, but these feelings are left undisclosed. Guilt, on the other hand, is associated with a desire to apologize, make reparation, and be forgiven for certain things that have been done. As Seneca once said, "Every guilty person is his own hangman." Guilt can be seen as a more moral and adaptive way of handling situations. Actually, experiencing guilt can make us feel virtuous. It motivates us to say, "I'm sorry," or to make amends in another way. The urge to relieve guilt may motivate a confession, but avoiding the humiliation of

"Experiencing guilt can make us feel virtuous."

shame may also prevent it. Thus, at times, shame and guilt may pull us in opposite directions.

Here again, family scripts play a role. Children learn moral emotional styles from their parents or caregivers. From a family-systems perspective, we can even discern inter-generational conti-nuities, in that shame-proneness or guilt-proneness will be acquired through direct modeling and other forms of identification between parent and child. Society in general, through our parents, teachers, religious leaders, friends, or work colleagues, intentionally or unin-tentionally ingrains in us the urge to feel ashamed or guilty for things at an early age.

In a family and cultural setting, repeated humiliation often leads to shame. When children grow up in an environment where they are ridiculed and humiliated and their needs are consistently frustrated, they may well begin to ask, "What is wrong with me that I deserve such treatment?" They will wonder whether they are defective or unworthy of love. This experience is the common relational backdrop for vulnerability and susceptibility to shame. Children who are repeatedly humiliated are likely to act out or shut down. Fearful of negative exposure, they react by humiliating others or becoming unable to function. Later in life, as adults, these feelings will linger on.

Some people come from families that put an unusually heavy burden of responsibility on them when they were young. The down side of this is that throughout life, even a trivial infraction noted by some authority figure (parent, teacher, employer, etc.) may spark a sense of failure, guilt, and diminished self-worth.

It is even possible to distinguish between shame-oriented and guilt-oriented cultures. Societies that rely heavily on public disci-pline and ostracism will instill greater shame in children than those that emphasize private discipline. Many non-Western cultures emphasize an interdependent self, one that is tied to group membership and tends to be more shame prone; while contemporary Western cultures tend to emphasize an independent self, separate from group membership and hence are more prone to feelings of guilt.

Shame and guilt proneness will play a major role in group settings. Depending on their intensity, it may be difficult for some executives to open up. To change this pattern, it is critical to create a safe space. Only when people preoccupied with feelings of shame and guilt feel safe will they be willing to lower their guard and feel free to participate. If such an ambiance of safety is not created, however, whoever is the catalyst in fostering team dynamics may have to deal with serious resistance.

EMOTIONAL CONTAGION

Another important issue in group settings is emotional contagion. Recent research has shown that our moods are far more strongly influenced by the people around us than we might think [25]. All of us, as part of our Paleolithic heritage (where we needed to be on the lookout for predators at all times), have a tendency to converge emotionally. We all seem to be programmed to be receptive to other people's emotions. And we all have a tendency to recognize and feel emotions that are similar to our own.

We can even hypothesize that the urge to mirror others is hardwired into our brain through a neural feedback mechanism, which probably developed because cooperation leads to more food, better health, and economic growth for a community. Like present-day herd animals that benefit from the ability to rapidly disseminate messages about risks and rewards, we automatically mimic and synchronize facial expressions, vocalizations, postures, body language, and other behaviors with those of other people. We also experience the emotions associated with the particular behavior we are mimicking [26, 27, 28, 29, 30, 31, 32].

How susceptible are you to emotional contagion?

- Do you recognize how you automatically mimic and synchronize your facial expressions, vocalizations, postures, and movements with those of other people (yawning, smiling, etc.)?
- Do you realize how quickly you are influenced by other people's mood states?
- Are you (consciously) aware of how swiftly and completely you are able to track the expressive behaviors and emotions of others?
- Do you consciously engage in emotional labor—that is, intentional emotional impression management consistent with organizational or occupational rules (such as smiling, using polite phrases, etc.)?

We use conscious and unconscious means to gain information about others' emotional states. Greater awareness of emotional contagion (including mirroring) helps us obtain invaluable information about what makes other people tick. It will also be very useful for understanding better the behavior and mood states of teams.

Some researchers have argued that the moods of friends of friends, and of friends of friends of friends (people three degrees of separation away from us whom we have never met) can influence us through our social network like a virus. A diverse range of phenomena are transmitted through networks of friends in ways that are not entirely understood: happiness and depression, obesity, drinking and smoking habits, ill-health, the inclination to turn out and vote in elections, a taste for certain music or food, a preference for online privacy, even the tendency to attempt or think about suicide [33]. According to social scientists Nicholas Christakis and James Fowler, these feelings ripple through networks like pebbles thrown into a pond.

"Much of who we are and what we do is determined by forces beyond the little circle we draw around ourselves." From a group dynamics point of view, we should acknowledge the fact that we are inherently social creatures and that much of who we are and what we do is determined by forces beyond the little circle we draw around ourselves. We influence others, and are influenced by them. In group or team situations, such contagious processes can be harmful or advantageous, depending on how they are managed. Knowing what we know about emotional contagion, the challenge is whether, to quote Rudyard Kipling, "you can keep your head when all about you are losing theirs and blaming it on you." Given the contagiousness of moods, this will not be easy. In a team situation, it is often the mood of the leader that sets the tone. If the leader is upbeat, the mood of the other team members will rise. But if he or she is down, everyone is down. And these changes in mood can occur very rapidly.

MIMICRY AND MIRRORING

As well as these rapid mood changes in group situations, there is also a close relationship between social contagion and our talent for mimicry and mirroring. The mirror is often used as a metaphor for the image of ourselves that we obtain from others, both within personal relationships and in society at large. Mirroring is common in social interactions, and awareness of the process is a powerful way to influence other people's behavior. From a clinical point of view, mirroring (like mimicry) refers to the original parent–child relationship, the mirroring responses that influence the development and maintenance of self-esteem [34, 35, 36, 37]. Mirroring seems likely to begin in the womb, when our body functions and heartbeat match the rhythms of our mother's body. These early mirroring processes establish the foundation for later mirroring reactions.

When we say that we "feel right" around another person, we are unwittingly acknowledging mirroring and synchronous behavior. When we meet others for the first time, we assess quickly whether they are positively or negatively inclined toward us, just as most other animals do for survival reasons. We mirror each other's body language and posture as a way of bonding, being accepted and creating rapport, but we are usually oblivious to the fact that we are doing it.

"We mirror each other's body language as a way of bonding but we are usually oblivious to the fact that we are doing it."

The ability to pass on emotions to each other helps us to adapt to social situations, including teams. We have come to recognize that social networks cannot merely be understood in terms of the behavior or psychology of the individuals within them. Networks can also acquire an emotional life of their own. Social network contagion processes, mimicry, and mirroring will (unconsciously) affect how we work as a team.

At first sight, however, the idea that we can catch the moods, habits, and state of health not only of those around us, but also those we do not even know, may seem alarming. It implies that rather than being in charge of where we are going in life, we often seem to be little more than back-seat drivers, since most social influence operates at an unconscious level.

The power of these mirroring processes and social contagion in groups reminds me of a folk tale from India that tells of a flock of birds that was peacefully pecking seeds under a tree. A hunter came along and threw a heavy net over the birds, saying happily, "Aha! Now I have my dinner!"

All at once the birds began to flap their wings. Up, up they rose into the air, taking the net with them. They came down on the tree and, as the net snagged in the tree's branches, the birds flew out from under it to freedom.

The hunter looked on in amazement, scratched his head and muttered, "As long as those birds cooperate with one another like that, I'll never be able to capture them. Each of those birds is so frail and yet together they can lift the net."

As this tale illustrates, an understanding of mirroring and social contagion in teams can be very beneficial if directed wisely. It explains why there is a place for "cloud" comments—why group-as-a-whole phenomena need to be taken into consideration in a group setting. But, as the discussions earlier in this chapter about double-bind communication, attachment, shame, guilt, emotional contagion and mirroring suggest, such comments need to be made with care. It is not easy to create an ambiance in a group coaching setting that allows group members to develop interpersonal trust, reciprocity in self-exposure, and personal risk taking. Making cloud comments may be perceived as threatening by some group members who find such observations bizarre and intrusive. If the members of the group (or team) are not in the right space, cloud comments will not contribute to an attitude of openness and responsiveness vis-à-vis the group process. On the contrary, such a comment may lead to defensive reactions and even withdrawal (emotional or otherwise) from the group. The ability to open oneself up to others and to make personal disclosures, however, is a crucial element in establishing authenticity and credibility. Being prepared to present oneself in an open, honest manner is essential to conveying authenticity to others.

What embarrasses you most?

What is the one thing you would be most disinclined to share with the members of your team?

Our most common secrets are:

- a deep conviction of personal inadequacy—feeling like an impostor
- a deep sense of personal alienation—despite appearances, you really do not, or cannot, care for or love another person as deeply as you pretend to
- a sexual secret.

Generally, all clients in coaching or psychotherapy experience a deep concern about their sense of self-worth and their ability to relate to others.

The essential task of people who want to create more effective team dynamics is to create and facilitate safe spaces in which feelings can be brought into the open in a constructive manner, rather than left stewing under the surface. For example, for change agents like group coaches, the challenge will be to help team members take chances and realize that pushing their emotional life underground can be a very costly strategy. In group (or team) situations, they need to be aware of the power of double-bind communication, attachment behavior patterns, the role of shame and guilt, emotional contagion, mirroring, and mimicry.

In spite of these formidable challenges, and in spite of the risks of opening up emotionally, talking about who we are and how we feel can also be a form of catharsis. Individuals who have been in team building sessions often say they experience a sense of relief, finally to be able to talk about sensitive issues, and to tell their own story. The advantage of such a session is that, through hearing the stories of others, people realize that they are not the only ones with problems or worries. We have all experienced moments when discharging pent-up emotions has been beneficial. The process of self-disclosure can be a form of emotional learning (as opposed to intellectual understanding) that can contribute to immediate and long-lasting change. While the team intervention takes place, the group coach needs to possess some of the qualities of a Zen master, using him- or herself as an instrument, enabling both the experiencing and observing egos to be operational.

To illustrate, a student went to his Zen master and said, "I cannot meditate properly. I feel so distracted. I think about other, more earthly things. My legs ache. I'm constantly falling asleep. It's terrible."

The Zen master looked at him, and said matter-of-factly, "It will pass."

A week later, the student came back to his teacher and said: "My meditation is wonderful. I feel so aware, so peaceful, so alive!"

"It will pass," was the response of the Zen master.

This Zen master stands above emotional contagion. He knows that everything is transitory. He has concluded that there is an emotional, cyclic nature to life. As this vignette illustrates, the challenge is not to become caught up in emotional waves. As change agents, we need to realize that our emotional responses take place within a bigger context. We need to have the ability to both experience and to observe. We also need to have the understanding that our emotional responses inevitably follow one another. Life has its own cycles.

REFERENCES

1. Martin D. J., Garske J. P., and Davis M. K. (2000). "Relation of the Therapeutic Alliance with Outcome and Other Variables: A Meta-Analytic Review." *Journal of Consulting and Clinical Psychology*, 68: 438–450.
2. Eagle, M. N. (2000). "A Critical Evaluation of Current Conceptions of Transference and Countertransference." *Psychoanalytic Psychology*, 17 (1), 24–37.
3. Etchegoyen, H. (2005). *The Fundamentals of Psychoanalytic Technique*. London: Karnac Books.
4. Hodgson, R. C., Levinson, D. J., and Zaleznik, A. (1965). *The Executive Role Constellation: An Analysis of Personality and Role Relations in Management*. Boston, MA: Harvard Business School Press.
5. Kets de Vries, M. F. R. (2007). "Decoding the Team Conundrum: The Eight Roles Executives Play." *Organizational Dynamics*, 36 (1), 28–44.
6. Kets de Vries, M. F. R. (2009a). *Reflections on Leadership and Career Development*. New York: John Wiley & Sons Inc.
7. Bateson, G., Jackson, D. D., Haley, J., and Weakland, J. (1956). "Toward a Theory of Schizophrenia." *Behavioral Science*, 1, 251–264.
8. Bateson, G. (1972). *Steps to an Ecology of Mind: Collected Essays in Anthropology, Psychiatry, Evolution, and Epistemology*. Chicago: University of Chicago Press.

9. Bowlby, J. (1969). *Attachment*. 2nd edn (Attachment and Loss Series, Vol. 1). New York: Basic Books.
10. Ibid.
11. Bowlby, J. (1973). *Separation: Anxiety and Anger* (Attachment and Loss Series, Vol. 2). New York: Basic Books.
12. Bowlby, J. (1980). *Loss: Sadness and Depression* (Attachment and Loss Series, Vol. 3). New York: Basic Books.
13. Ainsworth, M. (1967). "Suicidal Behavior and Attachment: A Developmental Model." In B. M. Sperling and H. W. Berman (Eds), *Attachment in Adults: Clinical and Developmental Perspectives*. New York: Guilford Press, pp. 275–298.
14. Ainsworth, M. and Bowlby, J. (1965). *Child Care and the Growth of Love*. London: Penguin Books.
15. Ainsworth, M., Blehar, M., Waters, E., and Wall, S. (1978). *Patterns of Attachment*. Hillsdale, NJ: Erlbaum.
16. Ibid.
17. Collins, N. and Read, S. J. (1994). "Cognitive Representations of Attachment: the structure and function of working models." In D. Perlman and K. Bartholomew (Eds), *Advances in Personal Relationships*, Vol. 5. London: Jessica Kingsley, pp. 53–90.
18. Hazan, C. and Shaver, P. R. (1990). "Love and Work: An attachment theoretical perspective." *Journal of Personality and Social Psychology*, 59, 270–280.
19. Byng-Hall, J. (1999). "Family and Couple Therapy: Toward Greater Security." In J. Cassidy and P. R. Shaver, *Handbook of Attachment: Theory, Research, and Clinical Applications*. New York: Guilford Press, pp. 707–731.
20. Nathanson, D. (Ed.) (1987). *The Many Faces of Shame*. New York: Guilford Press.
21. Goldberg, C. (1991). *Understanding Shame*. Northvale, NJ: Jason Aaronson, Inc.
22. Kaufman, G. (1996). *The Psychology of Shame*. 2nd edn. New York: Springer.
23. Tangney, J. P. and Dearing, R. L. (2002). *Shame and Guilt*. New York: Guilford Press.
24. Tracy, J. L., Robins, R. W., and Price Tangney, J. (2007). *The Self-Conscious Emotion: Theory and Research*. New York: Guilford Press.
25. Christakis, N. A. and Fowler, J. (2009). *Connected: The Surprising Power of Our Social Networks and How They Shape Our Lives*. Boston, MA: Little, Brown & Co.

26. Hatfield, E., Cacioppo, J. T., and Rapson, R. L. (1993). "Emotional Contagion." *Current Directions in Psychological Science*, 2, 96–99.
27. Hatfield, E., Cacioppo, J. T., and Rapson, R. L. (1994). *Emotional Contagion*. Cambridge: Cambridge University Press.
28. Showalter, E. (1997). *Hysterical Epidemics and Modern Culture*. New York: Columbia University Press.
29. Barsade, S. G. (2002). "The Ripple Effect: Emotional Contagion and Its Influence on Group Behavior." *Administrative Science Quarterly*, 47, 644–675.
30. Brower, L. (Ed.) (1988). *Mimicry and the Evolutionary Process*. Chicago: The University of Chicago Press.
31. Ruxton, G. D., Speed, M. P., and Sherratt, T. N. (2004). *Avoiding Attack. The Evolutionary Ecology of Crypsis, Warning Signals and Mimicry*. Oxford: Oxford University Press.
32. Thornton, C. (2010). *Group and Team Coaching*. London: Routledge.
33. Christakis, N. A. and Fowler, J. (2009). *Connected: The Surprising Power of Our Social Networks and How They Shape Our Lives*. Boston, MA: Little, Brown & Co.
34. Bowlby, J. (1969). *Attachment*. 2nd edn. (Attachment and Loss Series, Vol. 1). New York: Basic Books.
35. Bowlby, J. (1973). *Separation: Anxiety and Anger* (Attachment and Loss Series, Vol. 2). New York: Basic Books.
36. Bowlby, J. (1980). *Loss: Sadness and Depression* (Attachment and Loss Series, Vol. 3). New York: Basic Books.
37. Kohut, H. (1971). *The Analysis of the Self*. New York: International Universities Press.

CHAPTER 5

THE SECRET LIFE OF GROUPS

In much wisdom is much grief, and he that increaseth knowledge, increaseth sorrow.

—Ecclesiastes 1:18

Each thing is of like form from everlasting and comes round again in its cycle.

—Marcus Aurelius

Action and reaction, ebb and flow, trial and error, change—this is the rhythm of living. Out of our over-confidence, fear; out of our fear, clearer vision, fresh hope. And out of hope, progress.

—Bruce Barton

Three can keep a secret, if two of them are dead.

—Benjamin Franklin

On becoming a monk, a young man was given the task of delivering a sacred sword to another monastery. His journey would be a test, after years of dedicated study, to see how astute he was at applying his knowledge. His journey took him along a wild and desolate road, where great dangers lay. Would he be able to carry out his duty? Would he be observant enough to assess the dangers along the way and recognize when action was needed?

Late in the morning of the first day, the young monk realized that three very disreputable-looking strangers were following him. He became anxious for the safety of the sacred sword, which was encrusted with silver and gold. But then he remembered an old Zen saying that strangers are simply friends not yet met. His fears dissolved, leading to his resolve to pay little attention to the men behind him. When he stopped for his midday meal and the strangers joined him, he found them full of joy, asking him many questions about the way of Zen.

After lunch, the four continued their journey together. While walking the young monk reflected on the old Zen tale of a farmer who, thinking his neighbor's son a thief, saw thieving in his every movement. But when he found his lost axe under a pile of straw, he suddenly saw his neighbor's son transformed into an honest lad.

That evening as they ate their simple meal the monk's new friends became insulting and quarrelsome. At first, he was worried but then remembered an old Zen story about a Zen warrior who would impress potential opponents with his skill at picking flies out of the air with his chopsticks. Preoccupied with these thoughts, the young monk focused his attention on a fly buzzing around his head and at just the right moment reached for the fly with his chopsticks. And at exactly that moment, one of his fellow travelers, not knowing any of these old Zen tales, cut off the young monk's head and stole the sword.

As this story warns us, when we deal with groups, we have to watch out for interpersonal forces on multiple levels, or like the young monk, we risk trouble. We not only need to pay heed to the forces of fantasy but also to those of reality. The context in which things take place should never be forgotten. In the interpersonal field, there are many levels.

The same can be said about organizational life. In organizations, groups operate at a number of levels simultaneously. For example, there is a content level and a process level. Content is, of course, the task or objective at hand. Process regulates what group members need to do to accomplish the group goals, including how personal needs and emotions are handled; authority and power themes, determining who is in charge, how formal and informal leadership issues are played out, and how the group's various stakeholders are dealt with. Other process issues include decision-making methods, the quality of communication, and the role each individual plays. An important part of process is the dynamics of the group-as-a-whole (which I also described as "cloud" interactions in Chapter 2), most of which exists out of conscious awareness.

One of the founders of social psychology, Kurt Lewin, coined the term "group dynamics" to describe the way groups and individuals act and react to changing circumstances influenced by these forces [1]. His definition of a group was two or more individuals connected to each other by social relationships. Because they interact and influence each other, groups develop a number of dynamic processes that separate them from a random collection of individuals. Among these processes, Lewin included norms, roles, relations, need to belong, social influence, and other social effects on behavior, some of which I will describe in this chapter.

A popular perspective on the life of a group or a team is the longitudinal one, which assumes that groups go through different developmental phases. It takes time for a team to assemble, agree on process, accomplish objectives, and then disband when the goal is achieved. This suggests that groups have a lifecycle with a beginning, middle, and an end. We can also say, with a slight stretch of the imagination, that groups have a life narrative, in which they embark on a journey that leads them to their goal. However you look at it, it appears that groups also have a secret life, an existence somewhat independent of the lives of their members.

"Groups have a secret life, an existence independent of the lives of their members."

LINEAR THEORIES OF GROUP BEHAVIOR

One of the best-known progressive development theories is a four-phase one developed by Bruce Tuckman [2]. Tuckman's theory of group behavior consists of the following phases: forming, storming, norming, and performing. According to his theory, the path to high performance followed by most groups will develop according to this sequence. Subsequently, in collaboration with a colleague, Tuckman added a fifth stage, called adjourning, or mourning [3].

> **Review the different stages of your team's development and assess the greatest needs (individual, team, or task) for each stage.**
> **On which needs will you put the greatest emphasis?**
> **Circle "high," "medium," or "low" for the three needs at each stage of your team's development.**

	INDIVIDUAL NEEDS	TEAM NEEDS	TASK NEEDS
Forming	high	high	high
	medium	medium	medium
	low	low	low
Storming	high	high	high
	medium	medium	medium
	low	low	low
Norming	high	high	high
	medium	medium	medium
	low	low	low
Performing	high	high	high
	medium	medium	medium
	low	low	low

During the forming (or polite) stage, group members behave very positively toward each other. This is the initial stage in the development process, when members get to know each other, address requirements, structure, expectations, and the challenges ahead. In this phase, individuals make an effort to orient themselves within the group, and identify the boundaries of interpersonal and task behaviors. As they test one another interpersonally, they also develop dependency relationships with emerging leaders and other group members. There may be some discussion about process, which, if it goes on too long, can be frustrating for those who simply want to get on with the task at hand. This stage is usually short, possibly concluded in just one meeting.

The group (or team) moves into its storming phase, when harsh reality may set in. This part of the sequence is often characterized by conflict and polarization around interpersonal issues, with concomitant emotional responses related to content (the task) as well as process. This is probably the most turbulent phase, when team members struggle for airtime to present their own ideas and figure out which direction to take; it is often marked by intense debate, critique, and confrontation fuelled by group-as-a-whole dynamics. Storming is a form of resistance to the influence of selected group members and the nature of the team's task. At this stage of development, there is often a (chaotic) struggle for leadership and experimentation with various group decision-making processes. Coalitions may form.

Moving on successfully requires the group to remain true to its original mandate and avoid becoming distracted or stuck. Compromises may be required to advance decision processes and enable progress. Group members may feel that they are on an emotional roller coaster as they try to focus on the task at hand without the support of agreed structures, established processes, or specific relationships with their colleagues. Unfortunately, many groups remain stuck in this phase—in the case of organizational teams, this situation will lead to failure to reach goals.

In a best case scenario, gradually the group will reach more clarity and cohesion, despite unresolved uncertainties. They move into a norming stage, as agreement is reached on how the group will operate. During this third phase in the group process, previous resistances are overcome, new standards evolve, and new roles are adopted. By this stage, people have begun to understand each other's work habits and ethics, and can work together satisfactorily as a team. Responsibilities and roles are more clearly defined, expectations are set, and collaboration is more effective, including facilitation and direction by the leader. Members know each other better (possibly even socializing outside of the group setting), are able to ask each other for help, are prepared to accept constructive criticism, and engage in courageous conversations. They develop a strong commitment to team goals, and are aware of the progress they are making. Commitment and unity are strong, with members of the team experiencing a sense of "flow," of working at their best [4]. That said, there can be a prolonged overlap between storming and norming: as new tasks arrive, the team may revert to a typical storming stage. In normal circumstances, however, a team will work its way through it.

When the team reaches the performing stage, interpersonal structure becomes the catalyst for task activities. The team now has a shared vision and group identity that requires less facilitation. Intervention by the leader is minimal. The team is increasingly self-managed, and positional authority is less relevant. Decisions are made by consensus. Roles are flexible and functional, and most of the group's energy is channeled into the task. Structural issues have been resolved, and the prevailing structure is supportive of the required task performance.

Changing needs focus in the development of a team			
STAGE OF TEAM DEVELOPMENT	INDIVIDUAL NEEDS	TEAM NEEDS	TASK NEEDS
Forming: defining the task	high	medium	low
Storming: conflict about the task	high	high	low
Norming: setting the ground rules	medium	high	medium
Performing: task resolution	medium	medium	high

Although not all teams will reach this phase, advocates of the linear theory of group behavior maintain that many teams do succeed in getting there. This is the stage where a high performance team really starts to work at full capacity and deliver superior results. The team works toward achieving its goals, attending to relationships, style, and process issues along the way. Team members look out for each other. Disagreements may occur but they will be resolved constructively within the team. Team members, if required, make changes to processes and structure. Changes to processes and structure are made by team members if required. Individual members join or leave the team without seriously affecting the performance culture. Being part of the team at this stage feels easy compared to the earlier developmental stages.

The phase of adjourning involves the dissolution of the group: terminating roles, completing tasks, and reducing dependency. This stage might also be called transforming, or un-forming, as people begin to let go of the group's structure and move on to other tasks and objectives. The break-up of a group can be particularly hard for members who like the satisfaction of successfully performing repetitive tasks. Others may miss the regular contact with people who have become like friends. They experience pangs of separation anxiety. Uncertainty about future roles or job prospects might add to their reluctance to let go. Some students of group behavior have labeled this the "mourning" phase, since group members often experience loss—especially when a group is dissolved suddenly or splits with little planning.

The problem with a linear model is that it does not fully address the emotional experience of group members; in a sense, it labels symptoms of group dynamics, such as storming, but it does not suggest how to deal with the effects. In reality, group development may be more like a spiral than a series of clearly defined steps. Human behavior can sometimes be too erratic to be modeled linearly. To complicate matters, not only are the boundaries between stages quite fuzzy, but the stages themselves are also frequently non-sequential. In reality, group development does not necessarily proceed in a linear fashion. Stages can overlap; for example, a group might have moved into norming or performing, but the addition of a new member might force it back into storming. A group can develop successfully, but it can also regress, reverting to earlier stages of development. In trying to paint a universal picture of group dynamics, we can think of the linear model of group behavior as a guideline, but we should not over-generalize.

In fact, as with all human processes, groups often deviate from stage theory predictions. Some groups even appear to be in a permanent state of flux—or, worse, chaos. Individual members come and go; expectations about team output or purpose change; relationships break down or improve. Typically, people consciously or unconsciously try to balance their own needs with the needs of the group. The focus between these two balancing acts can shift constantly.

"People consciously or unconsciously try to balance their own needs with the needs of the group."

MONOMYTHICAL THEORIES: HEROIC JOURNEYS

Another way of making sense of how groups evolve is to take a different perspective, studying the ways in which outside forces can shape, forge, or destroy a group. A helpful way to conceptualize this perspective is to use the metaphor of a heroic journey. The monomythical narrative—the way of understanding events through story telling—can be a powerful way to capture the group experience over time.

Have each member of your team tell the story of a well-known heroic figure. They might choose a comic-book character (e.g., Superman) or a religious, mythological, or historical figure (e.g., Odysseus, Moses, Siegfried, Boudicca, or King Arthur).

The team members should consider the following questions:

- What patterns do you see when you map this person's heroic journey?
- Do you recognize any similarities?
- Do you see any differences?
- Can you explain what the hero or heroine is struggling to overcome?
- How do you compare your heroic story with the story of your own life?
- Think of a team of which you have been a member, and explore its particular journey.

Making sense of your own journey is a way to bring meaning to your life and create purpose and passion. Comparing your own story with the hero or heroine you have chosen can enable you to take a fresh perspective on your own life.

In his seminal, cross-cultural study of the mythology of the hero's journey, *The Hero with a Thousand Faces*, Joseph Campbell put forward the theory that significant myths from around the world, which have survived for millennia, all share a fundamental structure that he termed the *monomyth* [5]. According to Campbell, the monomyth carries universal themes, and fundamental structures and stages. The story usually goes as follows: "A hero ventures forth from the world of common day into a region of supernatural wonder: fabulous forces are there encountered and a decisive victory is won: the hero comes back from this mysterious adventure with the power to bestow boons on his fellow men" [6]. All our great stories, songs, and works of art follow this heroic path, usually culminating in a happy ending or the accomplishment of a greater good.

The monomyth sequence represents the general pattern of adventures that mythological heroes encounter during their quests (and we need to bear in mind that myths should be considered metaphors for a life we long to experience). The journey that the hero or heroine of a story takes is a process of self-discovery, self-integration, and self-fulfillment. As with any process of growth and change, this journey can be confusing and painful, but it also brings opportunities to develop confidence, perspective, and a new way of being in our world.

We can extrapolate this journey pattern to the journey made by a group—only, in this instance, we can consider the dragons, warlords, witches, and elves encountered along the way to be symbolic representations of the different (sometimes fearful) stakeholders encountered in organizations. Similarly, larger-than-life hurdles in the monomyth also represent adversaries and challenges as applied to organizational life.

Campbell describes 17 monomythical stages or steps. Some myths contain several of them, others contain fewer, and a very small number of myths contain them all. For simplification, these 17 stages can be organized into three sections, *departure* (sometimes called *separation*), *initiation*, and *return*. Departure deals with the hero or heroine's adventure prior to the quest; initiation deals with the hero or heroine's many adventures along the way; and return deals with the hero or heroine's return home with knowledge and powers acquired during the journey.

As I suggested, the monomyth story line can also be applied to organizational life, with the team representing the hero. Let's imagine that life is moving along normally in the organization when something happens to disturb this stable state. A team is put together to confront this threat. The members of the team—or seen at a meta-level, the organization itself—are the heroes and heroines in the narrative. They cannot rest until their task has been completed.

The most common scenario is that, as individuals, team members are reluctant to rise to this call. Their hesitation may be due to fear, insecurity, or a sense of inadequacy. However, refusal is not an option, as far as the powers that be are concerned. To survive this threat, the group is forced to create a sense of engagement and esprit de corps that is more powerful than members are capable of individually. Strengthened by cohesiveness, they move from a familiar world and begin their quest.

This departure represents only the beginning of the long and genuinely perilous path of initiatory conquests and moments of illumination. In this early phase, there will be a series of trials, tests, tasks, or ordeals for the team to undergo to begin its transformation. Symbolic dragons will have to be slain and unexpected barriers will have to be crossed—again, and again, and again. This is a pivotal stage of the myth-adventure.

Once the team has committed itself (consciously or unconsciously) to the quest, a guide and magical helper often appears to support them, especially if the adventurers have been wounded or weakened by their trials. In our organizational analogy, this guide might be a senior executive who assists team members in one way or another. Or the guide might be outside the organization—an external board member, consultant, or coach. More often than not, this protector will present the members of the team with artifacts (for example, a plan, or more resources) that will later aid them in their quest.

Once the goal is reached, the team enters the final phase, the return. The return can be just as adventurous and dangerous as the outward journey. The final factor that makes the adventure a monomyth is the hero's success in bringing the reward back to the normal realm of humanity, where it will contribute to renewing the community—in this instance, the organization. In an organizational setting, the reward can be a new product, a process discovery, an acquisition, or even a talented, highly sought after individual. To complete their adventure, the returning heroes must survive the impact of their return home—their re-entry into the organization. Many failures attest to the difficulty of returning to that threshold. The old guard in the organization may not like the new way of doing things, taking on the role of spoilers, and rejecting whatever innovations the adventurers want to introduce.

THE HELICAL POINT OF VIEW

An alternative to looking at groups as progressive communities or heroes engaged in quests is to take a deeper look at the more regressive aspects of group dynamics. A serious contribution to the helical view of systems psychodynamics was made by one of the founders of social psychology, Kurt Lewin, whom I mentioned earlier and who revolutionized the study of psychology by showing empirically that human behavior is not only a product of a person's internal psychological make-up but is also greatly affected by his or her dynamic environment [7]. The whole psychological field, or life space, within which people function—the interplay between environmental and personal psychological forces—needs to be taken into consideration in order to understand why we do what we do. Specific kinds of behavior are the outcome of tension between an individual's self-perceptions and the environment. Lewin's analysis provided a framework for looking at the tensions (forces) that influence social situations. He identified "facilitating" or "blocking" forces that affect the achievement of a specific goal.

Force field diagram

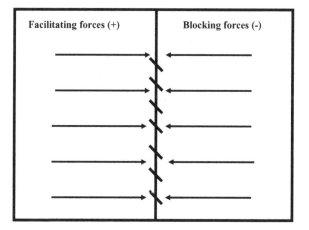

| Facilitating forces (+) | Blocking forces (-) |

Conduct a force field analysis to examine the forces facilitating and blocking change in your team.

In the template above:

1. List the forces currently driving you toward making these changes.
2. List the restraining forces (i.e., what is preventing your team and team members from making these changes?).
3. Assign a number to each item on a scale of 1 to 5, where 1 is the weakest and 5 the strongest.
4. Discuss with the members of your team how to
   a. strengthen the forces for change
   b. minimize the forces blocking change.

Lewin's classic force field diagram is useful in that it helps a group to create a mental picture of the tug-of-war between the opposing forces that influence a given issue. The simplified diagram above lists facilitating forces in the left-hand column, and blocking forces in the right. Arrows point toward the middle. Longer (or thicker) arrows indicate stronger forces.

Lewin's observations also set the stage for the idea that groups have a helical character. To be more precise, each phase of group activity depends upon the forces currently influencing it—themselves defined by all preceding activities. The helical point of view implies that all group members' experiences contribute to current activity; there is no break in the action, no fixed beginning, and no real closure. As they move forward, groups are simultaneously doubling back on themselves, absorbing the effects of their past behavior—the emerging curve of the helix is fundamentally affected by the curve from which it emerges.

Like a helix, groups are constantly moving forward, yet are always to some degree dependent on the past, which informs the present and the future. The helical perspective underscores the integrated aspects of all human communication as an evolving process that is always turned inward in ways that permit learning, growth, and discovery.

As the evolutionary helical point of view implies, groups can be compared to primitive tribes, as advocated by Wilfred Bion [8]. According to Bion, groups under pressure can regress to more primitive, unconscious beliefs or needs, which continue to exist in human societies as relicts of much earlier behavior patterns that evolved as group responses to danger. He termed this "basic assumption" functioning. Bion identified three basic assumptions: dependency, fight/flight, and pairing, a trio of concepts that has become a cornerstone of the study of group dynamics. These basic assumptions—which manifest themselves at an unconscious level—make it much harder for people to work together productively. The result is often delusional ideation—ideas completely detached from reality—that become fertile ground for the proliferation of rigid, dysfunctional patterns of organizational behavior.

Although groups are normally set up to pursue sensible and realistic goals, inevitably, from time to time, they deviate from actual work and fall into a kind of madness, driven by a regression to basic assumptions functioning. They can become entities preoccupied with primitive, archaic fantasies. Such primitive, powerful emotional processes will block and sidetrack real work activities. For example, a group can be completely derailed by the notion that there is a "traitor" among them, giving rise to paranoia and destructive anger; or, feeling lost, they may be looking for a "savior" that will get them out of their mess. Each of Bion's three basic assumptions interferes with task performance, and each contains its own logic, as we shall see.

> "Although teams are normally set up to pursue sensible and realistic goals, inevitably, from time to time, they fall into some kind of madness."

Dependency

People often assume, at an unconscious level, that the leader or organization can and should offer the protection and guidance our parents offered us in our early years. Groups subject to this dependency assumption are searching for a strong, charismatic leader to give them direction. The members of such groups are united by common feelings of helplessness, inadequacy, neediness, and fear of the outside world. In contrast to their own feelings, they perceive the leader as omnipotent and omniscient. They are readily prepared to give up their autonomy when they perceive help at hand. Some typical remarks of groups subjected to this regressive dynamic include, "What do you want me/us to do?" and "I can't take this kind of decision by myself; you'll have to talk to my superior." Such comments reflect team members' anxiety, insecurity, and professional and emotional immaturity, albeit imposed or learned over time in a stifling organizational setting. While unquestioning faith in a leader contributes to goal-directedness and cohesiveness, it also impairs the followers' own critical judgment and leaves them unwilling and unprepared to take any form of initiative. Although they are willing to carry out the leader's directives, they require the leader to do all or most of the thinking for them. Once a leader on whom followers have leaned is gone, bureaucratic inertia may take hold. People may be frozen in the past, going through the motions, wondering what their departed leader would have done.

Fight-flight

Another common unconscious assumption among teams can be that the organizational world is a dangerous place, and organizational participants must use fight or flight as defense mechanisms to cope with emerging threats. In teams subjected to the fight–flight assumption, a stance of avoidance or attack predominates. When the fight–flight mechanism takes hold, there is a tendency to split the world into friend or foe. Fight reactions manifest themselves in aggression against the self, peers (in the form of envy, jealousy, competition, elimination, boycotting, rivalry, fighting for a position in the group, and privileged relationships with authority figures), or authority itself. Flight reactions include avoidance of others, absenteeism, and resignation (that is, giving up). Remarks typical of people in a fight–flight situation include, "Let's not give our data to our finance people; they'll just use them against us," or "Our organization would be in good shape if it weren't for some of the idiots who run the place." Us vs. them language indicates that fight–flight assumptions have gained the upper hand. Instead of taking personal responsibility for problems, blame is routinely (and vindictively) assigned elsewhere. Subscribing to a rigid, bipolar view of the world, a group in a fight-flight position is fixated on protecting itself or conquering "the enemy," in various ways.

In some cases, group leaders fall victim to the fight-flight assumption, and encourage the team's tendency toward this kind of good-bad, with us or against us, us vs. them splitting. Externalizing their internal problems, they inflame their followers against real or imagined enemies, using this division to motivate people and to channel emerging anxiety outward. The shared search for and fight against enemies results in a strong and impenetrable conviction of the correctness and righteousness of their cause, and energizes them to pursue it. It also enforces the group's identity [9, 10]. Leaders who encourage fight-flight mechanisms by radiating certainty and conviction create meaning for followers who feel lost. The resulting sense of unity is highly reassuring. As followers eliminate doubters and applaud converts, they become increasingly dependent on their leader.

Pairing

Bion's third unconscious assumption describes the desire to pair up with an individual or a team perceived as powerful. It is the most difficult of his basic assumptions. In pairing, two people in a small group may come to dominate its process by talking to each other, and are allowed to continue doing so by the other members. The other members rely on a pair within the group for all creative efforts. This association can help group members cope with feelings of anxiety, alienation, and loneliness.

Wanting to feel secure but also to be creative, people who experience the pairing assumption fantasize that the most effective creation takes place in pairs. Two group members pair off and engender hope—perhaps in the form of some kind of messianic figure or symbol. Unfortunately, pairing also implies splitting up. The inevitable diversity within groups may result in intra- and inter-team conflict, which in turn may prompt individuals or pairs to split up the team.

In the pairing mode, grandiose, unrealistic ideas about innovation may become more important than practicality and profitability. Typical remarks heard within a team susceptible to the pairing assumption include, "Leave it to the two of us, we can solve this problem," and "If only the CEO and COO had a better relationship, our organization would be in really good shape."

Look at the way your team operates under stressful conditions. What patterns can you recognize? What is happening in your team?

Study the following statements and label them TRUE or FALSE

                             TRUE   FALSE

1. The members of our team seem to have stopped thinking for themselves.
2. The members of our team appear to be looking for a magical leader to solve all our problems.
3. The members of our team seem to come together to gratify their dependency needs rather than to do real work.
4. Fighting or withdrawal have become means to avoid dealing with the task at hand within our team.
5. The members of our team seem to be gathered to fight with leadership or to flee from it rather than to join in effective work.
6. The team seems to be preoccupied with some common enemy either within or outside the group.

TRUE   FALSE

7. Our team seems to be looking for some kind of messiah to solve all their problems.

8. Team development is frozen by the hope of being rescued by members who pair off and create new leadership.

9. The team seems to look for miraculous solutions to our problems instead of facing and overcoming difficulties through collaborative effort.

If you answered TRUE to statements 1, 2, and 3, your team has a dependency nature. If you answered TRUE to statements 4, 5, or 6, your team has a fight-flight nature. If you answered TRUE to statements 7, 8, or 9, your team has a pairing nature. Combinations of basic assumption groups are also possible. Furthermore, some teams move from one basic assumption to the other.

Bion also noted that the basic assumptions of a group may change, sometimes several times during a single session, even though the group may continue to work on the same topics or goals.

Social defenses

When the three basic assumptions prevail in the workplace, they offer strong proof that the organization's leadership is not dealing adequately with the emerging anxiety of working in a social setting. As people try to deny or to avoid these primitive fears and anxieties, the team's and the organization's primary task becomes distorted. One of the consequences may be that members of the organization develop specific communal mechanisms to defend themselves against the emergent basic assumptions and anxieties inherent in working within the system. When such defenses are adopted organization-wide, we call them social defenses.

Social defenses—systems of relationships reflected in the social structure of the organization—function like individual defenses but are woven into the fabric of an organization in an effort to assure participants that the workplace is really a safe and accepting place. But their real purpose is to transform and neutralize strong tensions and affect, such as anxiety, shame, guilt, envy, jealousy, rage, sexual frustration, and low self-esteem. Effective social defenses can help team members to deal with disturbing emotional experiences.

When the level of anxiety rises in an organization, executives typically rely on existing structures (rules, regulations, procedures, complex organization charts, elaborate job descriptions, and con-voluted organization-specific ways of solving problems) to contain it. When those structures offer insufficient containment—that is, when there are no opportunities to discuss and work through emerging concerns—people in organizations engage in regressive defenses, such as splitting, projection, displacement, and denial. Social defenses turn into bureaucratic obstacles. When these ways of dealing with the angst and unpredictability of life in organiza-tions become the dominant mode of operation (rather than an occasional stopgap measure), they become dysfunctional for the organization as a whole and contribute to emotional disengagement.

When they take the shape of bureaucratic routines and pseudo-rational activities, social defenses gradually obscure personal and organizational realities, allowing people to detach themselves from their inner experiences. Task forces, administrative procedures, rationalization, intellectualization, and other structures and proc-esses are increasingly used to keep people emotionally uninvolved and to help them feel safe and in control. While these processes do manage to reduce anxiety—their original purpose—they also replace compassion, empathy, awareness, and meaning with control and impersonality. Some teams show symptoms of the presence of social defenses. For example, under certain circumstances the formation of teams can be better understood as a ritualistic or routine response to anxiety-provoking situations, rather than as a rational response to a specific problem [11, 12, 13].

When social defenses become ubiquitous, the situation doesn't bode well for the effective functioning of organizations and teams. To prevent these defenses running wild, we need to understand them at a deeper level. The complexity of social defenses, however, means it is hard to disentangle them from the normal fabric of the organization. Defensive mechanisms are built into the way an organization functions and add to the challenges group coaches have to deal with.

> **"Defensive mechanisms are built into the way an organization functions and add to the challenges group coaches have to deal with."**

TWELVE ANGRY MEN

Director Sidney Lumet's 1957 classic film *Twelve Angry Men* dramatizes the linear, monomythical, and helical theories of group dynamics in the story of an all-male jury deliberating the guilt or innocence of a man accused of killing his father. They are asked to deliver their verdict "beyond a reasonable doubt." What, at first glance, seems to be an open-and-shut case turns out quite differently.

At the outset, 11 of the 12 jurors vote in favor of convicting the accused without even discussing the evidence presented at the trial. Only Juror 8 (played by Henry Fonda), refuses to walk into the groupthink trap; he is not ready to send a young man to the electric chair without careful consideration. He openly admits to the other jurors that he does not know whether the accused is guilty or innocent but that he needs to spend time discussing the case. He has what he considers to be a reasonable doubt.

Twelve Angry Men provides an in-depth view of the various stages of group development, breaking down each stage and revealing the intricacies and difficulties of uniting people from different walks of life into a unified and unanimous team. We recognize the various turning points as the group goes through the phases of forming, storming, norming, and performing. In the forming stage, before the first jury vote, we see how the members of the jury get acquainted and organized, and select a foreman. In the storming phase, conflicts arise as the members of the team determine goals and priorities. This phase starts when the vote turns out to be 11–1—Juror 8 is the only dissenting voice—creating turmoil among the jurors. In the norming phase the members of the jury choose the rules to coordinate the way they will deal with each other in the decision-making process, and begin to discuss the case in earnest. At this stage they reject the observations of bigoted Juror 12 and a second vote is six to six. Finally, in the performing phase, the jury members work well together. This phase appears to start when the three jurors who still think the accused is guilty are asked to explain why.

Taking a monomythical point of view, we follow Juror 8 on his quest for truth and justice. He is, at first, the sole juror prepared to stand up against the other 11 because the evidence doesn't sit right with him. He is the lone hero on a heroic quest for a fair, thoroughly deliberated verdict. Juror 8 convinces the others that it is possible for one person to be right, and everyone else to be wrong. In many ways, his quest is a celebration of justice. And he succeeds in bestowing this boon on the accused.

From the helical perspective, we can see all three basic assumptions—dependency, fight-flight, and pairing—at work through the various coalitions that are formed among the leading members of the jury. Very soon after the real deliberations start, Juror 8 and the cool calculating broker, Juror 4 (an intelligent, calm, and controlled man who is open to reasoned argument), become the *de facto* leaders of the group. As they gain stature, the others begin to defer to them in various ways. Although Juror 1, a rugby coach, is supposed to be the foreman, he is quickly usurped by the other two. During the course of the film, the reasons why one jury member after another joins the "not guilty" group become clear. Most of the jury members are mere followers, who change their vote under Juror 8's persuasion—the dependency assumption. Some of the other jurors withdraw or fight; still others form pairs.

The film is also an intense examination of the personal baggage, or internal theater, that each jury member brings into the room. The 12 men in the film all have different personalities and backgrounds. Personal agendas come into play. Prejudices or personal issues that have influenced the initial decision of "guilty" are uncovered. Juror 7, an uninterested, self-centered individual has only one thought in his head: not to miss that evening's baseball game. Juror 3, a tough businessman who is convinced of the guilt of the accused and wants to see the teenager sentenced to death, lets his own deep personal anguish cloud his reason. "Killing sons" seems to be a theme that haunts his inner theater, reflecting his ambivalent relationship to his own son. Only when this theme is brought into consciousness is he prepared to join the "not guilty" group. Encouraged by Juror 8, each juror comes to grips with the role their personal biases play in their decisions. The externalization of individuals' internal theater-influenced behavior eventually allows their perspectives to coalesce into a shared conclusion.

The personality conflicts, the joint efforts of the jury, and the functioning of several minds together in search for the truth are just a few characteristics of group dynamics illustrated in the film, with each interaction drawing on the different inner scripts that each member of the jury is dramatizing. Among these 12 men, the whole spectrum of humanity is represented, from the bigotry of Juror 10 and the cold analysis of Juror 4, to the courage of Juror 2 who finally takes responsibility for his own opinion, and the integrity of the lone dissenter, Juror 8. A meta-analysis of the secret life of this group shows that Juror 8's influence was grounded in his unconscious sense that below-the-surface currents were endangering the group's ability to reach a fair and honorable outcome and—fortunately for the young man accused of murder—Juror 8 was able to convince the others to re-evaluate their original verdict.

REFERENCES

1. Lewin, K. (1948). *Resolving Social Conflicts: Selected Papers on Group Dynamics.* New York: Harper and Row.
2. Tuckman, B. (1965). "Developmental Sequences in Small Groups." *Psychological Bulletin*, 63, 384–399.
3. Tuckman, B. and Jensen, M. (1977). "Stages of Small Group Development Revisited." *Group and Organization Studies*, 2, 419–427.
4. Csikszentmihalyi, M. (1990). *Flow: The Psychology of Optimal Experience.* New York: Harper & Row.
5. Campbell, J. (1949). *The Hero with a Thousand Faces.* Princeton, NJ: Princeton University Press.
6. Ibid., p. 30.
7. Lewin, K. (1948). *Resolving Social Conflicts: Selected Papers on Group Dynamics.* New York: Harper and Row.
8. Bion, W. R. (1959). *Experiences in Groups and Other Papers.* London: Tavistock.
9. Lasswell, H. (1960). *Psychopathology and Politics.* New York: Viking Press.
10. Volcan, V. (1988). *The Need to Have Enemies and Allies.* Northvale, NJ: Jason Aronson.
11. Menzies Lyth, I. E. (1960). "A Case Study of the Functioning of Social Systems as a Defense against Anxiety: A Report on a Study of the Nursing System in a General Hospital." *Human Relations*, 13, 95–121.
12. Jaques, E. (1974). "Social Systems as Defense against Persecutory and Depressive Anxiety." In G. S. Gibbard, J. J. Hartmann, and R. D. Mann, *Analysis of Groups*. San Francisco, CA: Jossey-Bass.
13. Hirschhorn, L. (1988). *The Workplace Within: Psychodynamics of Organizational Life.* Cambridge, MA: MIT Press.

CHAPTER 6

INTO THE CLOUD: THE PHENOMENON OF THE GROUP-AS-A-WHOLE

There are basically two types of people. People who accomplish things, and people who claim to have accomplished things. The first group is less crowded.

—Mark Twain

We could learn a lot from crayons: some are sharp, some are pretty, some are dull, while others are bright, some have weird names, but we have to learn to live in the same box.

—Anonymous

The unconscious is the ocean of the unsayable, of what has been expelled from the land of language, removed as a result of ancient prohibitions.

—Italo Calvino

Once upon a time when the world was young, an old Lakota spiritual leader sat high on a mountain and had a vision in which, Iktomi, the great trickster and teacher of wisdom, appeared in the form of a spider. In his vision, Iktomi spoke to the elder in a sacred language and, as he did so, picked up the elder's willow hoop, which was decorated with feathers, horsehair, beads and other offerings, and began to spin a web.

Iktomi talked to the elder about the cycles of life, how we begin our lives as infants, become children, and then adults. Finally, he said, we arrive at old age where we must be taken care of as if we were infants, completing the cycle. "But," said Iktomi, "in each cycle of life there are many forces: some good and some bad. If you listen to the good forces, they will steer you in the right direction. But, if you listen to the bad forces, they will steer you in the wrong direction and they may hurt you. These forces can help or hinder the harmony of Nature." And all the while the spider spoke, he continued to weave his web.

When Iktomi finished speaking, he gave the elder the web and said, "This web is a perfect circle with a hole in the center. Use the web to help your people reach their goals, making good use of their ideas, dreams, and visions. If you believe in the Great Spirit, the web will catch your good ideas and the bad ones will pass through the hole."

The elder took the web, left the mountain, and returned to his people where he passed on his vision. Ever since, many Native American peoples have hung dream catchers above their beds to sift their dreams and visions. The good is captured in the web and carried with them, but the evil in their dreams falls through the hole in the center of the web and is no longer a part of their lives. Some believe the dream catcher holds their future destiny.

Like the dream catcher in the Lakotan story, the group-as-a-whole is a very special kind of entity. It can also be compared to a net, web, or cloud, trapping the collective fantasies (conscious and unconscious) of all the individual members in a group or team. The group-as-a-whole catches verbal and non-verbal communication—it connects thoughts, moods, behavior and actions that may initially seem mysterious. And as the net contains diffused systems of interconnected mental forces, the ideas that are caught in it will display many different qualities—some influencing each other positively, others negatively. It is as if every group or team has a "cloud" hanging over it that contains partially metabolized material from its members.

This notion of the group-as-a-whole is one of the concepts that people interested in group dynamics can apply in making sense of what is going on in the group with which they are working. Other terms have been used to describe similar phenomena, such as social network, living system, group matrix, social unconscious, group mind, or reflective space, or, to use another term, collective "cloud" consciousness. All these terms have in common the concept that groups or teams can also be seen as highly complex, interactive entities in and of themselves. A group or team, therefore, is more than the sum of its parts; it is a place where people often **"A group is more** simultaneously meet on several levels, con- **than the sum of its** scious as well as out-of-awareness. **parts."**

From a historical perspective, group-as-a-whole theories can be traced back to 1896, when Gustave Le Bon, a French sociologist, published *The Crowd* [1], which studied the behavior of a group as a social system and individual members' relatedness to that system. According to Le Bon, people sacrifice part of their individuality when joining large groups and as a result large groups are easily influenced and susceptible to suggestion. To him, the group becomes a place of extremes where primary process thinking dominates. "An individual in a crowd is a grain of sand amid other grains of sand, which the wind stirs up at will" [2]. The wind Le Bon refers to could be any dominant force of authority—a charismatic leader, for example—able to coerce the group mind in one or another direction.

Sigmund Freud, influenced by Le Bon, concurred; people in a crowd respond differently to people and events than they would on their own. (Experimentally based social contagion theories were not yet known.) As Freud asserted, "The feelings of a group are always very simple and very exaggerated. So that a group knows neither doubt nor uncertainty . . . In groups the most contradictory ideas exist side by side . . . without any conflict arising from the logical contradiction" [3]. According to Freud, when primitive processes—originating from our archaic origins—are activated in groups, individual inhibitions fall away. Strange things can happen in groups, which can be very emotional, impulsive, and extreme in their behavior.

Of course all individuals do not react in exactly the same way in groups. Pierre Turquet, a serious student of group behavior, introduced the more nuanced notions of one-ness and me-ness concerning life in groups [4]. In his conceptual scheme, one-ness describes the search by some members of the group for a powerful union with an omnipotent force that would take care of their needs; given these people's mindset, they are prepared to surrender their identity for passive participation within the group, experiencing in this way a sense of feeling alive, wholeness, and well-being. In such instances, the prevailing fantasy is that existence is only possible within the context of the group.

Me-ness, on the other hand, is a contrasting fantasy based on avoiding the emerging anxiety of being swallowed up by the group. To some people, groups resemble threatening, cannibalistic monsters. They have the capacity to swallow up their members. Group members of this kind are concerned about loss of identity and may be troubled by feelings of annihilation when they are part of a group. A me-ness orientation, however, allows them to escape into their own safe, inner world and deny both the presence and existence of the group. When such an attitude dominates, however, there will be complete denial of outer reality; the focus is on the individual's inner reality [5, 6, 7].

Returning to Schopenhauer's hedgehogs, we can surmise that, in a group setting, people experience a fundamental need to draw closer to others but, at the same time, are reluctant to get too close. Each member of a group or team struggles, consciously or unconsciously, with these two dynamic forces, which are present at all times, with different degrees of intensity. This creates a sense of ambivalence about their specific place within the group—feelings that may be projected on the group-as-a-whole.

"In a group setting, people experience a fundamental need to draw closer to others but, at the same time, are reluctant to get too close."

It is to be expected that each member of a group will have a different attitude toward these opposing desires and each person's experience within the group will be played out in their own unique way. A group functions well when cohesive group processes regulate the need for separateness. Otherwise, interpersonal forces can lead to explosive behavior. When there is a short-circuit between different attachment patterns or desire for me-ness as opposed to one-ness, considerable tension is caused. One way or another, these opposing forces have to be metabolized, to protect the members of the group from paranoid or depressive anxiety.

THE COLLECTIVE AND SOCIAL UNCONSCIOUS

As these discussions illustrate, there are conscious and unconscious spheres in group processes. Some members of a group (or team for that matter) will be conscious of specific themes that remain unconscious for the group-as-a-whole. Others will be only subliminally aware of an unconscious "territory" in which they share ownership. Others again will have no clue what is going on.

To further understand the primitive processes that take place in a group setting, we can make an excursion to Jungian psychology. To Jung, the personal unconscious is a more or less superficial layer of the collective unconscious [8]. According to Jung, the personal unconscious contains themes that were once conscious but have disappeared from consciousness by being forgotten or repressed. In contrast, the contents of the collective unconscious have never been in consciousness, and therefore have never been individually acquired, but owe their existence exclusively to heredity. In other words, certain structures and predispositions of the unconscious are common to all of us: they are part of our evolutionary heritage. The collective unconscious is a basic biological reality. It consists of universal, deep structures and cultural belief systems; unconscious motives that drive a group, community, or society. Thus as humans, we all have a certain psychological as well as physical predisposition. Our DNA determines our physical predispositions; our psychological predispositions are stored in the collective unconscious. All of us draw on a common pool of ideas, images, and meanings. According to Jung, in this group-as-a-whole space something is created that goes beyond the individual contributions of its members.

A society, a people, or all humankind share this evolutionary heritage; to repeat, it is the product of ancestral experiences and contains concepts such as science, religion, and morality. To Jung, the basic forms we can find in the collective unconscious are archetypes, differing but repeating patterns of thought and action that reappear time and again across people, countries, and continents. These basic archetypes within us are defined as self, shadow, anima, animus, and persona.[1] Jung also noted that this collective unconscious can only be understood through an examination of the symbolic communica-

---

[1] The self is the product of individuation—the totality of the psyche; the shadow is a part of the unconscious mind consisting of repressed weaknesses, shortcomings, and instincts—the reservoir of human darkness; the anima and animus are the two primary anthropomorphic archetypes of the unconscious mind, both elements of the collective unconscious—the anima is the feminine image in a male psyche, the animus the reverse; and persona is the mask, the social role, we present to the world.

tions of the human psyche—through art, dreams, religion, myths, and the themes of human relational-behavioral patterns.

While Jung was hovering between genetics and social learning in his description of the collective unconscious, the psychoanalyst and social scientist Erich Fromm was more inclined to the latter. Fromm was the first person to have coined the term "social unconscious." He defined the "social unconscious" as "those areas of repression which are common to most members of society" [9]. According to Fromm, our beliefs, values and taboos are so engrained that they become unconscious over time—entering the social unconscious and limiting what we like to think of as our free will. Fromm argued that the family serves as the initiator of the social unconscious, or the psychological agent of society, staging societal requirements by molding children's character through culturally sanctioned child-rearing practices. Education, brainwashing, and propaganda, Fromm maintained, have much in common. Each society determines which thoughts and feelings will be permitted to arrive at the level of awareness, and which have to remain unconscious.

To further elaborate on Fromm's conceptualizations, we are expected to close our eyes to things the social group to which we belong claims do not exist [10]. However, we must accept as truth the things others say are true, even if our own eyes convince us that the information is inaccurate. Ultimately, what is determined as conscious or unconscious depends on the structure and patterns of feeling and thought produced by the society in which we are living. To Fromm, the social unconscious takes on a reality of its own, quite different from individual consciousness.

Both Jung and Fromm (like Le Bon, Freud, and Turquet before them) detected a powerful underground current within groups, containing a common pool of images, ideas, and meanings, based on the history of whatever society to which a group belonged. Other observers of group dynamics concurred, and suggested that forces beyond their control drive individuals in groups—as if a group as an independent entity has its own needs and exercises its influence quite separately from the individuals that would make up the group [11, 12].

For example, for Siegfried Foulkes (like Jung and Fromm), there is a social or interpersonal unconscious that precedes the emergence of individual consciousness. There is an entity called a "foundation matrix, based on the biological properties of the species, but also on the culturally firmly embedded values and reactions. These have been developed and transmitted, especially in the nuclear family, in the social network, class, etc. and have been maintained or modified by the intimate plexus in which the person now moves" [13]. This group matrix acts both as a container and as a holding environment for the psychic processes of the individual members of the group. It can be viewed as the hypothetical basis of all group transactions, providing the group's capacity for containment and holding.

This notion of being covertly affected by social cultural facts and forces in the group-as-a-whole has been further elaborated by Earl Hopper, another student of group dynamics, who argues that "the concept of the social unconscious refers to the existence and constraints of social, cultural and communicational arrangements of which people are unaware. Unaware, in so far as these arrangements are not perceived (not 'known'), and if perceived not acknowledged ('denied'), and if acknowledged, not taken as problematic ('given'), and if taken as problematic, not considered with an optimal degree of detachment and objectivity" [14]. Thus, according to Hopper, the social unconscious resides in all of us. However, we are "unconscious" or unaware of it. Usually, we take it for granted.

THE REALITY OF THE SOCIAL UNCONSCIOUS

Building on these various observers of group dynamics, I suggest that the social unconscious can be seen as a bridge between the social and the psychological. Each member of a group (or team) is a contributor to the social unconscious. He or she will co-create this shared unconscious of members of a specific social system. And this social system can be a team, a group, an organization, a community, a society, or a nation, or all of the above. These co-created social constructions are the recipients of shared anxieties, fantasies, defenses, myths, memories, and shared cultural prohibitions, the remnants of memorable, even traumatic experiences— representations that have been accumulated across the generations. This cultural "baggage" will invisibly influence the behavior and interactions of a team or group.

> **"Cultural 'baggage' invisibly influences the behavior and interactions of a team or group."**

Given the ever-present social unconscious, all of us are embedded in a highly complex, inter-related web of relationships, not always with much awareness that this is the case. Thus all of us have to deal not only with an inner psychological reality but also with an external one. Most commonly, however, we are unaware of these unconscious forces and factors that influence us.

What kind of emotional processes do you recognize in the group-as-a-whole?

- Attachment behavior—feelings of love and wanting to be close
- Fear of emotional closeness
- Feelings of pain and grief
- Feelings of shame
- Feelings of anger
- Feelings of guilt
- Feelings of envy

Reflect on the ways these feelings express themselves. Recall incidents—what thought processes were taking place?

In groups (or teams), the astute observer may notice the interface of (at times) conflicting dramatizations of each group member's unique inner script. When such interconnections occur, members of a group—apart from having to deal with their own peculiarities—also need to tap into a shared unconscious territory, with all its archaic assumptions, remnants of previous transference reactions, and a multitude of possible unresolved conflicts. It also implies that, when involved in a group coaching activity, we cannot disregard the social unconscious. We need to be aware of its presence when dealing with groups (or teams). Furthermore, the existence of the social unconscious will enable us to make a "cloud" observation (see Figure 6.1).

1. Physiological concerns (hunger, thirst, elimination/sleep, breathing, etc.)

2. Sexual/sensual concerns (lust)

3. Attachment/affiliation concerns (wanting to care/wanting to be loved/fear of abandonment/fear of loneliness/fear of emotional closeness: engulfment/dealing with mourning/grief)

4. Fearful concerns (self-esteem issues/not feeling worthy of approval/fear of being hurt/being shamed/feeling embarrassed/ feeling guilty/not feeling safe/being fearful/being distrustful)

5. Anger concerns (rage/resentment/envy/ jealousy/getting out of control/panic)

6. Exploratory concerns (play/social joy)

Figure 6.1   Basic concerns of people: the "cloud" issues

To take an example, one member of the executive team I was working with, reflecting on the previous day's activities, mentioned that he had had a frightening dream that night:

I was looking at myself in a mirror and barely recognized myself. I looked as pale as a corpse, but what really bothered me, seeing my mirror image, was that I had become almost bald. It was like I had had cancer radiation treatment. A few clumps of hair were still sticking to my head but most of the hair had fallen out. I got so upset that I smashed the mirror. I woke up immediately. The combination of the fright about what I had seen in the mirror and my violent reaction resulted in feelings of anxiety when I woke up.

This executive told the team that he had been thinking about the dream in the context of what had happened the previous day, when—although he had kept quiet—he had been very upset about what was going on in their organization. (The previous day's discussion had been about whether their mandate in the organization was being threatened by a number of powerful sub-groups.) Some time before, the team had been asked to set up an entity comparable to a skunk work, a project that had become extremely successful. But with success came envy from some of the more established departments in the company. A number of powerful interest groups in the organization felt threatened by their success. During the previous day's discussion, some of the team members had said that they felt a number of senior executives in the company were colluding against them. These people wanted to kill the project. If they succeeded, it would mean the end of the team.

I pointed out to the group that the dreamer, as spokesperson for them all, may have dreamt this dream (and presented it) to symbolize their sense of impotence about the situation. I wondered how angry the other members of the team were feeling, as what was happening was extremely unfair. Yet during that discussion there was not much anger shown. Instead, they circled around the topic of what would be good for the organization, as if they were sidestepping their anger on the matter. The dream could be interpreted as a representation of what was being done to them—a cancerous attack that made them feel "castrated" (castration

represented by the baldness)—but it also contained the growing anger felt by the members of the team.

This example illustrates what drives the social co-creation process: the individual's dynamic unconscious contains many basic desires that may not be realized at a conscious level, for fear that they may get out of hand. Consciousness has been withdrawn for defensive reasons. Since individuals are socialized in relatively similar societies, it is reasonable to assume that some of these warded-off conflicts are common to us all. This holds true no matter how heterogeneous our concerns are, because of the common biological properties of our species and our culturally embedded values and reactions. But these unconscious concerns can easily be activated.

But to view the group-as-a-whole as a completely separate entity dominated by regressive forces (as some scholars have done), detracts from the reality in the here-and-now. Focusing on the archaic parts of ourselves is only helpful when tied to the group's real-time exchanges, by working through the themes and issues that preoccupy us. What happens in the here-and-now remains essential.

THE QUESTION OF AUTHORITY

"Many teams get stuck because they fail to discuss and agree on the question of authority."

One of the typical themes to be found in a group's "cloud" concerns authority. In the group-as-a-whole container, one main concern is who is going to have authority over whom? Who will be dominant and who submissive? Many teams get stuck because they fail to discuss and agree on the question of authority, decision-making methods, and boundaries. The internal authority structure within the team needs to be clarified and, if necessary, continuously renegotiated.

Authority issues have been with us since the dawn of human-kind. In our distant Paleolithic past, alpha males had the important role of assuring the survival of the species. Like the silverback gorillas we can observe today, the chief of a tribe had to take care of direction (finding food), protection (against predators), and the creation of order—keeping the members of the group in line. If we fast-forward to the modern corporate world, we see that senior executives are expected to play similar roles.

Jockeying for authority is an inevitable part of group life, affecting the dynamics of the group-as-a-whole. The desire to overthrow authority and the temptation to rebel are ever-present. The roles executives play in a team setting are clear signifiers of some of these inevitable processes. All of this can be seen as reruns of the scripts that played out in their families of origin. They are part of the hotchpotch of mood-states and behavior patterns found in the team cloud.

SCAPEGOATING AND ALTERATIONS OF MOOD

Paranoid and depressive anxieties are major emotional drivers within a group-as-a-whole [15, 16, 17]. At the core of these primitive regressive processes is a basic feeling of helplessness, a state of mind that produces the deepest source of anxiety in human beings (evoking memories of our earliest, infantile anxiety about our dependency).

If these regressive forces are not dealt with, the group-as-a-whole falls victim to a paranoid mindset, expressed as mistrust, untruthfulness, suspicion, hostility, immoral behavior, rivalry, jealousy, envy, spite, and fear. This level of discord can contribute to a break-up of the social relations between members of a group or team, regardless of how effective each member (operating on his or her own) might be.

When paranoia raises its ugly head, some members of the group or team may behave destructively toward fellow members. Along with demonstrations of fear, mistrust, suspicion, anger, and caution, paranoid group members may even attribute secret meanings and messages to the coaches' comments. Some members of the group may also try to establish "unholy," collusive bonds with other members in order to defend themselves against their common enemy, the leader.

Paranoia may be accompanied by depressive reactions, so that some group members feel lonely, isolated, and even ostracized by other members. One result is that they may direct their anger inwards, and adopt a hypercritical attitude toward their own mistakes or achievements, seemingly unable to stop blaming themselves for imagined wrongdoings. Such strong self-criticism can contribute to a vicious, self-destructive circle that interferes with task performance—without even mentioning the harm it does to the functioning of the group.

Within this paranoid framework, scapegoats will be targeted within the group or team. Scapegoating is a way of deflecting our aggression onto safer targets, instead of directing it toward the target we are really frustrated with. People who become scapegoats act as receptacles for the projections of the unacceptable impulses experienced by the group-as-a-whole. Temporarily projecting unwanted parts of our self onto the other relieves anxiety while justifying the displaced aggression. As an additional "benefit," this act of projection may bind "good" group members closer together, by creating a common enemy.

"People who become scapegoats act as receptacles for the projections of the unacceptable impulses experienced by the group-as-a-whole."

In many instances, scapegoats are chosen because of some special or unique characteristic that makes them different from the other members of the group, for example: their status, or their position as the sole representative of a function in the organization, or being on the boundary of an organizational system. An individual's personal history can also become the lightning rod for projective processes; given a personal predisposition to be a victim or black sheep, some low-status individuals frequently become associated (forced by the group) with the unacceptable, unseemly, or foolish aspects of the group.

THE GROUP-AS-A-WHOLE AS A FORCE FOR CHANGE

In spite of its complexity, a group-as-a-whole consciousness can bring a team or a coaching group to more advanced insights about themselves [18, 19, 20]. Through various kinds of group intervention, group coaching among them, group members develop solidarity, realizing that there is a degree of universality to their problems. Being part of a coaching group is also an opportunity to exchange information about different challenges and solutions. The group-as-a-whole container can encourage this by bringing repressed feelings and fears to consciousness. Sharing and accepting the inner worlds of others helps to create a virtuous circle of trust, self-disclosure, empathy, and acceptance. Helping others—offering support, reassurance, suggestions, and insights—can have a therapeutic effect, contributing to a sense of self-respect and well-being. Groups also allow the emergence of role models. Hence, imitative behavior—or identification with the other—within the group is an important force for change.

> "Sharing and accepting the inner worlds of others helps to create a virtuous circle of trust, self-disclosure, empathy, and acceptance."

The kind of dynamics that take place in the group-as-a-whole may resemble those that took place in participants' families of origin. Given the durability of some patterns, group members cannot help but engage in family re-enactment.

The dynamics of the group-as-a-whole offer an opportunity for members to understand better past relationships with parents, siblings, and others. Together with the coach, participants can help point out different ways of dealing with conflicted situations and breaking rigid patterns.

To illustrate, in one executive team in which I was intervening, one of its members, the VP marketing, continually complained about being excluded. Her complaints were not restricted to missed invitations to a number of social occasions; she maintained that she had been left out of important meetings in the company. In one team coaching session, she suggested to a few of the other members of the team that they should include her regularly in meetings of their own teams (in order, she said, to make the executive committee function better). She mentioned a number of specific meetings to which she had not been invited and which she viewed as important. From their facial expressions and comments, it was clear that the other members of the team found her complaints tiresome, particularly because, as they tried to point out, most of these meetings were not part of her mandate. One team member, the VP finance, reminded her forcefully that she had frequently asked to be left out of sessions since she was already overloaded—a statement she denied. At one point, the discussion became so intense that the CEO intervened to try to calm things down.

While this was going on, I was asking myself a number of questions. Was the exchange just part and parcel of a typical day's work for this team? Was this simply a misunderstanding between two people? Or was there more to their argument than met the eye?

As it happened, I knew something about the personal history of all three, which supplied another level of understanding about the clash. I (and some others in the team) realized that all three were re-enacting specific family dramas. The VP marketing was the middle child in a family of three very competitive sisters. She had always felt that her elder sister was the favorite of her father, and the younger of her mother, which left her with a perpetual feeling of being left out, or excluded. Although being left out can be a reality, as an adult she was unconsciously going out of her way to recreate situations where she could righteously declare that people had done it to her again—that she had been excluded. As for the VP finance, his colleague's moaning reminded him of his older brother, who was always trying to push himself forward and get the better of him—small wonder that the behavior of the VP marketing grated on him and that he reacted so irritably when she went on automatic pilot. In fact, the VP finance was on some kind of automatic pilot himself, since he too failed to recognize his own unconscious dramatizations when provoked. Clearly, both parties had a negative transference to each other—easy to ascertain from their body language and verbal communication. To complete this messy picture, the CEO would never allow conflict within the team to work itself out and always stopped it prematurely, leaving everyone highly dissatisfied. His preference was to push difficult issues under the carpet and leave things unspoken. Although he was only subliminally aware of this behavior pattern, he had unconsciously cast himself in the role of peacemaker—a role familiar to him from his childhood when he had been the peacemaker between two parents who fought like cats and dogs. All three parties were acting out inner scripts that may have been fairly relevant in childhood but were no longer effective or appropriate in the here-and-now. I realized it was high time that they recognized the extent to which they were caught up in scenarios of the past, made new beginnings, and selected more appropriate and constructive scenarios.

How good are you at reading the team-as-a-whole?
Answer the following questions YES or NO

                                                           YES   NO

- Are there times in a team when you experience bizarre fantasies and ideas that help you make sense of what is really going on?
- Are you effective in expressing and deciphering these fantasies and ideas in a time-appropriate manner?
- Do you recognize quickly that certain people in your team act out specific roles?
- Do you know how to deal with silences when you are engaged in team work?
- Are you astute at assessing the mood of the team, and effective at getting it unstuck?

If you answer YES to most of these questions, you possess cloud consciousness and have the talent to move a team forward.

As this example shows, the shared unconscious territory of the group-as-a-whole brings with it all the unconscious assumptions brought into a team by individual members, assumptions that manifest themselves as transference patterns from important family relationships in the past. It is reasonable to assume that some unresolved, unconscious "theater pieces" linger on into adulthood. But some of the themes contained in the dynamic unconscious of each team member contain desires that, if fulfilled, can lead to serious interpersonal conflicts. For this reason, consciousness is withdrawn from these desires by means of defensive operations.

Negative capability

Deepening the coaching experience is easier said than done. There are going to be many occasions when change agents running a team building exercise will be puzzled by the team's dynamics. When that happens, they will need to be able to draw on a capacity to suspend their disbelief and withdraw into their inner world of self-reflection and analysis while they figure out what is really going on. The most effective people interested in creating high performance teams are unafraid of incertitude and unresolved issues and are able to remain open-minded. They are prepared to accept a condition that the poet John Keats termed "negative capability": "when a man is capable of being in uncertainties, mysteries, doubts without any irritable reaching after fact and reason" [21]. Keats was writing about Shakespeare, but many years later the psychoanalyst Wilfrid Bion drew on his definition when cautioning analysts against rushing into interpretations of their clients' behavior. It is important to maintain a state of deliberate open-mindedness—the ability to keep the imagination alive without having the urge for closure.

Assessing negative capability
Answer the following questions YES or NO

                                                    YES   NO
- Can you handle mysteries without becoming over-anxious?
- Are you able to suspend your disbelief when you encounter puzzling situations?
- Are you willing to remain in a state of uncertainty?
- Are you naturally open to impressions and ideas?
- Do you have the ability to play with your imagination without needing greater specificity?

If you answer YES to most of these questions, you may have this capability.

THE BLIND MEN AND THE ELEPHANT

"In the interchange between the team-as-a-whole and the individual, the inside affects the outside, and the outside the inside."

In the interchange between the group-as-a-whole and the individual, the inside affects the outside, and the outside the inside. The part is always connected to the whole, and the whole determines what happens in the parts. In terms of the "sum" (the group-as-a-whole) and its "parts" (the individual members), there is an interesting exchange between the inner theater of the individual and the "acting out" of individuals' scripts within the group-as-a-whole. The drama made up by the group-as-a-whole affects individual members, and individual dramas affect the group-as-a-whole [22, 23]. Similarities between the members of the team are constantly disrupted by differences, and differences constantly disrupted by similarities, creating a constant state of flux and tension.

People interested in building high performance teams would do well to remember the parable of the blind men and the elephant. Six blind men were asked to determine what an elephant looked like by feeling different parts of its body. The man who felt a leg said the elephant looked like a pillar; the man who felt the tail stated that the elephant was like a rope; the one who felt the trunk announced that the elephant was like a branch of a tree; the one who felt the ear thought the elephant was like a fan; the one who rubbed the belly stated that the elephant was like a wall; and the man who felt the tusk maintained that the elephant was like a solid pipe.

Of course, each of them was right, but none of them was completely right—and none of them was completely wrong. The tale illustrates the inadequacy of traditional human reasoning. It points out that people will understand only a tiny portion of reality and then extrapolate from it, each claiming that their interpretation is the correct version.

As humans we have a tendency to define our own realities. But it is all too easy to fall into the trap of believing we know the truth, when all we can ever hope to grasp at an intellectual level is merely an aspect of it. If we approach life solely on a conscious level, we inherently restrict our opportunities for understanding ourselves. However, blind seekers can transcend their own partial knowledge, and, like the six blind men comprehend the totality of the elephant—the mysterious whole—by pooling their individual knowledge of each part and working toward a better understanding of the whole. All of us who are interested in the dynamics of groups or teams need, at times, to have our head in the clouds.

REFERENCES

1. Le Bon, G. (1896). *The Crowd: A Study of the Popular Mind*. London: Ernst Behler.
2. Ibid., p. 33.
3. Freud, S. (1921). "Group Psychology and the Analysis of the Ego." In J. Strachey (Ed.) (1950), *Collected Papers of Sigmund Freud*, Vol. V. London: Hogarth Press and the Institute of Psychoanalysis, pp. 78–79.
4. Turquet, P. (1974). "Leadership: The Individual and the Group." In G. S. Gibbard (Ed.), *Analysis of Groups*. San Francisco, CA: Jossey-Bass.
5. Ibid.
6. Lawrence, W. G., Bain, A., and Gould, L. (1996). "The Fifth Basic Assumption." In *Free Associations*, Vol. 6, part 1 (37), 28–55.
7. Lipgar, R. M. and Pines, M. (2003). *Building on Bion Roots: Origins and Context of Bion's Contributions to Theory and Practice* (International Library of Group Analysis, 20). London: Jessica Kingsley Publishers.
8. Jung, C. G. (1964). *Man and His Symbols*. New York: Doubleday and Company.
9. Fromm, E. (1962). *Beyond the Chains of Illusion. My Encounter with Marx and Freud*. New York: Simon & Schuster, p. 88.

10. Fromm, E. (1941/1969). *Escape From Freedom*. New York: Avon Books.

11. Ezriel, H. (1952). "Notes on Psychoanalytic Group Therapy: II Interpretation and Research." *Psychiatry*, 15, 119–126.

12. Whitaker, D. S. (1985). *Using Groups to Help People*. London: Routledge, Kegan & Paul.

13. Foulkes, S. H. (1975). *Group Analytic Psychotherapy, Methods and Principles*, London: Karnac, pp. 131–132.

14. Hopper, E. (2002). *The Social Unconscious: Speaking the Unspeakable*. London: Jessica Kingsley Publishers, p. 127.

15. Jaques, E. (1974). "Social Systems as Defense against Persecutory and Depressive Anxiety." In G. S. Gibbard, J. J. Hartmann and R. D. Mann, *Analysis of Groups*. San Francisco, CA: Jossey-Bass.

16. Menzies Lyth, I. E. (1960). "A Case Study of the Functioning of Social Systems as a Defense against Anxiety: A Report on a Study of the Nursing System in a General Hospital." *Human Relations*, 13, 95–121.

17. Menzies Lyth, I. E. (1992). *Containing Anxiety in Institutions: Selected Essays*. London: Free Association Books.

18. Yalom, I. D. (1970). *The Theory and Practice of Group Psychotherapy*. New York: Basic Books.

19. Yalom, I. D. and Leszcz, M. (2005). *The Theory and Practice of Group Psychotherapy*. New York: Basic Books.

20. Rutan, S. and Stone, W. (2000) *Psychodynamic Group Psychotherapy*. 3rd edn. New York: Guilford Press.

21. Wu, D. (2005). *Romanticism: An Anthology*. 3rd edn. London: Blackwell, p. 1351.

22. Foulkes, S. H. (1990). In E. Foulkes (Ed.), *Selected Papers*. London: Karnac.

23. Dalal, F. (1998). *Taking the Group Seriously*. London: Jessica Kingsley Publishers.

PART THREE

CREATING AUTHENTIZOTIC ORGANIZATIONS

CHAPTER 7

TOWARD SYSTEMIC CHANGE IN ORGANIZATIONS

God, grant me the serenity to accept the things I cannot change, the courage to change the things I can, and the wisdom to know the difference.

—Reinhold Niebuhr

He who rejects change is the architect of decay. The only human institution which rejects progress is the cemetery.

—Harold Wilson

If you don't like something, change it. If you can't change it, change your attitude.

—Maya Angelou

I couldn't find a group that wanted to do what I wanted to do. No one was really up for it.

—Tom Jenkinson

If it were as easy to design and carry out a change process as it is to prescribe and swallow a pill, there would be no need for leadership coaching or any other form of intervention. However, as the discussions in the previous chapters have indicated, change is exceptionally difficult, for individuals and for organizations. If the primary objective of group coaching is to establish a more effective organization through the creation of a sustainable coaching culture, then it should be helpful to add to our discussion of group coaching by looking closely at the process of change in individuals and organizations.

CHANGE WITHIN A SYSTEMIC CONTEXT

Apart from paying heed to psychodynamic processes, we should also look at organizations in a more systemic way, as organisms that are shaped and driven by specific elements of which they are composed. This perspective becomes even more compelling if we acknowledge that although organizations still float or founder as a result of individual and team actions, the wider system in which they operate is becoming increasingly diverse and virtual in terms of time zone, place, culture, nationality, gender, age, functional background, industry history, and so on.

While these complex, global, matrix-like structures present many advantages, they also create another challenge: diversity and virtual connections reduce the team's ability to meet individuals' desire for affiliation and trust, and as a result, may increase the likelihood of paranoid "me versus the world" thinking. The dissimilar backgrounds of team members, which can be more easily addressed if the group meets regularly in person, are more likely to be directly related to silo formation, turf fights, and slow decisions in virtual teams. To be avoided, these problems should be identified and addressed systemically—keeping in mind, as I mentioned earlier, that technical solutions are not sufficient; the human factor must be taken into consideration as well.

Systems theory is an interdisciplinary theory about the nature of complex systems in nature, society, and science, and is a framework by which we can investigate and/or describe any group that works together to produce some kind of result. Elements of systems theory can be very illuminating in thinking about organizational change and group coaching, especially for obtaining a more holistic view of an organization.

The theoretical basis of systemic intervention (like the interpersonal psychodynamic point of view) is to view people in relation to each other rather than to focus mainly or exclusively on what is happening within the individual (the purely intrapsychic orientation). A systemic approach fosters a better understanding of how all the parts of a system interact with one another, and take on a holistic shape. Students of systems theory are apt to point out that when we only look at the component parts of a system, we miss important information that can only be discovered by looking at the system overall. In many instances, the whole has properties that cannot be found in its constituent elements. To tie this to my earlier discussion of group-as-a-whole, we can say here that we are talking about the group-in-a-system.

Systems theory came to the fore as a specific discipline in the 1950s [1, 2, 3, 4]. It brings together theoretical principles and concepts from a number of disciplines, including the philosophy of science, physics, biology, and engineering. Applications of the systems approach can now be found in numerous domains such as sociology, political science, organizational theory, health administration, management, economics and psychotherapy—in particular, family systems theory. The understanding of systems theory has now evolved to the point where we incorporate many of its concepts into our everyday language without even being aware of it (as indeed we do with many psychoanalytic concepts). For example, we talk about a health care system, a body system, an information system, a banking system, a political system, and a family system. And notwithstanding its biological origins, systems theory has proved very effective at explaining the behavior of the individual in the context of organizations. These concepts help us understand people in relationships, provide the insights needed to decipher the complex interactions within groups, and help us understand resistance to change.

Homeostasis, the capacity to self-sustain, is an important concept in systems theory. Over time, despite temporary fluctuations, systems always seek to return to a stable, constant condition— and thanks to a system's ability to self-correct and self-regulate, it is able to return to its homeostatic state. This concept helps to explain why change—which fundamentally means a disruption of homeostasis—can be so difficult. For desired change to take place, therefore, the various parts and people in an organizational system need to be connected through positive and negative feedback loops. Helped by these feedback systems, a change in one part of the system will affect the other parts—which, in turn, will affect its original (in this context, less desirable) condition.

Taking a systemic approach, people engaged in team and organizational intervention focus on the complex network of relationships through which people function and the context in which problems arise. This perspective helps change agents discern specific patterns of behavior, how they came to be established, how they can be understood in the light of team interaction, and how feedback loops can be implemented to support change. A systems perspective makes us more aware of the intimate links between the intrapsychic, interpersonal, and social elements of the group-as-a-whole in relation to individuals. Systemically-oriented practitioners explore not only how people communicate, but what they communicate, aiming to identify and explore the patterns of values, beliefs, attitudes, and behaviors in roles and relationships that seem to have become set over time, and to enable people

> "A systems perspective makes us more aware of the intimate links between the intrapsychic, interpersonal, and social elements of the group-as-a-whole in relation to individuals."

to decide where change would be desirable. Many of the problems that block organizational change are systemic, that is, not only do individuals naturally resist change, but in addition, the organizational architecture (especially social defenses) may well be constructed in such a way as to make change very difficult.

THE PROCESS OF INDIVIDUAL AND ORGANIZATIONAL CHANGE

One day a young Buddhist making his journey home came to the banks of a wide river. Staring hopelessly at the obstacle in front of him, he pondered for hours how he would cross it. Just as he was about to give up and turn back, he saw a great teacher on the opposite bank. The young Buddhist yelled to the teacher, "Oh wise one, can you tell me how to get to the other side of this river?"

The teacher thought for a moment, looked up and down the river, then called back, "My son, you are on the other side."

As this story suggests, change very much depends on the kind of perspective we take toward it. Because we may find it difficult to take the perspective of others, change does not come naturally. We are often very reluctant participants in the change process. Change disturbs our equilibrium, and is a threat to our homeostatic, predictable, and stable world. We avoid situations that upset order, threaten our self-interest, increase stress, or involve risk. To quote the economist John Kenneth Galbraith: "Faced with the choice between changing one's mind and proving that there is no need to do so, almost everyone gets busy on the proof."

In most instances, change is not a comfortable process, and not without conflict. At the same time, we know that change is inevitable. It is a truism to say that the only constant in life is change. Evolutionary psychology has made it clear to us that it is not the

"It is not the strongest who survive, nor even the most intelligent, but those who are most responsive to change." strongest who survive, nor even the most intelligent, but those who are most responsive to change. Whether we like it or not, to exist is to change. Although change means leaving things behind—and letting go of what seems secure—there is no real security in things that are no longer meaningful.

Openness to change. How do you view change?
Answer the following questions YES or NO

YES   NO

- Do you make an effort to learn at the same pace as the world is changing?
- Do you have a good understanding of what drives change in your world?
- Do you know how to create buy-ins for change?
- Do you think you have the skills to deal with change?
- Do you know how to help people to become positive about change?
- Do you understand why most change management efforts fail?
- Are you good at handling surprise and fear of the unknown?

If your answer is YES to most of these questions, you may have some of the qualities needed to be an effective change agent.

President Woodrow Wilson once said, "If you want to make enemies, try to change something." We resist change for a wide variety of reasons, ranging from having a straightforward intellectual disagreement over the reasons for the change, to deep-seated psychological prejudices. Frequently, making a change requires a leap of faith. We are asked to move in the direction of the unknown on the promise that the unknown, once we know it, will be better for us. But we will only take active steps toward the unknown if we truly believe that the risks of doing nothing are greater than those of moving in a new direction.

Social relations play an important role in our reluctance to change. As a social species, we like to be connected to people and to associate with people we know. A request for change frequently means a questioning of these old connections, and disruption of cultural traditions and group relationships. Change may be associated with the fear that we are going to lose something we value— not a great incentive to embrace change or to explore new relationships.

Change may also create new and unfamiliar situations, conditions over which we no longer have control. This may lead to concerns about losing power, or infringement of our position and status. This fear of loss is very real. Change can affect our power base, meaning that we have to build another, with all the stress and strain that is involved. Under certain circumstances, a change effort can even be perceived as a personal attack, or "turf battle." No wonder that suggestions for change are met with such hesitancy and resistance; and no wonder that people argue against change— they clearly, and in some instances correctly, view the change as contrary to their best interests.

Self-doubt is another complicating factor in the change process. People may have the will to change, but question whether they have the skills to do so. They are concerned about the demands and responsibilities placed on them by the new business processes, systems, or technologies that accompany many changes. They wonder, perhaps rightly, whether they have what it takes.

"People may have the will to change, but question whether they have the skills to do so."

Others suffer from change fatigue. If an organization has been through a lot of upheaval, some people may resist change because never-ending change processes have overwhelmed them. They may decide to keep their head down until it passes. When we look at the success ratios of change processes, their attitude is not so hard to understand.

Related to this is reluctance prompted by inadequate explanation of the need to change—"If it ain't broke, don't fix it." People need to understand what is not working, what the proposed change will address, and the implications of changing or not changing, otherwise they will see only the trouble change will bring rather than its potential benefits and rewards. If there is no evidence of a real problem, calls to "fix" it will be ineffective.

Resistance can also be expected from people who are overworked, struggling with the limited resources available in the organization, and feeling that they already have enough on their plate. For them, change will be perceived as just one more burden, creating extra work and resource strain when they are already dealing with the highly exhaustive pressures of their daily activities. The expectation that they will have to implement change while continuing with their current duties is too much to take.

In some cases, the problem is less resistance to change than resentment at suddenly being presented with it. People do not like to be kept in the dark; but far more damaging is the perception that they have not had any input in the decisions made about change. People want voice.

Although the world is full of earnest people who really believe that change is for the better—that everyone will profit from the change initiative—there are many others who are not so sure. They may have a more skeptical, even paranoid outlook. They may question the change agents' motives. Is there more to the suggested change program than meets the eye? Have they seen the full deck of cards? Is the change initiative an attempt by some factions in the organization to increase their power base, or to eliminate potential rivals? Furthermore, people with some experience of organizational life know that change is like shuffling the cards, and brings both winners and losers. Some people will gain status, job security, and quality of life, and others will lose them. Whatever the reason, resistance to change is inevitable, and has to be anticipated and dealt with accordingly.

Almost all of the organizational consulting and coaching assignments I have been involved in were influenced by three factors: the individual and group dynamics I wrote about earlier, and resistance to change. Here is a "simple" example.

I was asked to help a board of directors of a privately owned company that was in a transformation process, attempting to reinvent itself, from a British former heavy industry fossil fuel equipment supplier, to a high-tech, green energy, consulting firm. To help make the transition, the CEO had hired a brilliant serial entrepreneur from Silicon Valley as the new Chief Innovation Officer. Within several months of his arrival, however, war had broken out between him and other members of the executive team. Aside from the CEO, the team complained to me bitterly about the CIO's impossible behavior. He was unorganized, rude, rarely answered emails, and missed many important meetings without any warning. I decided to organize an event—a high performance team intervention. I interviewed the participants before the team event, and most of the people I questioned admitted that the CIO was brilliant and had presented some truly innovative yet pragmatic ideas, but was an extremely difficult person to work with.

At the beginning of the event I asked the members of the team to do a self-portrait (described in Chapter 2). When all the self-portraits were hanging on the wall, I began to question the CIO about his drawings. As he talked, I learned that his grandfather had been a tremendously successful entrepreneur, but his father had gone from one low-paying job to another. The CIO had spent a great deal of time with his beloved grandfather, who clearly had seen the grain of brilliance in him that the CIO's father appeared to be lacking. The CIO told the other members of the team that his identity as an inventor and entrepreneur was the most important thing to him. And yet, he admitted, he had learned that creativity is a very fragile thing, so he did whatever he could to protect what he called the "spark." Listening to him, it became quite clear that his father represented some kind of "negative identity." There was this underlying fear that he would become like him. I could see that two systems—family and organizational—were in conflict. The CIO's family system supported and rewarded his persona of the absent-minded genius, whereas the organizational system he had just joined was trying, from his perspective, to stifle that genius. He had reacted fearfully, seeing his fellow members of the executive team as a threat, and as a result, he resisted all requests to change his behavior. After discussing this with members of the team, the CIO realized that his obstructive behavior was making the situation worse. At the same time, the other participants gained a better understanding of how to make the most of the genius in their midst who did not think the way they did, but who was as dedicated as they were to turning the company around. The outcome of the team intervention was that the CIO realized that he was part of a larger system. His actions created a short-circuit. It resulted in problems in other parts of the organizational system.

The CIO agreed to make specific behavior changes to facilitate communication with the other team members, and the others voiced their understanding and support of his need to protect the "spark." When I followed up with them several months later, I saw that the CIO had been able to make significant alterations in his behavior. Talking to him, he mentioned to me that, inspired by the event, he decided to see a psychotherapist. He felt that it had been a very good decision. The therapist had helped him explore the many positive sides of his father. Surprisingly, seeing his father in a different light had contributed to a much better mental state. He had been much less irritable these days; he had been more at peace with himself. Having a less stressed state of mind had helped him improve his relationship with the other members of the team. It also created a new equilibrium in the organizational system.

DEALING WITH RESISTANCE TO CHANGE

As this story shows, dealing with resistance to change means challenging and changing other people's perceptions and beliefs. It implies creating systemic changes. Changing opinions requires a lot of effort and people don't change overnight. Change also carries considerable psychological impact. Large-scale change efforts—especially those involving cultural change—are even more difficult to manage.

Let's look now at the five Cs of change—the essential components of any individual or organizational change effort—concern, confrontation, clarification, crystallization, and change [5, 6, 7].

Concern

If our human tendency is to resist change, how does the change process ever get underway? Under what conditions does our resistance start to weaken? Given the relative stability of individual personality, getting the process of change into motion usually requires a strong inducement in the form of a modicum of pain or distress—discomfort that outweighs the pleasure of secondary gains (psychological benefits such as sympathy and attention) that can create resistance to change) [8].

> "Getting the process of change into motion usually requires a strong inducement in the form of a modicum of pain or distress."

Change is often triggered by a sense of concern about our present situation. There will be disequilibrium in the system in which the person is operating. The most common triggers are family tensions, health problems, negative social sanctions, an accident, feelings of isolation, helplessness, and insecurity, problem behavior, distressing incidents occurring to someone close to us, daily hassles and frustrations, or problems at work. Many of the executives in the different programs (or management interventions) for which I am responsible report a high level of negative affect (emotions) in the period just prior to change, generally precipitated by triggers like these. These emotions make people aware of the serious negative consequences that will follow if their current dysfunctional behavior continues. This creates the conditions for a tipping point, that is, preparedness finally to break the status quo [9, 10]. People who have experienced major change in their lives have said that the change happened when they found the status quo increasingly difficult to maintain: their situation unsettled their psychological equilibrium.

Confrontation

When people are confronted with the fact that their bad days are turning into a bad year—in other words, that an isolated occurrence of occasional discontent has morphed into a steady pattern of unhappiness—they are no longer able to deny that something has to be done. Initially, they may brush others' observations and concerns aside, but eventually continued negation will no longer be tenable (although some people's efforts at denial can be quite heroic). From this point on, every new disturbance is recognized as part of a general pattern of dissatisfaction. Complaints coalesce into a coherent entity. At this stage, many people have what is commonly referred to in therapy circles as

"When people are confronted with the fact that their bad days are turning into a bad year, they are no longer able to deny that something has to be done."

an "Aha!" experience, a moment when they are finally able to see that neither the passage of time nor minor changes in behavior will improve the situation—indeed, the situation is likely to become worse unless something drastic is done.

However, the insight that drastic measures are required does not automatically compel people to take action. Nonetheless, it typically sets in motion an inner dialogue whereby they inwardly begin to consider alternatives to their current adverse circumstances. Having made the transition from negation to beginning to realize that all is not well, they are then able to move on from a situation in which every alternative appears more frightening than the status quo, to a position where they can undertake a reappraisal process. They start to play with their ambivalence, and their inner dialogue debates the advantages and disadvantages of taking some form of action.

Confrontation with the need for change is a necessary first step, but on its own is no guarantee of action. Some kind of focal event is required. Focal events are incidents that trigger change; however, they are not necessarily obvious—indeed, they can sometimes seem completely insignificant. Only in retrospect can they be interpreted as a milestone or a tipping point, the moment when the momentum for change becomes unstoppable. The focal event is often a minor occurrence—an ugly incident at the office, an argument with a child, a careless comment by a friend—that is seen as focal simply because it enables a discontented person to take the first, long-delayed step toward change. It becomes the catalyst in the change process, whether it is perceived as major or minor by an outside observer. A focal event, however trivial it may seem at first glance, can be an indicator of a whole range of incidents symbolic of the problem being experienced. Although objectively perceived as minor, subjectively

"A focal event, however trivial it may seem at first glance, can be an indicator of a whole range of incidents symbolic of the problem being experienced."

it is significant, because it calls attention to a problem that has existed for a long time.

The distinction between confrontation and clarification, which I discuss next, is not clear, because a clarification can be a confrontation. For example, a coach/consultant or other change agent might ask a member of a team if she can clarify a particular point. This apparent request for clarification is really a subtle and indirect confrontation. Confrontation is more emotionally loaded, while clarification seems more detached. The two approaches can overlap significantly, blurring their differences.

With both confrontation and clarification, we need to separate the self from the other. How do these processes start? Are they initiated by the individual concerned, or by others who point out that all is not well? There will be other- and self-confrontation, and other- and self-clarification; the latter has a high probability of deteriorating into an exercise in rationalization and intellectualization. Real clarification—the development of greater insight about what is happening to the self—is often initiated externally, and has to be accepted internally.

Clarification

When we are really confronted with stressful issues or focal events that precipitate moments of insight, we may be led to reinterpret what is happening in our life. Of course, some focal events—such as divorce, death, or illness—are objectively as well as subjectively significant and serious events. Others are less obvious, such as a caustic remark from a colleague or boss, or a request to run an operation in another country. It is at this point in the change process that we start to become ready to take action. We have a clearer idea of what is happening to us and what we need to do. Our resistance to change is breaking down. We have acquired new insights about our situation and see new possibilities, as opposed to our previous state of acceptance, helplessness, and hopelessness. Our emotional energy has been transferred from concerns of the past (such as dysfunctional behaviors) to the possibilities of the present and the future. We feel as if a heavy burden has been lifted, and are mentally ready to tackle a more constructive future.

"Change is so difficult that, even with the best of intentions, we can rarely manage it on our own."

Change is so difficult that, even with the best of intentions, we can rarely manage it on our own. Help may be needed from a family member, a trusted friend, another confidant, a psychotherapist, or a coach. The third step of the individual change process can be a public declaration of intent, which research suggests is a sound indicator of a high degree of commitment to change [11, 12]. Telling others what we plan to do, in a more or less public context, indicates that we have achieved a certain degree of acceptance of our problems. It shows that traditional defense mechanisms (such as denial, projection, and rationalization) have largely run their course. We are ready to take new initiatives.

Making a public commitment can be very helpful because it doubles momentum: it influences not only the individual making the commitment, but also the environment in which that individual functions. A dialogue has been set in motion that will lead to further insights. If, in a team intervention, someone states his intention to stop being a micro-manager, it is less likely that his colleagues will let him get away with any sign that he is reverting to his previous behavior. A public declaration of intent to change the current situation indicates a willingness to assume a more vulnerable position and to move the problem from a private to a public stage. People making public declarations during a team coaching session are expressing a wish to establish a new way of working—to establish a distance from their former, less desirable self.

Crystallization

By the time we get to the crystallization stage, the toughest challenges of the change process have been met. The personal resolutions of the clarification stage have laid the groundwork for a thoughtful, detailed reappraisal of goals and for experimentation with the new alternatives that have been envisioned. Cognitive restructuring has occurred. It is like the famous Gestalt exercise of young-or-old woman (see Figure 7.1)—an initial perception blocks another way of looking at things. Suddenly, new ideas and plans become clear and more definite in form. Reorganization has taken

Figure 7.1 Old woman–young woman as an example of cognitive transformation
(The cartoonist W. Hill originally drew the figure, and published it in the journal *Puck* on November 6, 1915.)

place, leading to a very different perception of a person's life situation.

But the destination of this sometimes painful inner journey is increased self-knowledge and a new beginning. As people progress through the various phases of successful personal change they demonstrate a growing ability to give up their old identities and roles and are able to adopt new ones. To get there, they may have the help of a coach, or, in a group coaching context, of the members of the team present when they made their public commitment. They begin to reorganize the world in which they live in a significant way. They re-evaluate their life's goals and meanings, letting go of the old and accepting the new.

Change: a never-ending journey

We all tend to talk big when it comes to change. But how many of the hundreds of new leaves we promise to turn over have even been looked at? The only true sign that change has been achieved is a new way of behaving. Inner transformation only takes place once a new way of looking at things has been internalized. The final part of the individual change process (see Figure 7.2) also involves proactively reshaping our internal world and the acceptance of a new way of doing things. We discard past patterns of thinking, feeling, and acting as we begin to turn towards the future. A shift in attitude and behavior culminates in the redefinition, and even reinvention, of our self.

THE PROCESS OF ORGANIZATIONAL CHANGE

For many organizational psychologists, organizational change and transformation are embedded in the process of individual change.

The five Cs of the individual change process

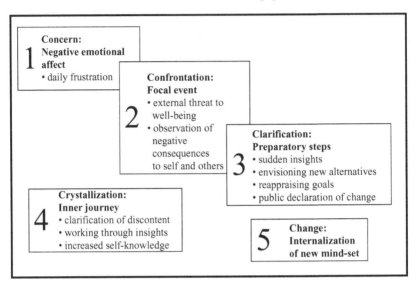

Figure 7.2 The individual change process

They argue that because organizations are made up of collections of people, the successful implementation of organizational change is dependent on understanding individual reactions to the change process. Organizations change because individuals change.

A maturing industry, increased competitive pressures on growth or profit margins, financial demands that are difficult to resolve, an economic crisis, or misalignment between shareholder and stakeholder expectations should all act as signals to management and boards of directors that their organization needs to revise its strategic plan for the future. However, even when there are clear signs that change is required within an organization, it is often resisted because people know it will involve moving into the unknown. Some of these resistances can be unconscious, and can even contribute to self-defeating acts of sabotage. For any organization to change, the degree of dissatisfaction has to be greater than the degree of resistance.

Corporate transformation and personal change

- What changes do you worry about most concerning your job and career?
- What do you fear doing, but will probably have to do, to survive these changes?
- If you risk doing nothing about them, what dangers might these threatening changes create?
- If you risk doing something about them, what opportunities might they create?

Reflect on these questions and ask yourself what your best options will be.

My model of change, as shown in Figure 7.3, provides a roadmap that can help management (and change agents) overcome organizational resistance by using a participative approach to engage the entire organization in change. The role of the senior team in leading an organizational change process is to provide

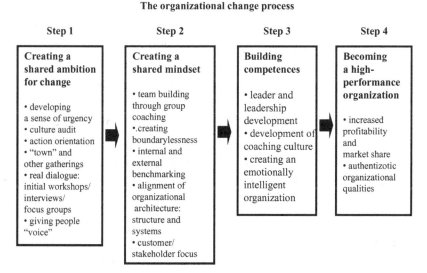

Figure 7.3   Creating an organizational change process

leadership that fosters a shared mindset and new behaviors, and ensures that the changes are institutionalized within the culture. Balanced leaders who can develop long-term strategies that align their organization's capabilities will be doing their company an invaluable service.

As many of the resistances to change are emotional in nature, change agents (including coaches and consultants) have to try to make targeted people realize that change can be advantageous. Cognition alone is not enough to prepare people for change, however. To win commitment for change, people must also be engaged cognitively and emotionally; in other words, people's heads and hearts have to be won.

> **"To win commitment for change, people must be engaged cognitively and emotionally—their heads and hearts have to be won."**

Nelson Mandela said, "Education is the most powerful weapon which you can use to change the world," but it can take time to educate people about the benefits of the change process. The company may have been drifting—with many employees feeling like helpless bystanders, watching the situation— and now is the time to give them "voice," to make them feel that they can be involved in making a difference.

Let me end this chapter with the parable of the six monkeys and the bananas. It is a good example of learning and unlearning, of rules and norms that have become institutionalized, to the extent that team members can no longer trace their origins.

Once upon a time there were six monkeys living in a cage. One day they awoke to find that a ladder had been positioned right in the middle of the cage and from the top of it a bunch of bananas dangled invitingly from a rope. One of the monkeys immediately climbed the ladder, but as soon as it reached the bananas, ice-cold water was sprayed down on all the other monkeys. This happened every time a monkey climbed the ladder and tried to grab the bananas. Very soon each monkey was on the lookout for one of its companions to climb the ladder. Whenever one of them tried, the other monkeys would stop it. As time went by, the monkeys simply learnt to ignore the bananas. Nothing would tempt them to try to get them, even after the bunch was lowered and within easy reach. The monkeys stayed well away: the last thing they wanted was another freezing shower.

Then one day a new monkey arrived in the cage. When he saw the bananas and tried to scale the ladder, all of the other monkeys attacked him and thrashed him severely. The new monkey quickly discovered that the bananas were taboo. As time went by more monkeys from elsewhere found themselves in the cage. Each in turn learned their lesson: stay away from the bananas. When they tried to climb the ladder, the others (including the newcomers) would attack them. Typically, it was the most recent victims that punished the new transgressor most.

In fact, the monkeys were so busy punishing each other that they failed to notice that despite the regular appearance of newcomers, their numbers mysteriously remained the same. For every new monkey that appeared in the cage, one of the originals was removed. It didn't take very long before all the six original monkeys had been replaced. Nevertheless, no monkey ever tried to climb the ladder again, despite the fact that all the original monkeys had gone and none of the remaining ones had ever received the icy shower. Ignoring the bananas had simply become a fact of life. If the monkeys could have replied, when asked why they attacked anyone who went for the bananas, their answer would almost certainly have been: "Well, I don't really know—it's just the way we do things around here." As can happen to many of us, the monkeys had gotten stuck in their ways, and change was no longer an option. They had reframed the situation and the organizational system had gotten the better of them.

REFERENCES

1. Von Bertalanffy, L. (1968). *General Systems Theory: Foundations, Development, Applications.* New York: George Braziller.
2. Churchman, C. W. (1968). *The Systems Approach.* New York: Laurel.
3. Miller, J. G. (1978). *Living Systems.* New York: McGraw-Hill.
4. Neumann, J. E. and Hirschhorn, L. (1999). "The Challenge of Integrating Psychodynamic and Organizational Theory." *Human Relations*, 52 (6), 683–695.
5. Kets de Vries, M. F. R. and Miller, D. (1984). *The Neurotic Organization.* San Francisco, CA: Jossey-Bass.
6. Kets de Vries, M. F. R. (2001). "Creating Authentizotic Organizations: Well-functioning Individuals in Vibrant Companies." *Human Relations*, 54 (1), 101–111.
7. Kets de Vries, M. F. R. (2006). *The Leader on the Couch: A Clinical Approach to Changing People and Organizations.* New York: John Wiley & Sons Inc.
8. Kegan, R. and Laskow Lahey, L. (2009). *Immunity to Change.* Boston, MA: Harvard Business Press.
9. Kegan, R. and Laskow Lahey, L. (2002). *How the Way We Talk Can Change the Way We Work: Seven Languages for Transformation.* San Francisco, CA: Jossey-Bass.
10. Kegan, R. and Laskow Lahey, L. (2009). *Immunity to Change.* Boston, MA: Harvard Business Press.
11. Maxwell, M. (1984). *The Alcoholics Anonymous Experience.* New York: McGraw-Hill.
12. Stall, R. and Biernacki, P. (1986). "Spontaneous Remission from the Problematic Use of Substances: An Inductive Model Derived from a Comparative Analysis of the Alcohol, Tobacco, and Food/Obesity Literatures." *International Journal of the Addictions*, 21, 1–23.

CHAPTER 8

BEING AN EFFECTIVE CHANGE AGENT

Only the wisest and the stupidest of men never change.

—Confucius

If there is anything that we wish to change in the child, we should first examine it and see whether it is not something that could better be changed in ourselves.

—Carl Jung

Without accepting the fact that everything changes, we cannot find perfect composure. But unfortunately, although it is true, it is difficult for us to accept it. Because we cannot accept the truth of transience, we suffer.

—Shunryu Suzuki

A person going nowhere can be sure of reaching his destination.

—Florian Houtman

In 333 BCE, Alexander the Great invaded Asia Minor and arrived in Gordium in the central mountains. He was only 23. Undefeated, but without a decisive victory either, he was in need of an omen to prove to his troops and his enemies that the outcome of his mission—to conquer the known world—was possible.

In Gordium, by the Temple of the Zeus Basilica, was an ox cart, which had been placed there by Gordius, King of Phrygia, over 100 years before. Gordius had tied the staves of the cart together in an extremely complicated knot. According to legend, whoever was able to release the knot would conquer Asia. Many came to Gordium to try to undo the knot, but all failed.

Having arrived at Gordium it was inconceivable that the impetuous and ambitious young king would not try to tackle the legendary Gordian knot. His generals gathered round as he struggled with the knot for a few minutes. After searching unsuccessfully for the hidden ends of the bindings, Alexander became impatient. He turned to Aristander, his seer, and asked, "Does it matter how I do it?" Aristander couldn't say, so Alexander pulled out his sword and sliced through the knot.

Alexander then went on to conquer Asia, thus fulfiling the oracle's prophecy. Ever since, the term "cutting the Gordian knot" has referred to solving a complicated problem through bold action. This is the task assigned to change agents like group coaches. Asking for help in making change is very hard for successful executives. And although "change" is an easy mantra for boards and top executive teams, or any management team to impose, a shift in the organization's collective conscious is particularly difficult. Change agents need to be prepared for (at least temporary) stalemates; however, if they know what they are doing, change agents like coaches can be highly instrumental in defusing such stalemates. They can help create tipping points—to create disequilibria and find new equilibria. Like Alexander the Great, they have to find innovative ways to cut the Gordian knot of group processes. They must take bold action to help the team progress. In doing so, they need the courage of their convictions—and a thorough understanding of their role and responsibilities.

INTO THE ZEITGEIST: A LOOK AT THE CHANGE AGENT'S WORLD

As I have already suggested, change agents who select leadership group coaching as their intervention of choice should realize that this option is not for the fainthearted. Group coaches have a very demanding task. They need to be masters of many things. They have to be quick, in the sense that they may only have one day with their clients to make some kind of difference, unlike a coach or therapist who meets with a single individual for a greater number of sessions. They should also be capable of using a clinical lens, tying together developments in the here-and-now with possibly outdated behavior patterns from the past. In addition, they need to have a solid understanding of the business context in which they are operating.

"Leadership group coaching is not is not for the fainthearted."

Throughout the group coaching process, leadership coaches need to maintain an aura of detachment and neutrality to be able to be a confidant to all the members of the team. Group coaches need to be prepared to identify the overt but also the covert issues of each individual participant. In taking this stand, however, they also have to be able to do so without over-identifying with goals that could blind them, and prevent them from seeing the problems with different eyes to arrive at new solutions. The coach needs to represent the salient issues of the (client) organization without becoming partisan to any one individual.

Faced with working with a group of Schopenhauer's hedgehogs—all jostling for the most comfortable position—a group coach has to make choices. Does she want to focus on each member of the team one at a time? Or does she tackle the vagaries of the group-as-a-whole? Or both? The choice is not easy. Some group coaches prefer to concentrate on direct issues concerning each individual member of the team. But this option inevitably leaves some hedgehogs out in the cold—and several elephants in the room. To be truly effective as catalysts of change, leadership coaches must pay attention to the "sum" as well as its "parts."

The imperative to make choices—to move constantly from a focus on the individual, to the group, and back again—also requires the group coach to possess the elusive quality of "negative capability," the ability to contain the confusion and anxiety about what is happening in the team. They must be able to switch between object and subject—keeping a close eye on what is happening to the group-as-a-whole—as well as monitor what is happening to each team member. And they need to encourage the team to think holistically, always keeping the general interest of the organization in mind.

Essentials of group coaching

- Focus on the emotions
- Explore the avoidance of distressing thoughts and feelings
- Identify recurring themes and patterns
- Have a developmental focus
- Discuss past experiences
- Focus on interpersonal relationships
- Pay attention to transferential issues
- Explore wishes, fantasies, and dreams

The challenge for group coaches as agents of change is to provide leaders with the kinds of intrapersonal, interpersonal, team, and leadership skills that enable them to help them and others expand their levels of responsibility and their capacity for taking initiative and action. In incorporating the perspectives of psychodynamic/systemic theories, the group coach also has an educational function in making organizational participants aware that there is something beyond a rational-structural mindset; there is more than meets the eye. They have to create a safe, transitional space where group members can communicate in a constructive way, where they can "play," and be more creative. The group coach sets the stage, models, and teaches the fundamental skill of daring to have what I call courageous conversations. In the group coaching session, people experience the way courageous conversations can, in effect, cut the Gordian knot. Understanding the power of courageous conversations is a key objective of group coaching sessions because it is a skill that, applied in organizations, lays the groundwork for change.

CREATING A TRANSITIONAL SPACE IN GROUP COACHING

Engaging in group coaching interventions is like creating a collaborative, therapeutic community. I use this analogy because these communities are characterized by a group-based approach to deal with personal problems. Simply stated, a therapeutic community is a program that relies on interactions within the peer group to help members confront the reality of their mental problems, and to subsequently commit themselves to a lifestyle change. The responsibility for the daily running of the community is shared among the clients and the staff.

Therapeutic communities

Therapeutic communities form a microcosmic society in which residents and staff assume distinctive roles and adhere to clear rules, all designed to promote the mental health of the community's members. This is a safe environment with clear boundaries and expectations, in which members have the opportunity to come to terms with their past through re-enactment of their problems within a treatment setting involving other members and staff. Group psychotherapy and psychodynamic interventions are often integral to the treatment, but therapeutic communities also offer the individual experiences to awaken dormant creative and social capabilities.

The essential elements of a therapeutic community are setting behavioral limits, creating sanctions and rewards, and using the power of role modeling. It is a framework that relies on positive change agents in people's lives, including family members, staff, peers, and others. The treatment community becomes a therapeutic agent, advocating self-help and mutual help, with rules, structures, and protocols to help people develop more acceptable, healthy lifestyle choices.

In therapeutic communities, it is made clear to the participants that they have to own their own life. The motto is: "You alone must do it but you can't do it alone." Clients are expected to be active participants in their own and each other's mental health treatment. As with group coaching, peer influence plays a central role. The therapeutic community is a powerful treatment approach. Its goals are to effect a complete change of lifestyle, take responsibility for one's own actions, acquire useful social skills, and eliminate antisocial attitudes and behavior. Not surprisingly, therapeutic communities have gained some reputation for success in rehabilitation and patient satisfaction all over the world [1, 2].

Some of the same principles applicable to a therapeutic community are applied to successful group coaching intervention. As with a therapeutic community, interpersonal learning becomes an essential vehicle for change. Individuals are taught to use their peers' observations to learn more about themselves, to make changes to their lifestyle, and to have a more balanced life. While self-help stands central, the peer community is used to facilitate social and psychological change, through confrontation of certain issues by other members of the team, and the coach.

In group coaching, like in the therapeutic community, participants are encouraged to take a fearless and searching moral inventory of themselves and others. In both intervention methods, self-reflection is crucial. Group coaching has some resemblance to "the cult of confession" (a public admission of personal shortcomings) that is often found in therapeutic communities. Opening up, for whatever reasons, can be a cathartic experience if the audience is a respectful recipient of these revelations. In addition, in group coaching (like in therapeutic communities) there is usually an element of "love bombing," implying the warm acceptance without strings attached, offered by the others. Containment also plays an essential role.

"Peer pressure will often be the catalyst that converts criticism and personal insight into positive change."

As I have suggested, in both therapeutic communities and group coaching, peer pressure will also often be the catalyst that converts criticism and personal insight into positive change. Peers can have a persuasive influence on others' desire to become more responsible and accountable. Importantly, they will often interpret painful incidents in different ways—emotionally and cognitively reframing it, and creating a new reality. Generally, whatever structure is being used, viewing our own behavior through a group lens is a very powerful experience. Peer pressure can play an essential role in creating real tipping points.

Trust is, of course, essential and the old Hippocratic dictum—"Do no harm"—needs to be stressed emphatically. As the intervention unfolds, helped by the coach, participants develop the trust necessary to be able to open up and learn from each other. Generally, I prefer interventions consisting of several modules that give the participants an opportunity to interact with each other in a structured psychological way over a longer period of time. Such interventions have a significantly higher chance of making a lasting impact on executives than the often temporary highs created by one-shot events.

A playful space

For this level of trust, group support, and experimentation to occur, a kind of "transitional space" needs to be created. For executives, this transitional space is a protected time for reflection away from the office. It is most effective when physical surroundings are comfortable but neutral, away from the distractions of the organizational world.

But more importantly, the transitional space is a figurative, or mental, one, where we can deal with a duality of internalization and externalization—the conflict between the internal world of thoughts, fantasies, feelings, and fears, and the external, real-life world of organization and society [3]. The group coaching setting offers a transitional space where these two worlds can meet and be explored. It can be compared to an arena in the interstices between our inner and outer worlds in which we can experiment, temporarily, with new behaviors or ways of thinking. In this space, team members can "regress in the service of the ego," retire from the stress of life, and replenish themselves in order to continue to function well, be playful, and arrive at new life solutions [4].

From a conceptual point of view, the notion of transitional space is symbolized by the contained or protected interaction between mother and infant. Children need to play with what they know to be true in order to find out more, and then use what they learn in new forms of play. Through play, children have a chance to practice what they learn; play becomes a multi-purpose vehicle for adapting to the real world, a major avenue for learning how to manage anxiety about real and perceived dangers, a place where they can test their fears. In this safe space—this intermediate area of experience, shared by parent and child—children can experiment at will, suspending the rules and constraints of physical and social reality.

As a developmental tool, play is not only useful for children; it continues to be important throughout life. And adults can relearn how to play. When working with teams and organizations, group coaches can recreate a similar transitional space, providing the conditions for innovative shifts and new developments in organizations. As play is associated with unconscious processes, it provides the raw material for conscious engagement in the real world with new ideas, experiences, and interpersonal relationships. It also allows players to transcend passivity and to become active doers, involved in what is happening around them. Like children, they can explore themselves, their emotions, and their behavioral patterns through play.

A safe space

Effective change catalysts (and particularly group coaches) recognize that full team engagement will not be achieved unless each member of the team can trust that their conversations will not result in harm to their objectives or their future prospects. They will make a great effort to recreate a safe, supportive, warm, and neutral atmosphere for the team. They will attempt to create a place where difficult matters can be addressed with more freedom or safety than would be possible within the formal organizational structure. If people have a safe area to "play," they are more likely to reveal more about themselves, and have a greater readiness to learn about new ways of functioning. Coaches will attempt to create a place where difficult matters can be addressed with more freedom or safety than would be possible within the formal organizational structure.

> **"If people have a safe area to 'play', they are more likely to reveal more about themselves, and have a greater readiness to learn about new ways of functioning."**

Establishing a safe, transitional place where opinions can be expressed will create a climate of interpersonal trust and preparedness to engage in social reciprocity, as far as exchange of information is concerned. Support and acceptance are essential if the members of the group are to risk exploring and revealing more of their inner and outer worlds. If there is no trust, it is unlikely that team members will be transparent. But when there is enough interpersonal trust, group members will be willing to engage in constructive conflict resolution and to make commitments, and are more likely to be accountable for their decisions.

As far as opening up is concerned, although a change agent like a group coach should not be a blank sheet, at the same time, the members of a team aren't embarking on a group intervention to hear about the coach's successes and failures. It is not appropriate for group coaches to share too much personal information. Self-revelation on the part of the coach needs to be minimal and limited to helping the participants gain insight into specific interactions in the here-and-now.

A transitional, safe space is rather like the web of the dream catcher—team members hover productively between the self and other selves, making experimental forays into alternate identifications in ways that, if all goes well, deepen and expand their capacity to take on the world in creative ways, and leaving behind the things that do not work.

The web of the dream catcher

In the dream catcher's web, we can also find material pertaining to the group-as-a-whole, another intermediate developmental phase between intrapsychic and external reality. As the repository of the unfinished business of many of the participants, it becomes a world of fantasy and make-believe, a playing field between the members of a team that needs constant attention. And astute group coaches will make good use of this playing field by making "cloud" obser-vations, when appropriate. Such interventions can be very helpful for breaking stalemate in a group process and moving a team forward. For example, if the group coach senses that the discussion among team members is stuck, or going nowhere, he or she can articulate this feeling in a gentle way, wondering whether this inability to move forward may be related to an elephant in the room—to some unfinished business nobody is prepared to deal with. Such an intervention could encourage one or more members of the team to find ways to break the impasse, one avenue being to tackle the elephant.

COMMUNICATION: LISTENING WITH THE THIRD EAR

Listening with the third ear, in psychotherapy, involves listening very carefully to what someone is both saying and *not* saying. It calls into action the listener's intuition and emotional intelligence, to capture what is going on under the surface. In a similar way, when a participant in a group coaching session is in the hot seat, relating his or her story, the group coach's role is to capture key points and peak moments from the various dialogues, posing ques-tions and making hypotheses that help move the dialogue forward to a more meaningful level. Team members are also encouraged to focus on what happens in the dialogue between the coach and the participant in the hot seat. In listening with the third ear, they are also asked to look for areas where further questions might be indi-cated, or propose other hypotheses about aspects that might not have been investigated sufficiently in the dialogue. Topics may include moods (the mood of the dialogue—joyful, surprised, reflective, sad, awed, fearful, irritable, angry, boring, disgusting, etc.), the relationship between mood and issues that are presented, and other themes. Coaches also need to pay attention to the general mood state of the executives in the team and be aware of their transference reactions.

In addition, given the influential role they play, change catalysts like group coaches should also be careful about what they can and cannot communicate. They need continually to reflect on what they know and what they don't know—and seek to know more. Group coaches also have to be perceptive about overt and covert, verbal and non-verbal messages. They should be prepared to talk about the elephants in the room when appropriate, but also know when to keep their mouth shut.

"Group coaches should be prepared to talk about the elephants in the room when appropriate, but also know when to keep their mouth shut."

Group coaches should also abide by the phrase "strike when the iron is cold." If the iron is too hot, observations will less likely be heard. At any given moment, there are exciting interactions within each individual, between individuals, within the group-as-a-whole itself. An awareness of these dynamics is based on a deep theoretical and practical understanding of team dynamics and team development, as well as significant coaching experience with individuals and groups. However, that awareness is only as useful as the coach's ability to listen deeply, to decide what really matters and when to draw attention to it properly.

"Group coaches should 'strike when the iron is cold.'"

THE YIN AND YANG OF EMOTION AND COGNITION

To be most effective, a group coach's primary focus needs to be affect (emotion), not necessarily cognition (intellect). The most important learning takes place emotionally. This means that if cognitive observations are made, they need to be tied to affect. For example, in the group session with the board of directors I described in Chapter 7, at one point I said to the CIO, "The group is telling you that you will have to change your attitudes toward meetings. You can't just not show up when you promised to do so." I then said to the CFO, "Would you want to have [the CIO] as your boss?" The CFO became visibly agitated at the idea, and said, "No way, he is far too disorganized. I'm not prepared to deal with his messes." This outburst had an effect on the CIO. After a moment, I asked him how he felt about what had been said. He responded, "That was embarrassing. I had no idea people see me that way. I don't like hearing that people don't want to work for me." He went on to agree that he would make a serious effort to show his respect for his colleagues by being at meetings when he promised. He added with a somewhat embarrassed smile, that he also would make an effort to be on time.

As this example shows, envisioning the possibility of, and finding the motivation for, behavior change needs both cognition and emotion. Repetitive experiences will be needed to help people work through the intellectual (cognitive) aspect of their dilemmas as well as to acquire a corrective emotional experience toward it—that is, the process by which the client gives up old behavior patterns and learns or re-learns new patterns by re-experiencing early unresolved feelings and needs.

RESISTANCE JUDO: CONTAINING CONFLICT

Change agents like group coaches must also be prepared to tackle interpersonal problems on the way, as it is more than likely that, at some stage or another, team members will display dysfunctional behavior. The conflicts with which each individual is struggling are likely to be repeated in a group setting. In such instances, it will be up to the coach to point this out, thus taking on what may be a necessary, therapeutically task-relevant, but socially taboo role. They also need to recognize when social defenses are in operation. To reduce their dysfunctional effects, group coaches have to find ways to replace the utility of defensive rituals with more constructive ways of containing anxiety and managing personal risk. Here the concept of resistance judo can be helpful: do not confront acted-out resistance head-on. This stance reminds me of a Sufi story.

An ancient story tells of a Sufi village that was attacked and captured by a group of warriors. The king of the victorious tribe called the Sufi leaders together. "Unless you can tell me what will make me happy when I am sad and sad when I am happy," he threatened, "the entire village will be put to the sword tomorrow morning."

The village people built a large fire and all night long their wisest men and women sat around it in deep discussion, trying to find the right response to the king's challenge. What could make a man happy when he was sad, and sad when he was happy?

The sun rose all too soon and the conqueror entered the village. Approaching the wise ones round the dying fire, he asked, "Have you found the answer to my question?"

One of the men reached into his pouch and presented the king with a gold ring. The king was enraged. "I have no need for more gold!" he shouted. "How can this ring make me happy when I am sad and sad when I am happy?" "My lord," said the elder, "look at the ring again." So the king looked more closely and saw there was an inscription inside the ring. It read, "This too shall pass."

The inscription in the Sufi ring tells us about something more than the transience of things; it also tells us about the need for emotional containment. Emotional containment can be thought of as a place—a physical or psychological space—within which we can face our fears and anxieties, calm our emotions, and withdraw to recuperate.

In dealing with teams with difficult participants, a change catalyst like a group coach must be supportive and take active steps to counteract an individual's propensity to feel unaccepted, rejected, and even persecuted. Responding empathetically and demonstrating interest in the person will largely counteract these tendencies but it is also critical to establish a working alliance with other members of the team. Positive reframing of uncomfortable feedback is a creative task. The coach should note similarities among members of the team and promote caring attitudes. This will help to facilitate the development of cohesion, provide a sense of belonging, and reduce feelings of alienation. In the process, the group coach can become a model of identification for the team.

Difficult team members need to have the opportunity to reveal and work on the disruptive aspects of their personality. They may even require the coach to create an illusion that an all-powerful, protective group-as-a-whole (including the group coach) will "rescue" them if necessary. Gradually, as these difficult aspects of personality are revealed, understood, and tolerated, these team members, like infants, will become more balanced and no longer need the protective quality of the group-as-a-whole.

In one high performance team exercise it became clear that the process was not working. The group was stuck. One of the participants, obviously bored, was staring out of the window. Another member of the team also seemed to be out of it, sneakily having a look at his iPhone. In the meantime, the discussion of the ratings of the 360-degree feedback questionnaires of yet another team member was quite perfunctory. Clearly, it was high time to make a group-as-a-whole interpretation.

The day before the intervention took place, I had had dinner with the CEO, John, during which he told me that the previous week he had been negotiating the possible sale of the company. He said that the other members of the executive team had been informed about these discussions but didn't know the outcome. They also knew that if the sale went through, John would most likely leave to spend much of his time teaching at a local university, something he very much enjoyed.

Keeping this information in mind, I wondered whether the anxiety of being deserted by their powerful, very charismatic leader could be an issue that might derail the team building process. Were they concerned about who would take care of their dependency needs if John were no longer there? Did they fear being deserted? Given the stalemate in the group process, the time had come for a "cloud" observation.

I said to the members of the team, "I somehow have this feeling that we are stuck. For a while we have been going around in circles. I don't feel that we are adding much value to Lionel [the person in the hot seat]. And I wonder why? Maybe we should take some time out and think about what is going on in the room right now. I wonder if some of you are thinking about a broader issue, like the possibility of the sale of the company—and what such a step would mean for you? How would each of you experience John's departure?"

This comment brought a burst of new energy into the room. Several team members said unequivocally that they felt that selling the company was a terrible idea, a mistake. One in particular said over and over again that it would be like a betrayal of the employees. I wondered whom he was talking about. Another executive belabored the point about John no longer being there. According to him, this would implode the executive team. Without John, how would they be able to move forward? A very meaningful discussion about this issue followed (leading to further discussions after the session), after which the discussion about Lionel continued.

As this example illustrates, when the dynamics of the group-as-a-whole seem to be working against the process, a change agent like a group coach can help members verbalize what is bothering them. In the previous example, I talked about the elephant in the room, that is, the team's feelings that the CEO would be deserting them, and their anxiety whether they would be able to manage without him. The possible departure of the CEO resulted in a burst of dependency associations among the members of the team, a process that resonated among everybody. I put into language what was floating in the cloud.

Verbalization

Language is the social medium for translating the dynamics of a team and giving meaning to what is happening. Without conscious verbalization, team members are prone to be driven by bizarre, out-of-awareness forces that may contribute to inappropriate behavior. The need "to act out," to engage in disruptive behavior, can often be attributed to the failure of the coach's interpretive work, or the team member's (or members') failure to assimilate the coach's interpretation. Some people prefer to act out, rather than remember and reflect.

> **"Language is the social medium for translating the dynamics of a team and giving meaning to what is happening."**

Verbalization is a robust tool. The purpose of language is to build a bridge between the visible and the invisible, the conscious and the unconscious. While dealing with group-as-a-whole issues, giving names to phenomena as they come to the fore is the first step in the process of demystifying and neutralizing the multiple forces at play.

However, it is not easy to ascertain the nature of conflict between specific members of a team, as it happens, because as humans we are masters at obfuscation. The defenses of negation, denial, and avoidance are very much part of the human condition. But notwithstanding the smoke and mirrors that accompany the dynamics of the group-as-a-whole, group coaches need to be prepared to monitor the level of anxiety in the team, and if necessary,

> **"The defenses of negation, denial, and avoidance are very much part of the human condition."**

confront unequivocally the major anxieties as they surface. These anxieties need to be addressed, clarified, and defined.

There will be times when group coaches have to act as gate-keepers, setting boundaries for members of the team because of their acting-out behavior. Their role is to guide the process, and help shape the norms that will make a team coaching intervention most effective. They have to watch the civility of behavior among team members. If the group consists of people from the same organization, coaches also need to have a deep understanding of that organization's culture, the related sub-cultures, and the general business context.

In sum, group coaches need to control the ambiance of the team by minimizing disruptive behavior, promoting cohesion, and creating a transitional space that facilitates interpersonal trust. Effective group coaches will encourage the expression of intrapsychic conflict (and its attendant emotional behavior) and its verbalization (as opposed to acting-out behavior). They will create greater tolerance for the *Sturm und Drang* of intra-group conflict, reassuring its members that conflicts need not necessarily be destructive and can be smoothed out.

COURAGEOUS CONVERSATIONS

One of the most important lessons a participant in a group coaching session can take away is an appreciation for the power of what I have described before as courageous conversations. This type of conversation is so rare that I make a point of wrapping up group (or team) coaching interventions with examples of courageous conversations that took place during the intervention, and encouraging the group members to think about how they could have courageous conversations in their organizations.

Courageous conversations are those less-than-pleasant exchanges (although these conversations can be reframed quite positively) that are necessary to move people in the organization forward and away from inappropriate behavior. Courageous conversations occur when people are prepared and unafraid to say what they honestly think and feel, to whom they need to say it, and to do so in a positive, constructive way so others can hear their message without judgment and respond to it in a similar manner. It is important to note that courageous conversations should be constructive and never hurtful.

The ability to communicate in a more open and honest manner is an important factor in the creation of high performance teams and high performance organizational cultures. In the best places to work, courageous conversations are part of the DNA of the workplace. The more complex the organization, the greater the negative consequences will be of not holding these conversations; when friction builds, people cannot work productively together.

Trust is a major dimension of organizational life and the glue of courageous conversations. But such trust does not appear out of nowhere. Establishing it requires substantial investment of time before members of a team (or any group) are prepared really to trust each other. Ironically, most people or teams who are in the room for group coaching interventions would probably not be there if someone had had a courageous conversation with them, or if they had the courage to speak honestly to one another. Thus the group coaching intervention becomes not only transitional space for change, but also a place to learn and experiment with holding courageous conversations.

Courageous conversations require us to engage in a dialogue with people we don't normally talk to about things we don't normally talk about. But the courage to have such conversations will help us to resolve relational conflicts. If we want the people we interact with to perform at an acceptable level, such conversations will inevitably come to the fore in both work and non-work situations. However, if we are unable or unwilling to have these conversations, the effect will spread beyond the immediate parties involved.

"Courageous conversations imply engaging in a dialogue with people we don't normally talk to about things we don't normally talk about."

But giving feedback on a sensitive issue can be very challenging. Most of us are reluctant to deal with troublesome areas and struggle with confrontation. Our natural inclination is toward avoidance, although (as we may have discovered to our dismay) negation of the issue may solve a problem only temporarily. If knotty issues are not dealt with and are left to fester, they become part of the team or organizational rumor mill, until they explode into damaging and hurtful conflict.

Do you engage in courageous conversations?
Answer YES or NO to the following questions

                                                            YES   NO

• Are you prepared (and unafraid) to say what you honestly think and feel about other people in your organization?
• Are you willing to have tough, difficult discussions about others' work?
• Are you prepared to address the "elephants in the room" without being afraid of negative repercussions?
• Do you speak your mind about performance issues that most others are tempted to avoid?
• Are you mentally strong enough to face your boss about difficult issues?
• Are you prepared to have courageous conversations to learn more about yourself?

If you answer YES to most of these questions, you are ready for courageous conversations.

Indeed, the mere act of beginning a conversation with people with whom we have an issue—never mind reaching a solution—can be extremely liberating. It can turn into a tipping point for the creation of better working relationships. We should not forget that the quality of our conversations reflects the quality of our relationships and our effectiveness at work. Having courageous conversations is a very effective way of conveying the right message, to the right people, at the right time.

Courageous conversations also help the parties involved to see things from a wider perspective. They present an opportunity to explore what the future might be if nothing changes and behavior patterns remain the same. If these conversations are conducted in an authentic, sincere, constructive way, however, they will contribute to the development of a basic sense of trust between those engaged in them. When we see things from another person's perspective, we can usually understand better why people behave as they do. We always seem to have difficulty understanding that others don't think like us. But if we take an emphatic stand, we gain more knowledge about complicated issues, clearing the way to take the next step. We can explore with others what a more desirable future might look like. We become more confident and resilient when facing challenging situations.

It is through courageous conversations that a team can address the undiscussables that have to be verbalized. Displaying hidden emotions or conflict in actions rather than words can create serious problems. If some of the exchanges within the team remain undiscussable, it will be hard for the team to progress. If covert psychological forces are not being dealt with properly, a team tends to become dominated only by the power relationships among its members. If the feelings that dominate the group-as-a-whole container are not dealt with, the original raison d'être of the team may dissipate. This nebulous psychological effect can be identified in the here-and-now in the group coaching session, and effective ways to hold courageous conversations back in the workplace can also be discussed.

THE VICISSITUDES OF CHANGE

Hope is a very powerful force and group coaches can encourage such positive expectations, by pointing out that their colleagues have been able to overcome the sort of problems they are struggling with themselves. Seeing others doing well is inspirational. By highlighting individual team members' achievements, and how well the team is working, coaches can aid the effectiveness of the team.

Leadership group coaching: facilitating factors
How many of these statements are TRUE of you?
   As a coach:

- I am focused on creating hope.
- I make it clear that many problems are universal.
- At times, I give guidance about personal and organizational issues.
- I hope there is an altruistic motive within the team.
- I may, at times, point out the family origin of specific seemingly irrational behavior patterns.
- I try to nurture interpersonal learning within the team.
- I am a great believer in the power of mirroring and mutual identification.
- I know that catharsis can be very beneficial, if timed properly.
- I try to foster a sense of belonging within the team.

If most of these statements are true of you, as a group coach you have a good understanding of the forces of personal change.

Through group interventions, the members or team realize that they are not alone in their confusion. They quickly figure out that they are all in the same boat and that there is a degree of universality to their problems. Their experience is not that different from others. This can be very comforting, if something of a letdown, given our wish to be unique, even in our misery. Sharing our inner world and accepting the inner worlds of others has a very positive effect. It creates a virtuous circle of trust, self-disclosure, empathy, and acceptance.

So "welcome to the human race" not only puts problems in perspective; it also contributes to a sense of cohesiveness within the team. It enhances the experience of feeling part of something, and adds to our sense of belonging and acceptance. It feels good, that we are still considered good enough, warts and all. Sharing intimate experiences has an additional positive influence in that it makes members of the team feel less alone. Predictably, given the investment they have made in each other, the members of the team want to maintain this sense of belonging—and will go to great lengths to keep these contacts live.

Being part of a team is an opportunity to disseminate information about different aspects of human functioning. While didactic instruction should be given sparingly in a group coaching setting (it is better for clients to make discoveries for themselves), it can be beneficial at times. But explanation, clarification, and even direct advice about certain incidents within the team can reduce anxiety, and establish a modicum of control over a troublesome problem.

It is not just coaches who might offer suggestions about specific life problems; members of the team will do the same. They might suggest taking a different approach to a difficult relationship in a fellow-member's life and exploring other ways of going about certain things. Within the team setting, information can be shared about psychological problems, illnesses, and recommendations for attaining a healthier work-life balance. All these guidance activities can make the team function better.

An additional positive force for change is the altruistic motive, or the desire to put the needs of others above our own. While helping for helping's sake—the genuine desire to make things better for others—may seem selfless, ironically it can have some "selfish" side-effects. The act of giving to others can have numerous personal benefits. It feels good to be important to the lives of others, but more than that, there seems to be a link between being helpful to others, and living a longer, healthier, happier life. Helping others—offering support, reassurance, suggestions, and insights—can have a therapeutic effect, contributing to our sense of self-respect and well-being. Having something of value to offer to others is a heartening experience. The initial rush from the "helper's high" may be followed by a longer-lasting period of improved emotional health.

Altruism will prompt team members to credit fellow-members for having helped them to deal better with life's adversities. Learning through the influence of interpersonal relationships plays an essential role in making teams and individual members more effective. The willingness of team members to have courageous conversations with each other can be extremely illuminating. Team members are very well placed to point out others' dysfunctional character patterns. Offering to help work on these with other members of the team can be a great incentive for change. Constructing our self-regard through the positive appraisals of others is an important component of learning.

This interpersonal learning process can also be instrumental in detecting and correcting distortions in self-perception. It can facilitate the discovery of new solutions and a degree of behavior modification. There are always going to be some team members whom we admire because of the way they deal with life's adversities. They will become our role models, the kind of people we would like to become. Imitative behavior—or identification with the other—is an important part of this interpersonal learning process and a force for change. Identification involves our associating with or taking on the qualities, characteristics, or views of another person or group. In this way we may assimilate an aspect, quality, or attribute of the other, and be transformed, wholly or partially, following the model the other provides. However, as a caveat, I should add that identification is not necessarily a conscious process.

Participating in a group or team intervention also provides an outlet for cathartic experiences. For some members, being part of a team is an opportunity to get things off their chest—a forum for figurative emotional cleansing. The members of the team can encourage this by helping to bring repressed feelings and fears to consciousness. Expressing the things that trouble us, instead of stubbornly holding them back, can be very powerful. Proper containment of these emotions by the group coach and other team members—when comments are received in a highly respectful manner—is essential to making catharsis a significant experience.

Engaging in a cathartic experience is also a way of practicing how to express feelings. However, catharsis alone might not in itself have a beneficial effect. There will be occasions when it can even be counter-productive, in particular if it occurs at the wrong time or place. Under the right circumstances, however, it provides an opportunity to re-experience and transform deeply troubling or repetitive life experiences, providing an opportunity to understand better why certain psychological wounds have been so troublesome.

As I have noted before, the kind of dynamics that take place in the group-as-a-whole will resemble those that took place in participants' families of origin. Given the durability of some patterns, team members cannot help but engage in the re-enactment of family patterns within the group. In deciphering activities within the group-as-a-whole screen, the group coach needs to be attuned to the fact that many actors are re-enacting old patterns: there will always be transferential echoes of parental figures, evoking memories of authority issues, or siblings, reviving problems of rivalry, jealousy, and envy.

"The dynamics of the team-as-a-whole offer an opportunity for team members to understand better their original family dynamics."

The dynamics of the group-as-a-whole offer an opportunity for team members to understand better their original family dynamics. The patterns we can identify in the group-as-a-whole will help clarify past relationships with parents, siblings, and others. Team members will have a chance to explore hang-ups they have never resolved with certain members of their family, and to relive deeply troubled family situations (with guidance from other members of the team) in a more corrective way—team members now acting as more accepting and understanding members of the "family." Together with the coach, team members can help point out different ways of dealing with conflicted situations and breaking rigid patterns.

Last but far from least, there are the beneficial effects of self-knowledge and insight. Discovering and accepting our previously unacknowledged or misunderstood personality characteristics can be very enlightening. It can be helpful to realize that certain ways of behaving—specific reactions and (unrealistic) expectations—may have been a survival strategy when we were younger, but are no longer applicable in our present. Arriving at this psychological realization allows us to take greater control over our life, stop blaming others, and take ultimate responsibility for what we do.

Overcoming ghosts from the past

Change agents like group coaches should take maximum advantage of these catalysts for change. In addition, group-as-a-whole experiences provide the material to decipher the various projections and transference reactions between individual team members.

The group-as-a-whole screen also provides an opportunity for group coaches to recognize their own counter-transference reactions toward the team and its members [5, 6]. The need for coaches to operate at numerous stages at the same time—while using themselves as an instrument—can make group coaching a messy process; there are so many confusing strands to tie together. But coaches who are willing to take this leap will deepen the coaching experience for themselves and their clients.

Leadership coaches are often engaged in activities that can be compared to a shadow play. In one-on-one coaching, difficult relationships with the various stakeholders in the organization will be explored; in group coaching within one organization, not only are all the team members present but so too are many ghosts from the past, including all the overt and covert dynamics that accompany them. Metaphorically, the people that make up the team are attached to *wayang* dolls (*wayang* is a Javanese word meaning "shadow" or "ghost") who re-enact, in a convoluted puppet play, their ghosts from the past. In group settings—which are microcosms of the "real" world—the members of a team are likely to bring their conflictual relationships with other people to the table. They need to be aware that a group mind has been created within the team through the interface of numerous personal scripts, making it possible through the experience of the group-as-a-whole to arrive (consciously and unconsciously) at collective sense making and collective action.

The group-as-a-whole needs to be viewed as a dynamic evolving social structure, created by all the members of the team, which they continue to modify through their participation and interaction. The members of a team have a great capacity for co-creating shared emotion and engage in emotional contagion—projections to be found in the group-as-a-whole. Given its complexity, however, there is always a risk that members of the team may not be consciously aware of their efforts to safeguard specific interactive patterns, even as the "*wayang* play" takes place right in front of their noses. This is where change agents like group coaches need to step in to clarify what is happening. By doing so, they may create corrective emotional experiences, basically by re-exposing team members (under more favorable circumstances) to emotional situations they were unable to handle in the past. The group-as-a-whole screen, guided by the group coach, will make it possible for its members to experiment with ideas and feelings, previously experienced as taboo and threatening. When people start to make sense out of past events they experienced as bewildering, they are learning to discriminate between past and present, between behavior that was appropriate then, and what is appropriate now. They are also unlearning helplessness, and achieving mastery. The flip side of this coin is that, at times, re-enactment of past experiences will evoke such primitive emotions that certain members of the group will withdraw defensively or respond in a very disturbed manner.

Making sense of the complex dynamics at play within a group (identifying the various "scents") will be easier for people who are not part of the system, who can be much more effective at providing clarity about what is going on. Group coaches are not socialized by one particular organizational system, which is one reason why they can play such a vital role in changing teams and organizations.

A FEW ADMINISTRATIVE DETAILS

Apart from being a sensitive observer of the psychological issues of the members of the group, and paying attention to the dynamics of the group-as-a-whole, a change agent like a coach has some more pedestrian issues to take care of. First and foremost, attention needs to be given at all times to the team's primary task—what it is the team actually needs to accomplish within the greater organizational context.

To do this, coaches must have a keen sense of business acumen, of how businesses operate and are profitable. Coaches gain the trust of client leadership teams not only because they know the ins-and-outs of individual and team psychological processes, but also because they understand the business a specific team is dealing with. They know the language of the business. Coaches who do not know the market conditions in the client's industry, the structure of the organization, its competitive advantages and its challenges, its labor and organizational circumstances (and much more), are not going to be able to assist the leadership team credibly.

Given the complexity and intensity of the group coaching process, I have found it useful (wherever possible) to work in pairs for a team intervention. Pair working enables each group coach to move in and out of the many entanglements that are part of the group intervention process, taking an active or passive (more observational) role as necessary. For the partnership to work best, both coaches need to get along with each other, have a fundamental respect for each other, and have some complementarity of styles.

Before group coaches decide to undertake a team intervention, they need to assess the support they have from the power structure in the organization. If the intervention is going to be taken seriously, the support of the CEO is a sine qua non—even more so if the CEO is also a major shareholder. Without the support of the CEO, the intervention is likely to be lackluster and disappointing. CEOs are role models and without their blessing, coaching interventions will be a waste of time and money.

When the decision is made to embark on a group coaching intervention, it is probable that some members of the senior team will be unenthusiastic about it, but these resistances can be dealt with. If the CEO is one of the participants (which is to be recommended), it is important that he or she is told to play a relatively low key role throughout the process. It doesn't take much for the other team members to be intimidated when the CEO is too forceful—as we shall see in the tale of M'bogo.

THE TALE OF M'BOGO AND SYNCERUS

There was once a buffalo herd led by a very forceful animal, called M'bogo. One day, M'bogo, lying on a grassy spot close to a stream and chewing his cud, bellowed to his followers, "How's it going down there?" and waited for the good news. Off at a distance, the younger buffalo debated what to say. Things were not going well. The supply of green grass was dwindling rapidly and there was not much left to eat.

But nobody had the nerve to break the bad news to M'bogo—they knew only too well what could happen when he became angry. Many had the scars to prove it and the last thing they wanted was to put him in a bad mood. "What shall I tell him?" Syncerus, his second-in-command, asked the others. M'bogo's last outburst of anger when another herd had moved into their best grazing grounds was still a vivid memory. Like most of the others, Syncerus knew that it was time to move on and look for better pastures. Most of the grass had been eaten to the roots, apart from the place where M'bogo was lolling. Syncerus asked himself, did he dare tell M'bogo that the herd was in danger of starving? Well, he realized, the answer was no.

Finally, Syncerus approached M'bogo. "Things are going quite well, boss," he called. "There is enough grass for everyone. Of course, rain would be helpful—but we are muddling through." M'bogo grunted, and said, "I'm happy to hear that things are going well." He closed his eyes and continued to chew.

The next day did not bode well. A new herd of buffalo had moved into the one area where there was still some green grass left. This unexpected arrival was catastrophic. Syncerus slowly made his way toward M'bogo and, after engaging in some small talk, said, "Oh, by the way, boss, a new herd has moved into our territory." M'bogo's eyes snapped open, and he got ready to give Syncerus a sweep of his horns. Realizing what was coming, Syncerus added quickly, "But it's no big deal. From what I've heard, they're just passing through." M'bogo calmed down immediately, and said, "Good. No point getting worked up over nothing, is there?"

But as the days passed, the situation worsened. One day, looking down from his spot on the hill, M'bogo noticed that there were very few buffalo left in his herd. Summoning Syncerus, he asked irritably, "What's going on? Where is everyone?" Syncerus could not bring himself to report that most of the herd had left with the newcomers to look for better grazing grounds. Very hesitantly, he said, "Boss, before the rains come, I thought it was a good time to sort out the herd and get rid of the dead wood, you know, the ones who can't defend our youngsters against lions and hyenas." "Very good," said M'bogo. "Superb thinking. Getting rid of shirkers will give us a bit more elbow-room. Buffalo need strong leadership. I'm pleased to hear that you are taking the right steps."

It was not long before Syncerus and M'bogo were the last buffalos left. The moment of truth had come. Syncerus could delay no longer; he had to tell M'bogo what was going on. He lumbered over to him and said, "Boss, I have terrible news. We are the last ones left. All the other buffalos are gone." M'bogo was so surprised that he forgot to swipe Syncerus with his horns. "They all left me?" he cried. "For what reason? What went wrong?" Syncerus just stared sheepishly at the ground. "I can't understand it," said M'bogo. "They left me, and just when everything was going so well."

As this tale illustrates, it is not always easy to give feedback. It can be difficult to get difficult messages across without upsetting people. A group coach is one of the few people who can step into the gap, and gently but firmly tell the M'bogos of the world the truths they need to hear, those that might affect the survival of the organization. And not to forget, the group coach, with the help of the group, can support Syncerus in discovering how he can change his behavior to become a more courageous, strategic-thinking second-in-command.

REFERENCES

1. Campling, P. and Haigh, R. (Eds) (1999). *Therapeutic Communities Past, Present and Future*. London and Philadelphia, PA: Jessica Kingsley Publishers.
2. DeLeon, G. (2001). *The Therapeutic Community: Theory, Model and Method*. New York: Springer Publishing Company.
3. Winnicott, D. W. (1951). *Transitional Objects and Transitional Phenomena. Collected Papers: Through Paediatrics to Psycho-analysis*. London: Tavistock Publications.
4. Kris, E. (1952). *Psychoanalytic Explorations in Art*. Madison, CT: International Universities Press, 2000.
5. Etchegoyen, H. (2005). *The Fundamentals of Psychoanalytic Technique*. London: Karnac Books.
6. Kets de Vries, M. F. R. (2009a). *Reflections on Leadership and Career Development*. New York: John Wiley & Sons Inc.

CHAPTER 9

THE ZEN OF GROUP COACHING

What is the sound of one hand clapping?

—Zen kōan

You cannot teach a man anything. You can only help him discover it within himself.

—Galileo Galilei

We make a living by what we get. We make a life by what we give.

—Winston Churchill

Leadership is the art of getting someone else to do something you want done because he wants to do it.

—Dwight Eisenhower

Once upon a time there was a stonecutter who was very dissatisfied with his lot. He wanted to be more powerful. One day, he passed a wealthy merchant's house, and through the open gateway glimpsed the man's numerous fine possessions and important visitors. "How powerful that merchant must be," thought the stonecutter enviously. "I wish I could be like the merchant and no longer a humble stonecutter."

To his great surprise, his wish was granted. Suddenly the stonecutter was the merchant, enjoying more luxuries and power than he had ever dreamed of, and was envied and detested by those less wealthy than himself. But soon a government minister passed by, carried in a sedan chair, accompanied by attendants, and escorted by soldiers beating gongs. Everyone, no matter how wealthy, had to bow low before the procession. "How powerful that official is!" said the stonecutter aloud. "I wish I could be a government minister."

And as suddenly as before, he was the minister, carried everywhere in his embroidered sedan chair, feared and hated by all around, who had to bow down before him as he passed. The stonecutter liked his new position very much.

One hot summer day, the minister was feeling very uncomfortable in his stuffy sedan chair. Looking up, he saw the sun shining down on the land. He realized that the sun that was more powerful than any minister—indeed it must be the most powerful thing in the world. It shone down on all things. Everything grew because of the sun. The sun had deadly powers. "I wish I could be the sun," said the stonecutter. And so he was.

A few days later, as he shone his power down on the inhabitants of the land, a large storm cloud passed beneath him, blocking his rays from the earth. Frustrated, the stonecutter realized that the sun was not the most powerful thing in the land if a simple storm cloud could diminish his greatness.

So he wished to become a storm cloud. And he pelted down rain and threw out bolts of lightning, thunder resounded all over the land, demonstrating his mighty power. He flooded the fields and villages and was cursed by everyone. But soon he found that he was being pushed away by a great force—the wind. "How powerful it is!" marveled the stonecutter. "I wish I could be the wind."

Then he became the wind, blowing tiles off the roofs of houses, uprooting trees, feared and hated by all below. But after a while, he ran up against something that would not move, no matter how forcefully he blew against it—a huge, hulking rock. He tried to move it but, despite all his efforts, it would not budge. "How powerful that rock is!" he thought. "I wish that I could be a rock."

So he became the rock, and was more powerful than anything else on earth. Then one day, he heard the sound of a hammer pounding on a chisel, and felt himself being changed. "What could be more powerful than I, the rock?" he wondered. He looked and saw the figure of a stonecutter.

The challenge for the stonecutter was to discover his inner power, beauty, creativity, and love. He would never feel totally happy until he fulfilled this inner need to be satisfied with who he really was. Would the stonecutter have realized his inner potential faster if he had had a wise guide? Who knows? Perhaps a sparring partner might have saved him from the complicated journey he embarked on, giving him the right advice at the proper moment, or just listening to his thoughts after each trans-formation. By asking open-ended questions, and pushing him gently, a well-trained outsider might have helped him recognize that he could achieve his goals in a much more straightforward way.

In some ways, the role of a change agent like a consultant or group coach is to accompany individuals on journeys of discovery. Think of what would have happened if the wise guide had been able to convene a group that included the stonecutter, a merchant, a government offi-cial, and so on. Each would have spoken about their own realities, and the stonecutter would have come to understand his own unique position in the world much sooner.

"The role of a change agent like a consultant or group coach is to accompany individuals on journeys of discovery."

In earlier chapters of this book, I have drawn on stories from many lands to illustrate that the right word, gesture, action, or even moments of silence can have a powerful effect when used just at the appropriate moment. In this chapter, I want to go into greater detail about the tools and techniques a coach might use during a group coaching session.

> "It is very difficult to keep a clear head when you are the 'garbage can' for powerful projections, projective identifications, introjections, mirroring, and transference reactions."

It can be hard to maintain emotional and psychological neutrality, to provide containment for the powerful feelings that can arise during group discussions. It is very difficult for the group coach to keep a clear head when he or she is the "garbage can" for the powerful projections, projective identifications, introjections, mirroring, and transference reactions that are part and parcel of the coaching day.

As I have mentioned, leadership group coaching has proven to be a highly effective intervention technique. Thousands of executives have gone through various forms of group (or team) coaching. I have worked with a large number of senior executive teams and boards of directors and I have heard it all, from difficult family histories, to vicious organizational turf fights, to belligerent resistance to change. But one thing is certain—the process seems to work. In the following sections, I will go through a leadership group coaching intervention elaborating on the vignette presented in Chapter 2. As the narrative of a group coaching journey unfolds, I will explain the procedures, methodologies, framing concepts, and techniques that underlie each phase of such an intervention process. Some elements are essential for creating the transitional, safe space in which the group (or team) can experiment with ideas. Other elements are helical, in that they ebb and flow under the control of the group coach; for example, using a paradoxical intervention, or searching for the hidden, competing commitments that can hinder motivation for change. By describing all these elements, I hope to illustrate an overall gestalt of this change technique, capturing the delicate balance of action and non-action that leads to a powerful, transformative event for participants.

SELF-PORTRAIT: CREATING THE TRANSITIONAL SPACE

I often start a group coaching intervention process (like the example given in Chapter 2) by asking participants to draw their self-portrait. This is a deceptively simple exercise. The instructions are to draw seven simple images that represent the way participants view their work, leisure, past, and future, what is in their head, their heart, and in their stomach (see Figures 9.1a and b). Although most people are pretty skeptical when given this assignment, they quickly become deeply involved in the exercise. When the team comes back together, I ask each participant to elaborate on their drawing. This is a fun but highly effective way to draw participants into the transitional space—and have them say important things about themselves.

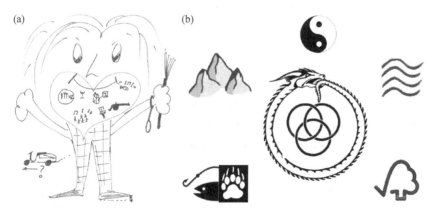

Figure 9.1a and b   Two examples of a self-portrait

If conditions of feeling safe are met, the members of a group (or team) will venture to share relevant personal information while explaining their self-portrait. Again, it is up to the leadership coach to construct safe boundaries for constructive confrontations and clarifications. Group (or team) members need to be able to see that it is helpful to share their reactions without being too concerned with politeness, rationality, and embarrassment. They are learning to use the right side of their brains more—the imaginative part that uses feelings, and is more fantasy-based. At times, serious affective reactions (like tears) might surprise the group (or team), but these manifestations of deeper emotions can be extremely helpful in moving the intervention forward. They will help team members acquire an appreciation of each other's strengths and weaknesses.

LIFE NARRATIVES: LETTING THE FOCAL ISSUE EMERGE

Another thing to be established early in the group coaching intervention is the identification of the focal problem(s) that each member of the group would like to work on. In order to change, people need to be clear about what it is that they want to change. For example, this might be a problem concerning micromanagement, abrasive behavior, conflict avoidance, excessive narcissistic behavior, or other matters. Of course, if we really want to dig, these are all manifestations of deeper issues such as faulty self-esteem, unresolved rivalry issues, and other matters. Helped by their fellow team members and the coach, participants need to identify their central problem(s) and need to be able to formulate explicit, tractable improvement goals.

In a group coaching intervention, in addition to the self-portrait exercise, I include a debrief of the results of a 360-degree leadership feedback package and a review of personal observer feedback from work and non-work environments (see the Appendix for a description of the instruments). I have found that these personality, behavioral, and organizational assessments are great tools for getting the group coaching process into motion. The feedback these tools provide can be an excellent icebreaker, providing the members of the team with greater understanding of themselves and others, and how the team and organization function. These questionnaires also enable executives to compare their self-perceptions with the observations of colleagues, subordinates, their boss, and others who know them well. There is frequently a serious gap between what many executives say (or believe) they do, and what really happens. These discrepancies give insights into how their behavior impedes their own and others' effective functioning in the organization. This new understanding helps them think about how they can relate to one another more effectively. At the same time, it encourages tolerance by indicating that different approaches may be valid in different situations. It contributes to insights about the best way to manage and work for people with certain dominant characteristics, which combination of styles works well, and which to avoid. The inclusion and analysis of developmental material is extremely helpful in creating greater awareness of why team members act the way they do.

Here again, a change catalyst like a group coach should be patient and open-minded. In many cases, individuals will talk about problems that they are already aware of. Although they may know that they are a micro-manager, conflict avoidant, or abrasive in their leadership style, the problem is that, as the years go by, they haven't done anything about it. The challenge for the coach is to help create a tipping point (using various techniques) so that something finally happens (one hopes for the better). The task of the group, with the guidance of the coach, is to uncover what the real issues are.

Over time, I have discovered that restricting a high performance team intervention to the information given by the multi-party feedback questionnaires was just not enough. It made the intervention process too sterile. Studies on story-telling have shown that the personal narrative can play a major role in structuring group interventions [1, 2, 3, 4, 5]. Narratives, touching crossroads in a person's life, can serve as an extremely helpful way to get to know the people behind the tables and figures, particularly in a multi-cultural organization that operates globally. What was their journey to their current organization? How would they describe their leadership style? What is it like to be brought up in Singapore, as opposed to France, or Abu Dhabi? What were the best and worst moments of their life? What people say, the stories they tell, about the significant events and experiences that made them who they are now will be extremely relevant.

The story-telling that begins with the self-portrait exercise often unlocks new insights. When people tell their history (and listen to the narratives of the other participants), they are often able to identify specific themes that began in their past and continue over time into the present. Their challenge (which is also a challenge for the coach and other participants) is to identify these themes. This means—during the group coaching intervention—not only having a better understanding their own story but also being able to make sense of other people's. Such an understanding will help them coach their colleagues effectively.

I have noticed that, more often than not, the stories people tell about their lives center on seemingly insoluble dilemmas grounded in misguided perceptions of their world and the world of others. These dilemmas are often associated with their organizational challenges. But problems that may seem unsolvable when faced alone may turn out to be quite solvable with the support of a group or a team.

"Telling stories is a way of working through internal crises and developmental challenges at home and at work."

Telling life stories is a way of exploring the self and can lead to some bigger existential questions such as: Who am I? Where am I going? How will I get there? Telling stories is a way of working through internal crises and developmental challenges at home and at work. It is also a way to arrive at meaningful personal life integration.

ANIMAL METAPHORS

A metaphor is another narrative device that can be viewed as a compromise between the choices of direct expression or concealing ideas or feelings. A change catalyst like a coach may generate and apply metaphors as part of the group coaching process. Difficult or emotional communications can be more easily expressed as metaphors, permitting a more gradual examination of the material, and exposing its covert meanings. Metaphors can inspire new, alternative perspectives of an issue. The use of metaphors often has a playful and vitalizing effect. Not only are coaches expected to use metaphors to make difficult messages more palatable; the other members of the team are expected to do the same. If the members of the team are able to work with metaphors, they can produce new and fresh perspectives. The process of free association is often very liberating for team, the coach, and the person in the hot seat.

Hence, after having dealt with the more factual information, derived from the various multi-feedback instruments, I often use metaphors to encourage the members of the team to start the process of giving courageous feedback. I ask the group to answer the question, "What animal does this person remind you of?" and the follow-up question, "Why does she remind you of that animal?" Typical answers are, an ostrich, a beaver, a labrador, a leopard, and so on. I find animal metaphor narratives, and the underlying message they convey, a very good method for getting the group coaching process underway, or for solidifying a message the group may be trying to get across to a particular individual.

Using animals is not a meaning-neutral process, however. Animals have many anthropomorphic characteristics—and using animal metaphors when describing people is a great way to ascribe leadership attributes. For example, monkeys are perceived as smart, active, and sometimes badly behaved. Tigers are considered dangerous and fierce. Turtles withdraw into their shells, so are viewed as timid and withdrawn. Saying someone is a donkey could mean that the person is stubborn, and not susceptible to the influence of others. A giraffe could signify someone with her head in the clouds; chameleons have a certain connotation; and comparing someone to a bull doesn't need much more clarification. Entire organizations can be mapped this way. The magazine *Rolling Stone* once described an investment bank as a "great vampire squid wrapped around the face of humanity, relentlessly jamming its blood funnel into anything that smells like money"—a powerfully revelatory metaphorical statement.

It will be up to the group coach to decipher the team's metaphorical language constructively and create the opportunity to extend reflection on its meaning. For example, the coach could ask, "What would it be like to have this person as a boss?" "If you were this person's boss, how would you manage her?" "As a friend, what advice can you give this person to become even more effective?"

PARADOXICAL INTERVENTION

In their seminal book *Pragmatics of Human Communication*, Paul Watzlawick and his fellow authors attempted to formalize Bateson's double-bind theory (described in Chapter 5) [6, 7]. According to Watzlawick, every communication has content and a relationship aspect: the latter classifies the former and can be considered a meta-communication. They propose that all forms of communication include more information than just the plain meaning of the words—that is, information about how the communicator wants to be understood and perceived.

In emphasizing the role of meta-communication, Watzlawick expanded the double-bind theory into a general theory of pragmatic paradoxes. This approach has been made more operational in strategic family therapy and techniques like paradoxical intervention. Like Bateson, adherents of this point of view look at pathological situations as a product of distorted communication patterns. To deal with them, they use paradoxical ways of intervention, attempting to break established, highly insular, and nonproductive family patterns. This type of intervention can also be effective in group coaching situations.

Paradox is a term for describing a directive that qualifies another directive in a conflictual way, either simultaneously or at a different moment in time. To take a famous example, the Cretan Epimenides made the immortal statement: "All Cretans are liars." Was he lying or telling the truth? If his statement is false, it is true, then it is false, which would in turn mean that it is actually true, but this would mean that it is false, and so we can go on *ad infinitum*. Thus a paradox is not merely a contradictory directive; it is also an assignment that gives a message on different levels, so that one message disqualifies the other.

"Paradoxical intervention involves prescribing the very symptom the client wants to resolve."

Examples of paradoxical intervention
Example 1 Two of your subordinates are always arguing. Nothing you say to get them to stop seems to work. Instead, you bring them to your office and tell them that you will leave them there to fight for 20 minutes each day. There are some rules, however: they are allowed to yell at each other, but no hitting, and no throwing things.
Example 2 During team meetings one person always monopolizes the discussion. The team leader is at her wits' end, trying

to find a way to get him to see that others would also like some airtime. Finally, at one of the team meetings, she decides to deal with the matter differently. When the meeting starts, she says, "John, since you have so many good ideas to contribute, can you help the discussion this time? I would like you to start and tell us all the things you have on your mind. Please, take your time, we have all the time in the world. Put whatever you think is important on the table."

Example 3 A valued member of the team told his boss reluctantly that he had decided to quit, having received an excellent offer from a competing company. His boss replied that he was smart to do so. He would have done the same, in his position. Clearly, the competitor was offering much better career opportunities. From what he could tell, the new job looked as if it could be much better than the one he had now. But, his boss went on, maybe he could help him get the best deal out of the other company? He started to explore the tempting new job with his employee, going into its pros and cons, and made his employee realize he would be much better off staying where he was.

Reflect on these three stories and figure out what is really going on. If possible, discuss them with someone else.

Paradoxical intervention involves prescribing the very symptom the client wants to resolve. It's a complex concept often equated with reverse psychology. For example: A client fears failure, so the coach asks her to fail at something; a man has problems with procrastination, so the coach asks him to schedule one hour each day to procrastinate. And so I could go on. The underlying principle is that we engage in behaviors for a reason, which is typically to meet a need (rebellion, attention, a cry for help, etc.). If a symptom is involuntary, having to do it voluntarily means the behavior can be controlled and is no longer a symptom. In prescribing the symptom the coach helps clients understand this need and determine how much control (if any) they have over the symptom. By choosing to make the symptom manifest, they may recognize that they can create it, and therefore have the power to stop or change it.

The primary aim of a paradoxical intervention is to acquire some kind of control over a relationship, so this intervention technique is particularly useful in bringing about change in rigid relationships. In these instances the way things are organized works against changes by maintaining control of how the present relationship is defined. A paradoxical intervention removes the locus of control to the person instead. The ultimate goal is to bring under voluntary control what has been involuntary—and therefore out of control [8, 9].

All coaching interventions (group and individual) may incorporate paradoxical strategies when dealing with resistance. Paradoxical intervention can be used as an integral component of a more comprehensive and complex intervention process. In a trusting relationship, symptomatic behavior can be dealt with through a humorous, paradoxical interchange. But, in my experience at least, paradoxical intervention is often used as a last-ditch effort after other, more traditional forms of intervention have failed. The success of the double-bind hypothesis, and more specifically the selection of specific paradoxical interventions, will depend on the resistance, or readiness, of the individual.

I remember the CEO-owner of a family business who responded to my question about what he would like to see in the future with the observation that he wanted his three children to work in harmony together in his company. His children, however, had become increasingly frustrated by his constant refusal to think about succession planning, and to give more responsibility for the business to them. He had sabotaged all the efforts they had made to change the situation. When I asked my client why he was not giving his children more responsibility, he said he felt they were not yet ready. "They have so much more to learn. Doing it now would be too risky for the business."

I agreed with him, and said, "You may be right. Your children may be complete incompetents. In fact, I wonder why you give them as much responsibility as you do now? It would be the last thing I'd do in your place. They have been in the company long enough; they should be ready by now. But from what you're saying, it seems the company would be much better off without them. Maybe you should look into that? Maybe you should let them do things they are really good at. And that may be outside the company. Perhaps they don't really want to be in the company." That really got his goat. He became highly irritated and protested that his children liked the business; I was totally wrong. He was clearly deeply disenchanted with me and I realized that he was thinking of firing me. But happily my comments started him thinking. He called me two weeks later, asking me to come and discuss the matter further. At our meeting, I mentioned that his procrastination about the succession issue had cast a dark shadow over the company. None of us is immortal. Wouldn't it be fantastic to see his children do a great job in the company? Wouldn't it be nice to have their gratitude, instead of the issue being a constant irritant? A month later, during a team workshop, he made the decision to step down as CEO, making his daughter, the oldest of his children, CEO, and himself remaining as non-executive chairman.

MOTIVATIONAL INTERVIEWING

Motivational interviewing is another highly effective technique in the change repertoire of change agents like leadership coaches.

Motivational interviewing is a specific client-centered, semi-directive counseling approach for eliciting behavior change [10]. In other words, motivational interviewing aims to help clients explore and resolve their ambivalences about behavior change. It combines elements of style (warmth and empathy) with technique (e.g. focused, reflective listening and pointing out discrepancies in behavior).

How do you deal with your people?

Study the following questions and answer them YES or NO

	YES	NO
1. When you listen to people, are you respectful about what they are saying?		
2. Do you tend to ask open-ended questions?		
3. Do you express empathy when you talk about difficult issues?		
4. Do you discuss their feelings of ambivalence about specific problems?		
5. Do you make an effort to allow them, rather than you, argue for change?		
6. When they become defensive about an issue, do you shift position, and take another tack?		
7. Do you emphasize to them how capable they are, whatever they are doing?		

If you answer YES to most of these questions, you (knowingly or not) practice motivational interviewing.

The operational assumption in motivational interviewing is that ambivalence or lack of resolve is one of the principal obstacles to be overcome in getting the change process started. The main strategy in motivational interviewing is to help clients examine their ambivalence about change, with the goal of increasing their desire for it, their recognition of its importance, and their belief in their ability to make change happen. The premises of motivational interviewing are:

• Motivation to change is elicited from the client, and not imposed from without.
• It is the clients' task, not the coach's, to articulate and resolve their ambivalence.
• Direct persuasion is not an effective method for resolving ambivalence.
• The coaching style is generally quiet and eliciting.
• The coach tends to be directive in helping clients examine and resolve their ambivalence.
• The coach explores discrepancies between clients' current behavior, their values, and their long-term goals.
• The coach does not challenge the resistance, accepting the client's reluctance to change as natural rather than dysfunctional.
• The aim of the coach is to support self-efficacy, and help clients move toward change successfully and confidently.
• The relationship between coach and client is more like a partnership or companionship than an interface between expert and recipient.

Motivational interviewing tries to be non-judgmental, non-confrontational, and non-adversarial. As an intervention technique, it should be used to increase the client's awareness of the causes of problems, their consequences, and the potential risks attending unchanged behavior. During the interface between coach and client, the ambivalence about the course of action to be taken is

dealt with subtly, with both parties exploring the perceived benefits and costs associated with different scenarios.

It can be helpful to explore the often confusing, contradictory,
and uniquely personal elements of the focal conflict. As people
steeped in the motivational interviewing technique emphasize, a
confrontational approach will usually increase client resistance and
reduce the probability of change. Change agents like coaches need
to draw out their clients' ideas, not impose their own; they need
to roll with the resistances. More significantly, the client needs to
be ready for change—and be the one to present the arguments for
change. Unsurprisingly, the motivational interviewing technique
can be frustrating for coaches accustomed to strong confrontation
and to giving direct advice.

In motivational interviewing, the coach needs to be highly
attentive and responsive to clients' motivational signs. Resistance
and negation of a problem should not be interpreted as a client's
personality problems, but as feedback regarding a too pushy
approach from the coach. The coach is expected at all times to
respect clients' options to make their own choices about their
own behavior. An atmosphere of collaboration is essential to
build a working alliance between coach and client, allowing
the client to develop trust toward the coach, something that is difficult to achieve in a confrontational atmosphere. No matter
how much change agents might want their clients to change
their behavior, change will only happen if the client wants it.
Open questions, reflective listening, affirming, and summarizing
are the principal features of the modus operandi between client
and coach.

In a group setting, motivational interviewing in which team
members discuss the advantages and disadvantages of different
choices and actions will help them make up their mind about how
to move forward. In this trusting, collaborative atmosphere, individuals can develop strategies based on their own needs, wishes,
goals, values, and strengths.

COMPETING COMMITMENTS

Another way to help people change is through what has become known as the four-column exercise. This is a way to help people recognize the tension between what they would like to do and the competing commitments that block them from doing so. They are looking for help because they feel stuck. But in spite of all their good intentions, they don't seem to get anywhere. Given this kind of stalemate, the question becomes whether there are other forces at play that prevent them from reaching their intended goal.

Sigmund Freud (1926) coined the term "secondary gain" to describe this process, in which the external and incidental advantages derived from an illness, such as rest, gifts, personal attention, and release from responsibility, prevent well designed and well intended change efforts coming to fruition. Freud suggested that secondary gain should be seen as an unconscious process, outside the awareness of the individual, which blocks them doing what they say they want to do. Until they gain some insight into this secondary gain, however, people who say that they want to change will often feel frustrated and fail in their attempts to sustain progress toward new goals.

In order to help individuals and groups address challenges associated with secondary gain, the developmental psychologists Robert Kegan and Lisa Laskow Lahey [11, 12] reframed Freud's notions of secondary gain, and developed a theory of "competing commitments" that enable people to deal with these challenges. They argue that difficulties experienced at work and life practices are often a result of underlying commitments that work against the very changes people are trying to undertake. According to Kegan and Laskow Lahey, in every change situation, there will always be resistances at work—forces that keep us from changing, both individually and organizationally. These forces can be seen as "competing commitments."

Kegan and Laskow Lahey argue that helping people to make initial progress toward a new goal or challenge can often be looked at as the easy part. But helping to embed new behaviors or new practices into a person's regular way of doing things is often much more difficult. This is when these hidden "competing commitments," which are often poorly articulated or even unconscious, pop up. Many of these "competing commitments" are based on long-held beliefs that are an integral part of a person's make-up, so they can be difficult to change.

Contrary to Freud, Kegan and Laskow Lahey offer a more cognitive behavioral-oriented approach to overcome what they label as "personal immunity to change." When people engage in behavior that thwarts their ability to achieve an outcome they say they genuinely want, the cause could be deeply held internal beliefs that act in opposition to conscious desires. In other words, when people are unable to see their good intentions come to reality, other forces may be at play and no matter how hard they try, their progress remains inexplicably stalled.

Competing commitments should not be seen as a weakness but as a form of self-protection arising from deeply rooted beliefs people have about themselves and the world around them. They are usually based on some big assumptions individuals have made about the world. We are rarely aware of the fact that we make these assumptions because they are part of our general make-up. We accept them as reality. It is only by bringing major assumptions out into the open that people can challenge these assumptions and take action to overcome this immunity to change. When these beliefs are uncovered, change is possible. And to tackle these various forces, Kegan and Laskow Lahey developed a four-column exercise to help people deal with competing commitments.

To make this four-column exercise work, people who undertake this activity need to ask themselves a number of questions. The first is to identify a commitment that is important and insufficiently accomplished. For example, "What would you like to see changed at work, so that you could be more effective or so your work would be more satisfying?" It is important that people name something that they are very committed to. Generally, responses to this question will be expressed in the form of a complaint. The outcome of this commitment should be written in the first column. The second question is, "What are you 'doing or not doing' that is keeping your commitment from being more fully realized? What commitments have you made to yourself that compel you to operate this way?" People list everything they are doing/not doing that works against their commitments. The fears that surface ought to point them toward a competing commitment. They should recognize their counterproductive behaviors and put these observations into column two. The next step (column three) is to reflect on what the action or inaction is suggesting, in that people might be more committed to something else (the competing commitment). Here they have to write down what they think their competing commitment(s)—fears—might be. Finally, in column four, people write the big assumption (fear) behind this competing commitment. They can then look at the various ways in which their assumption is preventing them from getting the results they really want. People can spend their lives living false assumptions that have their origin in childhood. It can take time to identify a competing commitment and its underlying assumption. However, after completing this process, the real work comes in changing deeply rooted assumptions, which also requires persistence and frequently the assistance of a coach or other change catalyst.

Figure 9.2 gives an example of the four-column exercise. It refers to a person who experiences difficulties in being part of a team. It lists all the steps in the process.

Kegan and Laskow Lahey's four-column exercise is a very helpful way of bringing to light some of the hidden competing commitments that block change. Going through the process with each member of a team can be a significant first big step to bringing about meaningful change that lasts. Changing behavior means being honest with ourselves or being willing to hold honest con-

Improvement goal/ commitment	Doing/ not doing instead	Hidden competing commitments (why this immunity to change?)	Big assumption: I assume that if I... then...(something awful) will happen: (picture of hell!)
Become better at being a team player.	Afraid if I am a team player I will waste a lot of time and money— and I am already stressed out. Also, I am likely to get into fights with others, fights that I may lose.

Furthermore, I always feel uncertain speaking in groups. I fear I will make a fool of myself.

but....by not being a team player I irritate the others. They see me as a prima donna. | Fear of wasting my time/fear of losing opportunities/fear of getting into fights and losing/fear of looking stupid/fear of being humiliated/fear of feeling inferior/fear of being helpless. | If I say yes to become a team player, I will never fulfill my full potential as an individual. I may even lose my sense of identity. I may lose my self-respect. |

Figure 9.2   Four-column exercise

versations with the people who make up our world. Through this process of uncovering competing commitments we put a label to very personal feelings that we are often reluctant to disclose, such as deep-seated insecurities, or highly simplistic views of human nature. In essence, uncovering a competing commitment makes all the sense in the world.

THE WAY OF ZEN

I also find that the gentle, non-confrontational approach of Zen can be very helpful in a change effort like group coaching. The true Zen way is not to tell people what to do; it is important that people take responsibility for their own inner journey and discoveries. Let me illustrate the Zen way, fittingly, with a story.

The Zen master Hakuin was known and praised by all who knew him for living a pure life. Near him lived a beautiful Japanese girl, whose parents owned a shop. One day, to their fury, her parents discovered she was expecting a child. At first, their daughter would not confess who the father was but finally, after much harassment, she named Hakuin. In great anger her parents went to the master and confronted him. "Is that so?" was all he would say in reply.

After the child was born the girl's parents brought it to Hakuin to look after. By this time Hakuin's good reputation had been destroyed, but this did not trouble him, and he took very good care of the child. From his neighbors he obtained milk and everything else the baby needed.

A year later the child's mother could no longer withstand the burden of her lie. She told her parents that the real father of the child was a young man who worked in the fish market. Her parents went immediately to Hakuin to apologize, ask his forgiveness—and get the child back. As Hakuin handed the child over to them, all he said was: "Is that so?"

What are the lessons of this tale for the coach? First, true character depends on how we respond to difficult challenges. Hakuin responded to an unwanted situation with calmness of mind and spirit. He did not allow an unexpected event to disturb his inner peace and happiness. He kept his head in difficult circumstances and showed great independence and indifference to the opinions of others. Second, the tale illustrates that we should not always jump to conclusions about other people's character, and we should be careful in giving advice.

STAYING ON COURSE TOWARD A POSITIVE OUTCOME

Change catalysts like group coaches are also responsible for making sure the group stays on course. Continuous clarification of both individual and team issues will be vital. The group coach must attend to the group-as-a-whole and its members' issues to ensure that negativistic, pessimistic, paranoid, and depressive attitudes will not inhibit the course of the group coaching intervention.

For some people, confrontation with certain issues can be traumatic. The team member may feel exposed, become defensive, or withdraw. At all times, it is important that the team member in the hot seat receives maximum support. When that is not forthcoming from the other team members, then the coach must intervene. Serious confrontation of individuals by the group coach should be avoided. The coach, more than any other person in the group, has the most power to leave a person feeling exposed, attacked, or mortified.

At times, however, gentle confrontations may be necessary to prevent scapegoating and to counter intractable resistances, particularly team-wide resistances. Elements of both support and confrontation need to be included to make the intervention effective. Interpretations need to be given within the context of support, so that they serve as a kind of corrective emotional experience.

To encourage a sense of trust and support (apart from the kind of interventions already mentioned), I use various techniques, including positive reframing, encouragement, and the anticipation or rehearsal of difficult situations. Reframing is a cognitive technique used to assist people in diffusing or sidestepping a painful situation, while enhancing self-esteem. An essential part of reframing is assessing people's strengths—looking not only at what has gone wrong but also at what has gone right in their life [13, 14]. Participants can then draw on their psychological strengths to deal with the areas of conflict. Encouragement, which is closely related to reframing, encompasses reassurance, praise (which, to be helpful, must affirm something that the recipient considers praiseworthy), and empathic commentary. Such observations contribute to a sense of self-efficacy. Anticipation allows people to move through new situations hypothetically and to weigh different ways of responding. Allowing someone to become better acquainted with a situation reduces anticipatory anxiety. Rehearsal allows people to practice more appropriate ways of engaging in future events, expanding their adaptive repertoire. The purpose of all these interventions is to help individuals acquire a greater sense of self-efficacy, a belief that they are capable of taking action [15].

ACTION PLANNING

Although the guiding philosophy in a change effort like group coaching is to allow the space and time for exploration, and not look for closure too early, it is equally important to crystallize a small number of points for action for each individual when the intervention comes to an end. I usually ask each person to identify two or three (no more) action steps related to change at the individual or organizational level. The group (or team) helps each person in turn to fine-tune the timing, resources, and support required for the change to occur. Within the holding environment of a team intervention, both the group coach and fellow participants can point out better ways of doing things, building on what they have learned listening to each other's stories.

Having played in the transitional space with new ways of thinking during the intervention, individuals feel more comfortable making a public commitment to the other members of the group (or team) about the changes they would like to make. This sort of commitment accelerates the personal transformation process, because it doubles momentum: It not only influences the person making the public commitment (cementing willingness to confront a difficult situation) but also enlists the cooperation of others for help and accountability, a strong reinforcement for change. By taking a public stance, the speaker issues a self-ultimatum: go through with the change, or lose face—and not be taken seriously. The chances of these steps being achieved are significantly improved if they are signed off by all the other members of the team. Ensuring that each member of the team has a stake in the others' action plans is a very effective way of helping the team accomplish its set purpose.

"Ensuring that each member of the team has stake in the others' action plans is a very effective way of helping the team accomplish its set purpose."

If the group is a natural working team, each member of the team will feel responsible for the others, and help the others to meet their commitments following a group coaching intervention. To reinforce these good intentions, one or more follow-up sessions should be scheduled to review individual progress. After all, many people are very good at making New Year's resolutions but most are abandoned before the end of January. A sense of mutual responsibility will also facilitate frank conversations about broader issues, such as organizational values, corporate culture, and future directions—a more boundaryless point of view. Facetiously, I sometimes say that our major allies in the change process are shame, guilt, and hope. Shame and guilt will hold team members to their promises, while hope channels each participant's desire for better personal, team, and organizational effectiveness. The role of a change catalyst like a group coach is to help each participant live up to his or her full potential.

Let me end this chapter by telling an old Zen story about a female lion cub who was lost in the savanna. After several days, by which time she was nearly dead from hunger and thirst, a ewe found the cub, took pity on her, and cared for her.

As the lioness grew up, all the sheep could see that she was not like them. She was bigger than the biggest ram and her coat was the color of the warm, summer sunset rather than the clouds. Also, her face was broad and her teeth sharp. Still, she ate the same grass and drank the same water as all the other sheep and was tolerated by the flock.

Although she was a lion, living her life among sheep, the sheep-lion only knew sheep. And the sheep, never having seen a lion, did not know the sheep-lion was a lion. They all lived together in the same meadow eating, sleeping, and moving as a herd. The lioness became very good at spotting dangerous animals, so she guarded the herd at night and moved in front of the herd during the day.

One day, an old male lion approached the flock of sheep. The sheep all ran, but the lioness held her ground and just looked at him. The lion led the lioness to a pool of water and they both leaned over to drink. When the sheep-lion saw her reflection in the water, she let out a mighty roar, and in that moment she was transformed. Yet there was still the temptation to stay with those she knew, in the place where she felt safe and comfortable.

The old lion told her, "Don't run away from who you are. You may have grown up with a herd of sheep, but you have grown into a beautiful lioness. Lions are strong, independent, and brave. There are many more things that lions do and places they can go than stay in this safe green meadow."

When the lion had gone, the flock of sheep returned. The ewe approached her golden child and said, "Many years ago, I found you dying under a bush and I could not let you starve to death. So, I nursed you and kept you warm in the safety of the herd. Now it is time for you to go your own way. Make your life your own; make your own choices, not those of the herd." The lioness rubbed her ewe-mother's head in gratitude one last time, then turned and left the flock.

"We may be lions but made to think that we are sheep."

As in this story about change, the question remains: what do the clients want to be, sheep or lions? All of us have to look into the pool to see who we really are. For all of us, it may be high time to reflect what we really see, and make a move to break out of whatever we have been conditioned by others to believe about ourselves. We may be lions but made to think that we are sheep. Time is very short; the clock is ticking, and it is high time to do something about it.

REFERENCES

1. Loewenberg, P. (1982). *Decoding the Past: The Psychohistorical Approach.* New York: Alfred A. Knopf.
2. Spence, D. P. (1982). *Narrative Truth and Historical Truth.* New York: Norton.
3. McAdams, D. P. (1993). *Stories We Live By: Personal Myths and the Making of the Self.* New York: William Morrow and Company.
4. Rennie, D. L. (1994). "Storytelling in Psychotherapy: the Client's Subjective Experience." *Psychotherapy*, 31, 234–243.
5. McLeod, J. (1997). *Narrative and Psychotherapy.* London: Sage.
6. Watzlawick, P., Jackson, D. D. and Bavelas, J. B. (1968). *Pragmatics of Human Communication: A Study of Interactional Patterns, Pathologies, and Paradoxes.* London: Faber.
7. Watzlawick, P. (1976). *How Real Is Real? Confusion, Disinformation, Communication.* New York: Random House.
8. Weeks, G. R. and L'Abate, L. (1982). *Paradoxical Psychotherapy: Theory and Practice with Individuals, Couples and Families.* London: Routledge.
9. Ballou, M. (Ed.) (1995). *Psychological Interventions: A Guide to Strategies.* New York: Praeger Publishers.
10. Miller, W. R. and Rollnick, S. (2002). *Motivational Interviewing: Preparing People to Change.* New York: Guilford Press.
11. Kegan, R. and Laskow Lahey, L. (2009). *Immunity to Change.* Boston, MA: Harvard Business Press.
12. Kegan, R. and Lasow Lahey, L. (2002). *How the Way We Talk Can Change the Way We Work: Seven Languages for Transformation.* San Francisco: Jossey-Bass.
13. Seligman, M. E. P. and Csikszentmihalyi, M. (2000). "Positive Psychology: An Introduction." *American Psychologist*, 55 (1), 5–14.
14. Cooperrider, D. L. and Srivastva, S. (1987). "Appreciative Inquiry in Organizational Life." In W. A. Pasmore and R. W. Woodman (Eds), *Research in Organizational Change and Development*, Vol. 1, Greenwich, CT: JAI Press, pp. 129–169.
15. Bandura, A. (1997). *Self-Efficacy: The Exercise of Control.* New York: W. H. Freeman.

CHAPTER 10

A HOLISTIC DESIGN FOR ORGANIZATIONAL INTERVENTIONS

Trust men, and they will be true to you; treat them greatly, and they will show themselves great.

—Ralph Waldo Emerson

Group conformity scares the pants off me because it's so often a prelude to cruelty toward anyone who doesn't want to—or can't—join the Big Parade.

—Bette Midler

It is amazing what can be accomplished when nobody cares about who gets the credit.

—Robert Yates

There was once a woman who prayed for a vision of what it would be like in Heaven and Hell. That night she had a dream that she was in Hell. She saw a huge table laden with delicious food. Sitting around the table were starving people with long forks tied to their arms. They could pick up the food with their forks, but the forks were too long for them to get the food to their mouth. They were all sobbing and moaning with frustration as they tried to eat the food they longed for.

The next night, the woman dreamed that she was in Heaven. To her astonishment, it was exactly the same—the same table laden with food, and people with long forks tied to their arms. But there was no sobbing or moaning round the table; everyone was smiling and enjoying their food. They had learned to feed each other. This parable highlights the essence of working in teams and provides a graphic image of good and bad teamwork.

ENGAGING PEOPLE IN THE CHANGE PROCESS

The best way to engage in a major organizational change effort is to do several things simultaneously—senior management has a number of levers it can operate. To start with, the top executive team must have a clear focus on what it wants to accomplish and agree on a shared vision of the future. Second, the Internet and other forms of IT can play a major role in influencing the culture by tapping into employees' needs—and making it more possible (especially in very large organizations) to create the opportunity to have voice. Third, structural rearrangements (including reward systems) need to give the right signals about the direction the organization wants to take. In particular, reward systems need to be aligned with organizational values, and behavioral measurements should be put into place.

These three changes are relatively easily to implement. But there is a fourth task: the most difficult assignment is to change the mindset of the people who have to carry out the changes. For this, top leadership needs to inspire people's collective imagination, so that they buy into a shared vision. Here is where a change technique like group coaching comes into place. (See Figure 10.1 for an overview of the organizational culture change process.)

The problem is that organizations, like the individuals in them, are creatures of habit. Once the rules and behavior patterns of

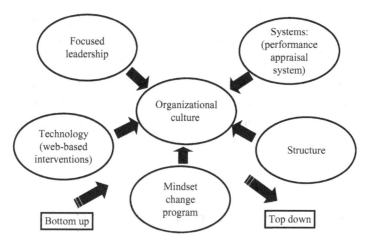

Figure 10.1   Creating an organizational change process

teams have been established (consciously or unconsciously), new-comers (as in the example of the monkeys and the bananas) are usually indoctrinated by existing members. In this way, organizational teams perpetuate the status quo. This is one reason why it can be so difficult for organizations to evolve, even when it is clear that things need to change. As with individuals, understanding the patterns and themes that influence old behavior in organizations, and the history behind them, can be crucial for counteracting these influences and keeping channels open for new beginnings. Organizational members need to be courageous and openly question when something doesn't make sense anymore.

> "Understanding the patterns and themes that influence old behavior in organizations can be crucial for counteracting these influences and keeping channels open for new beginnings."

It is a truism to say that improving performance takes time; however, improving organizational performance may involve doing more than merely changing team processes. Organizational systems—like reward and recognition, performance management, and training—may need to be addressed as well. A strategic reorientation may be needed. But to be able to make these strategic or structural alterations, teams and groups of people who make up the organization need to work well together.

As I have said many times before, this is where group interventions can be of great help. The expected outcome of any successful group intervention should be a team of people that shares a common purpose, has a clear direction, and demonstrates mutual understanding of roles, dependencies, and values.

ORGANIZATIONAL INTERVENTIONS

I usually start an intervention with a leadership audit to assess whether an organization is really ready for such a journey. The leadership audit allows me to judge the degree to which the senior team is committed to the process, and the existing problems between them (structurally and interpersonally), and to assess the participants' psychological maturity. The degree of psychological insight within the team will be important. Are they ready for group intervention and willing to engage?

One of the first, and most straightforward, things I do is to look at the physical premises—surroundings, architecture, office layout, and furnishings—all of which reveal something about an organization's culture. Inside the fabric of the organization, the language used, messages on bulletin boards, the dress code, and other organizational policies all provide further clues about the working life of the organizational participants.

An exploratory look at what senior management is all about adds another dimension to the organizational portrait. There are a number of questions I ask myself. What sort of impression do the organization's executives make? Do they seem to be a homogeneous group or are they very different from each other? Do my conversations with different executives reveal consensus about the primary task of the organization? Are executives clear about the criteria that determine how power and status are allocated? What sorts of people are identified as high potentials? How do employees perceive key power holders and the CEO? What alliances can I identify? What "basic assumptions" prevail, if any? More probing questions about employees, the executives' relationships to one another, meeting protocols, customs, and routines, will provide a fairly clear picture of the organization's culture.

When asking these questions, I always deploy a clinical/systemic lens. It is important to look beyond the official narratives (which might just be slogans) and listen carefully to what else is being said, as this often reveals a number of implicit cultural values. It is also essential to listen to what is not being said to get a sense of the "undiscussables" in the organization. These efforts can also be helpful to identify possible recurring social defenses.

Assess team members' coachability?

Study the following questions and answer them YES or NO

                                                            YES   NO

- Are they motivated?
- Do they have a self-reflective capacity?
- Do they have empathy/interpersonal connectedness?
- Do they have emotional management skills?
- Do they have a degree of psychological mindedness?
- Do they have a sufficient degree of mental flexibility?
- Do they have the capacity to link current to past problems?
- Do they have a high degree of frustration tolerance?

If you can answer YES to most of these questions, you will have an easier time coaching these people.

To create a safe coaching environment where people can play with ideas, emotions, and behavior, participants need to be prepared to engage in a modicum of self-exploration and self-experimentation. Given the stress that these group interventions can put on participants, only relatively well-adjusted people will have the psychological strength to participate and, importantly, be of help to themselves and others. When undertaking an organizational intervention, therefore, I am vigilant in assessing executives' capacity to gain from such interventions. I look for the level of motivation to learn and change; the capacity to be open and responsive; interpersonal connectedness; emotional management skills; a degree of psychological mindedness; the capacity for introspection; responsiveness to others' observations; the ability to tolerate depression; and flexibility. All these criteria need to be subtly assessed before the start of a change intervention.

The process of application and interviewing gives clients a sneak preview of the intervention they will be part of, and the opportunity to evaluate the initial fit between the intervention and the readiness of the members of the team. Through interviews, I assess whether the team members will be able to cope with the psychological demands of a team intervention and whether they will fit with the group coaching effort. This pre-program work of interviewing is the first step in the change process, as it brings many psychological issues to the surface; not the least of which is the anxiety generated during the waiting period before the intervention actually starts.

As I mentioned earlier, to continue my data gathering, I use a combination of specially developed 360-degree feedback instruments, focus groups, individual interviews, written surveys, and behavioral observations. One way to give people voice, set the stage for creating a shared mindset, and collect data about the organizational system is to conduct an organizational culture audit. One of the tools I have developed through working with organizations engaged in change efforts is the Organizational Culture Audit (OCA), a simple and easy to administer psychometric questionnaire that elicits employees' responses about 12 dimensions of organizational culture and produces a qualitative analysis of the data (see Appendix for a short description of the instruments).

A culture audit allows the organization's participants to map and assess organizational values, principles, and practices. It can also be used to measure how near or far from the mark the organization's actual behavior is compared to its desired values, in other words, whether executives and employees really practice what they preach. The group coach can use this knowledge of both the actual and desired state of the organization, working with the board and senior executives to determine the strategic manoeuvres, competitive actions, investments, new developments, organizational changes, and other actions needed to reorient the enterprise in the proper direction. In particular, a cultural assessment plays an important role in aligning behavior and performance indicators with the future vision for the organization.

The outcome of an organizational culture audit will be invaluable to both a change catalyst like a leadership coach and senior management as a source of data to inform the rationale for a change process, especially if combined with qualitative data gathered from observations, focus groups, web-based interaction, and interviews [1, 2]. Once the features of the organizational culture are mapped out and made visible through an audit, the senior executive team can compare existing employee values with the behavior they feel is needed to effectively implement the organization's strategy—and begin to map the changes needed to improve the organizational architecture (structure and systems).

After sharing the data with the top team, I usually leave it to team members to draw inferences. It is useful for them to discuss the current culture and identify the parts of it that are highly effective and need to be supported, as well as the practices holding the organization back. A vision of a more effective organizational culture can then be created, based on the audit's snapshot of the entire organization, using audit data and the outcomes of the qualitative analysis. Steps can be taken to develop a shared set of values that will be carefully aligned with the direction the senior executive group wants the organization to take. To start the change process and create an action plan, the senior executive team has to reach agreement on the areas that need attention. They need to tackle the cultural gaps that have the greatest effect on the ability of the organization to implement its strategic success model.

The data from the culture audit should also be presented to the organization at large, to help employees see the gap between where the organization is, and where they would like it to be. Exploratory culture workshops (facilitated by group coaches) offer an excellent opportunity for participants to gain a better understanding of the salient themes of the organization's culture. The initial interface between the change agent and the organization can be used to explore some of the latter's important underlying themes. From working with the top team in a group coaching session, further workshops or sessions can be developed to help desired change trickle down through the organization.

The information gathered during the initial intervention with the senior leadership team can be used for a series of further group interventions, cascading down the organization to create awareness of the cultural change process in the organization as a whole. If participation is mixed, including executives from different departments, divisions, or geographical areas, these sessions will also be instrumental in minimizing organizational silos and boundaries, and the symptoms of not-invented-here syndrome. Instead of turf fights, potential synergies between various parts of the organization can be discussed. Such activities set the stage for a more networked organization with a coaching, learning culture.

INSTITUTIONALIZATION OF CHANGE

If the various change measures are supported appropriately, the stage will be reached when there is emotional acceptance and recognition that the new behaviors are working and the new values being lived. As this happens, some people may need help to deal with letting go of the old practices and ways of thinking. And while senior management can support new ways of behaving through reward systems, embracing these changes emotionally is another matter. At this point, group (or team) coaching interventions at a middle management level, using the same process I have described throughout this book, can become very effective ways to help people deal with loss, and to start new beginnings. Supported by their peer group interactions, employees will accept the need to behave differently and recognize advantages to themselves and the organization, as well as supporting the organization and its new strategies. As the business's performance improves, people are likely to internalize new values and beliefs. Their roles and futures will become clearer, reinforcing their long-term commitment to innovation and organizational renewal.

A CASE IN POINT

But how does this work in practice? As a case in point, I was asked to help top management in a global bank to develop their leadership capabilities as part of a major organizational change intervention over a number of years. Well before the financial meltdown in 2008, this particular bank had been through turbulent times; a number of very poor decisions on the part of some senior executives resulted in large losses that endangered the bank's liquidity. The bank had been run in a highly autocratic manner, creating a dysfunctional dependency culture. When the liquidity crisis occurred, the country's regulator jumped in, an intervention that led to most members of the top executive team being fired and the board revamped. A new CEO was brought in, a recently retired executive of another bank in a different country. He had a fairly unattractive assignment. Apart from the bank's weak financial position, another danger on the horizon was a take-over threat by one of the bank's competitors.

The new CEO's number one priority was to calm the unrest among the bank's employees. As a first step to managing his own anxiety and that of the employees, he gathered the top 200 people for an initial meeting, where he introduced himself, told them something about his background, and made a few comments about the challenges ahead. He emphasized, however, that he needed their help and advice to create a better situation. For that purpose, he asked them to send him a personal email stating what they liked and disliked about the bank, what they could contribute to bring the company back to its original successful state, and what they personally could do to make it even better.

The CEO made it a point to respond to each email he received and had private conversations about the recommendations with the top 75 people in the company. During another meeting of the senior group, he fed back what he had learned from this exercise and, with their help, set priorities. He used podcasts to transmit critical turnaround themes and more generally to improve employee communication. In addition, he travelled around the various countries where the bank was located to visit offices and hold town hall-type meetings.

The information provided gave him an even better sense of what action steps were needed. Many complicated strategic issues had to be dealt with concerning resource allocation. Priorities needed to be set. The organizational structure needed to be clarified, in particular the role of the central office given the bank's wide geographical spread. Clearly, something needed to be done to turn around the dependency culture that was so prevalent in the bank and the embedded and costly silos. While all these things were going on, the bank's competitive position was deteriorating and threat of a take-over increasingly palpable. This too had to be stopped.

The CEO needed a capable executive team to help him take steps to stabilize the bank, and hold off the take-over threat.

Independent thinking had not previously been a behavior pattern in the bank. He hoped that with greater decentralization, many potentially talented executives would be "liberated," although in the past, talent management had never played a role in the bank. The CEO decided to hire an HR professional, who was made a member of the executive committee, a sign of the important role he was expected to play. Subsequently, the CEO and the new VP Human Resources/Talent Management brought a stream of high-powered executives into the company (a few of them from the CEO's previous company). They also began to assess the talent available within the organization.

At this point, I was asked to help create more of a team culture. The process started with two modular workshops called "The Leader Within." Starting with the top 24 people in the organization, intense group coaching took place in these workshops in groups of eight, which I facilitated with the help of a second coach. The first module included a presentation on high performing organizations and teams, followed by observations (refined after each workshop) about the issues they felt needed attention in the bank. This introduction was followed by two days of team coaching, using a number of multi-part feedback instruments to jump-start the process.[1] The second workshop included another multi-part leadership feedback questionnaire (the Leadership Archetype Questionnaire[2]), an organizational culture audit[3], and a culture exercise, followed by interactive team presentations of the kind of organization they would like to be (including

---

[1] The instruments used were the *Global Executive Leadership Inventory* [3], and the *Personality Audit* [4].

[2] The *Leadership Archetype Questionnaire* is another online questionnaire designed to help participants identify their salient leadership behavior through eight leadership archetypes: strategist, change-catalyst, transactor, builder, innovator, processor, coach and communicator [5, 6, 7].

[3] The Organizational Culture Audit was another online questionnaire used in the intervention [8, 9].

strategic and structural recommendations, timeline, and assigned responsibility).

The seminars were extremely well received. It helped that leadership development workshops—or more generally "dreaming about the future"—had previously been unknown in the organization. Not only did these workshops give each executive a very pragmatic professional and personal action plan, they also set the foundation for a networked team culture. They helped create a more boundaryless organization, reduced turf fights, and made for better information exchange. Most importantly, the participants felt they had voice within the organization, a perception that helped break down the existing dependency culture.

After each series of workshops, my colleague and I had an intense discussion with the CEO and VP HR to discuss systemic changes. The boundary management of these discussions had been clarified very specifically beforehand, ensuring that no personal information about the participants would be part of this interchange. In a few instances (agreed upon by these people beforehand), we signaled the possible loss of talented executives because of a misfit between them and their position. We also (again, after previous clearance by the people in question) made recommendations about executives' possible developmental needs. Subsequently, the top 75 executives had an intense career development conversation with the CEO and VP HR, as part of a search for greater congruence between their needs and the needs of the organization. For people lower down the organization, these conversations took place between the individuals and the senior figures in that part of the organization. The workshops were being cascaded down the organization for maximum effect.

The observations made in the workshops by the top 75 executives about the organization they would like to work for were transformed into meaningful action. The results of those workshops became the basis for important strategic and structural decisions, including geographic repositioning. A number of structural changes were made, including the introduction of a performance appraisal system to create greater alignment with the values to be espoused by the "new" bank. A number of people who didn't live up to those values or their leadership action plan were asked to leave. After three years of these group interventions the bank had regained an increasingly competitive position, and interestingly enough was relatively unaffected by the global financial meltdown.

The expressions "transformational" or "quantum change" are often used when discussing organizational change; however, many change interventions seldom reach that level of significance. Individuals will experience only a handful of transformational events that truly change the nature of how they interact with the world. When a toddler begins to walk, when a woman gives birth, or a teenager drives a car on her own for the first time, these experiences transform the individual's self-image and relationships in an indelible way.

"Individuals will experience only a handful of transformational events that truly change the nature of how they interact with the world."

If an organizational change process is going to become transformational in this sense, top management needs to do some deep soul-searching about the way people in the organization deal with each other—as a group they need to take novel actions and transform the inner fabric of the organization. In particular, the people in the organization need to acquire a new way of looking at things, to see what ordinarily is not seen, as this story of Nasreddin, the legendary satirical character of Sufi fiction, illustrates so well.

One day, Nasreddin saw a man sitting despondently by the side of the road and asked him what troubled him. The man responded, "There is nothing of interest in life, my brother. I have sufficient capital, meaning that I don't have to work, and I am only on this trip to seek something more interesting and entertaining than the life I have at home. So far, I haven't found it." As the traveler stopped speaking, and without uttering a word, Nasreddin seized the traveller's knapsack and made off with it down the road. Nasreddin knew the area very well, and was easily able to outdistance the traveler.

The road twisted and turned, but Nasreddin cut across several bends, so that he was soon back on the road, well ahead of the man he had just robbed. He put the knapsack down and waited by the side of the road for the traveler to show up. In due course the miserable man appeared, having followed the tortuous road, and unhappier than ever because of his loss. As soon as he saw his knapsack he ran toward it, shouting with joy. "That's one way of providing interest and entertainment," said Nasreddin.

For the executives in the bank I described above, who had lived in a dysfunctional culture for so long, breaking the old patterns of interaction—a habit they had invested in—was very difficult. The challenge for the new CEO and his team was to nudge their employees to regain an open mind and try a different way of looking at things. As Nasreddin demonstrated to the traveler, it is never too late to learn new lessons and make our life's journey more exciting.

REFERENCES

1. Kets de Vries, M. F. R. (2010d). *The Organizational Culture Audit: Participant Guide*. Fontainebleau, France: INSEAD.
2. Kets de Vries, M. F. R. (2010e). *The Organizational Culture Audit: Facilitator's Guide*. Fontainebleau, France: INSEAD.
3. Kets de Vries, M. F. R., Vrignaud, P., and Florent-Treacy, E. (2004). "The Global Leadership Life Inventory: Development and Psychometric Properties of a 360° Instrument." *International Journal of Human Resource Management*, 15(3), 475–492.
4. Kets de Vries, M. F. R., Vrignaud, P., Korotov, K., and Florent-Treacy, E. (2006). "The Development of The Personaity Audit: A Psychodynamic Multiple Feedback Assessment Instrument." *International Journal of Human Resource Management*, 17(5), 898–917.

5. Kets de Vries, M. F. R. (2006b). *Leadership Archetype Questionnaire: Participant Guide*. Fontainebleau, France: INSEAD Global Leadership Centre.

6. Kets de Vries, M. F. R. (2006c). *Leadership Archetype Questionnaire: Facilitator Guide*. Fontainebleau, France: INSEAD Global Leadership Centre.

7. Kets de Vries, M. F. R. (2007). "Decoding the Team Conundrum: The Eight Roles Executives Play." *Organizational Dynamics*, 36(1), 28–44.

8. Kets de Vries, M. F. R. (2010d). *The Organizational Culture Audit: Participant Guide*. Fontainebleau, France: INSEAD.

9. Kets de Vries, M. F. R. (2010e). *The Organizational Culture Audit: Facilitator's Guide*. Fontainebleau, France: INSEAD.

CONCLUSION

Very little is needed to make a happy life.

—Marcus Aurelius, *Meditations*

He is happiest who finds peace in his home.

—Johann Wolfgang Von Goethe

Our lives improve only when we take chances—and the first and most difficult risk we can take is to be honest with ourselves.

—Walter Anderson

It seems to me that people have vast potential. Most people can do extraordinary things if they have the confidence or take the risks. Yet most people don't. They sit in front of the telly and treat life as if it goes on forever.

—Philip Adams

A monk set off on a long pilgrimage to find the Buddha. He devoted many years to his search until he finally reached a river, beyond which lay the land where the Buddha was said to live. The monk took a boat to cross and looked around as the boatman rowed. After a while, he noticed something floating toward them. As it got closer, he realized it was the corpse of a man. The dead body drifted so close to the boat that the monk could almost touch it, and with a dreadful shock he recognized it—the body was his own! The monk lost all control and wailed at the sight of himself, still and lifeless, drifting with the river's currents. That moment was the beginning of his enlightenment. He realized that there was a deadness inside him that needed to be dealt with.

Providing insight, facilitating change, and reviving people who are in a rut are major parts of any kind of leadership intervention, of which group coaching is one. The group coaching intervention technique is more important than ever in our increasingly interconnected and rapidly changing world.

There is every reason to expect that a shrinking globe, an information-linked world, and the persistence of complex problems will require human teamwork to continue and to increase. Teamwork is a core competency in our knowledge society, in much the same way that it was once a core competency of Paleolithic society. Through group coaching, lateral bridges will be built, a sine qua non for making present-day, highly complex organizations work. Unfortunately, teamwork was supplanted by a focus on the individual in the reductionist, industrial world. Now, however, we seem to have gone full circle, realizing once more the importance and power of working in teams.

"Teamwork was supplanted by a focus on the individual in the reductionist, post-industrial world."

When an organization supports its executives in the development of high performance teams through leadership coaching programs, the individual, the team, and the whole organization will benefit. Leadership coaching complements existing leadership development programs and makes an essential contribution to the success of any change initiative. What's more, group or team coaching leads to increased self-awareness, and provides a better understanding of the kinds of obstacles that people have to deal with in their journey through life. It gives people a new lens through which to examine deeply confusing personal, team, and organizational problems. Whether these dilemmas are conscious or unconscious, leadership coaching can help executives to create tipping points, to make them more successful at managing their day-to-day responsibilities, meeting their goals, recognizing when they find themselves at crossroads, and, most importantly, creating a fulfilling life.

LEARNING AND UNLEARNING

One of the prime functions when embarking on a change process using group coaching is to deepen the connections among executives and between executives and their organizations. The aim of the group coaching intervention technique that I have described in this book is to liberate people from the hidden intrapsychic forces that prevent them from changing and from assuming a meaningful, authentic life in the organization.

I have suggested that one task-related function of change agents like leadership group coaches is not only to help team members acquire greater understanding of their own behavior (and how they are perceived by others) but also to make sense of what happens in the team-as-a-whole, that is, the interpersonal and transpersonal processes that occur within a team. If a leadership coach wants to set the powerful therapeutic factors of interpersonal and group learning into motion, the members of the group must learn to recognize, examine, and understand those processes. They need to examine themselves, study their own dialogues, and their relationships to others, overcome their inner resistances to change, and apply and integrate their learning into concrete behavioral changes. Similar pressures are put on group coaches, who have to maintain a stance of negative capability amidst the emotional and disquieting identity work and soul-searching that is taking place within the team they are working with, and to guide this team to greater self-awareness and capability.

I have emphasized that group coaches need to operate with the team at a number of different levels. First, they need to appreciate what is happening and being communicated within the team. They need to understand team members' preoccupations in the here-and-now—mostly conscious but sometimes unconscious. Second, at the level of hidden or meta-communication, they need to decipher unconscious communications—that is, what is really going on between people, the "snakes under the carpet" that are generally avoided in ordinary discourse. Leadership coaches will also have to use themselves as instruments by taking into account their relationships with and reactions to the team and the individuals within it. This rapid interchange at multiple levels will exert huge demands on leadership group coaches, but also make their work very exciting.

But in using themselves as instruments, change agents like group coaches also have to deal with the mystery that is themselves. All of us have to study human motivation from the inside, to truly understand what is happening on the outside. We all need to know our own strengths and weaknesses before we can be helpful to others. By turning the clinical lens onto oneself and exploring present realities in the light of one's own past experiences, coaches can learn from mistakes in a new way.

"All of us have to study human motivation from the inside, to truly understand what is happening on the outside."

If organizational leaders, consultants, or coaches see only the task rationale or social psychological purposes of team formation, and fail to consider the underlying psychodynamic factors—such as social defenses, hidden emotions, internal motives, shared anxieties, unexpressed conflicts, etc.—opportunities for improved effectiveness are missed. In incorporating the perspectives of the clinical paradigm, the organizational practitioner will move away from a purely evaluative and prescriptive mindset to one that is more reflective, and mindful of unconscious forces. I make a plea to coaches and their clients to look deeply and courageously into the defensive rituals and resistances within organizations and to transform them into more constructive ways of containing the anxieties and risks inevitably associated with life in organizations.

Creating high performance teams requires that we pay heed not only to the structures and processes that facilitate team working but also to the more messy aspects of teamwork. Leadership group coaches don't just look at what is happening on the surface; they try to make teams and team members more aware of what lies beneath, including their ability to navigate their own unconscious world. In order to get the best out of teams, coaches need to be comfortable with the worlds of fantasy and illusion that each of us carries within us. They should feel comfortable in the twilight world between fantasy and reality. They should be able to see and retain a reflective stand, as in the following Sufi story.

THE TEACHER AND HIS DISCIPLES

A renowned Sufi teacher was very ill and forced to rest in bed for a long period of time. One evening a number of disciples sat in silence with him for several hours—although nothing was said, many wonderful things appeared to the consciousness of everyone present, apparently from within. In due course the teacher seemed to become tired and indicated he was ready to settle for the night. Then, with no warning, he sat bolt upright up in bed and told his disciples that, as a boy, he had had a teacher who had always encouraged him "to get the best out of everything." With that he lay back down. The disciples understood that he wanted them to make more mental effort and remained with him for a little longer.

When they eventually took their leave of him to retire—though hardly any words other than his strange outburst had passed between them—the teacher turned smiling to his disciples, and said, "Well, we had a very productive session, didn't we?"

The moral of the story is that change can be a very subtle process. Although nothing seems to happen, much can happen. Groups and teams are both very complex and very abstract entities. They only become real because of the people that bring them to life. Experience has taught me that the group coaching method is not only extremely efficacious in furthering individual self-development, but has proven extremely effective in creating great teams, and highly effective, sustainable, authentizotic organizations—great places to work where people feel alive. At the risk of being too repetitive, organizational models of teamwork that proceed from predominantly structural-rational premises are incomplete without reference to the impact of unconscious dynamics on human behavior. An appreciation of the psychodynamic and systemic elements of group life can bring an added dimension to the understanding of teams at work. Using this lens in a team and organizational context will help executives deal with the most difficult leadership task they have to face: To change the world, they have to change themselves.

APPENDIX: INSTRUMENTS

The IGLC/KDVI 360-degree leadership assessment repertoire is composed of a number of distinct measurement instruments, including the *Leadership Archetype Questionnaire*, the *Personality Audit*, the *Global Executive Leadership Inventory*, the *Inner Theater Inventory*, and the *Organizational Culture Audit*. These individual and team-oriented instruments help to decipher various leadership competencies, personality dimensions, team roles, inner drivers, and the assessment of organizational cultures.

1. THE LEADERSHIP ARCHETYPE QUESTIONNAIRE

The *Leadership Archetype Questionnaire* (LAQ) characterizes the style in which leaders deal with people and situations in their organization, i.e., their specific leadership style, and what steps need to be taken to create a well-balanced team [1, 2, 3, 4]. A group of carefully selected individuals can become a highly effective team that delivers much more than the sum of its parts.

The eight leadership archetypes included in the LAQ are strategist, change-catalyst, transactor, builder, innovator, processor, coach and communicator.

- *Strategists* are good at dealing with developments in the organization's environment. They provide vision, strategic direction, and outside-the-box thinking to create new organizational forms and generate future growth.
- *Change-catalysts* love messy situations. They are masters at re-engineering and creating new organizational "blueprints."
- *Transactors* are great dealmakers. Skilled at identifying and tackling new opportunities, they thrive on negotiations.
- *Builders* dream of creating new organizations and have the talent and determination to make their dream come true.
- *Innovators* are focused on the new. They possess a great capacity to solve extremely difficult problems. They like to innovate.
- *Processors* like an organization to be a smoothly running, well-oiled machine. They are very effective at setting up the structures and systems needed to support an organization's objectives. They make the "train" run on time.
- *Coaches* are very good at developing people and getting the best out of them. They are instrumental in creating high performance teams and high performance cultures.
- *Communicators* are great influencers, and have a considerable impact on their surroundings.

The LAQ helps leaders understand the way they deal with people and situations in an organizational context, identify situations in which a particular leadership style could be most effective, and think about what it is like to work with people who demonstrate certain dominant behaviors (see Figure A.1). It also helps a team determine the best roles for each team member, the best way to manage and work for people with certain dominant character-

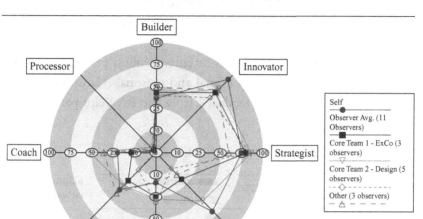

Figure A.1 Sample LAQ personal graph

istics, which combination of styles works well, and which to avoid. Finally, it helps leaders create teams of executives best suited to particular challenges, for example, merger integration, new product development, or helping an organization through a transition.

2. THE PERSONALITY AUDIT

To be effective leaders, executives must begin with an understanding of the reasons for doing what they do. They need to study their motivation from the inside to truly understand what is happening on the outside. This requires taking into consideration their relational world, paying attention to the forces of human development, and considering their emotional management. This approach creates a more three-dimensional appreciation (a 720-degree feedback system) of human behavior and helps executives obtain greater access to, and understanding of, their emotional lives.

The *Personality Audit* (PA) is oriented around personality traits that are influential in organizational and personal relationships (see Figure A.2) [5, 6, 7]. The feedback from the PA helps participants

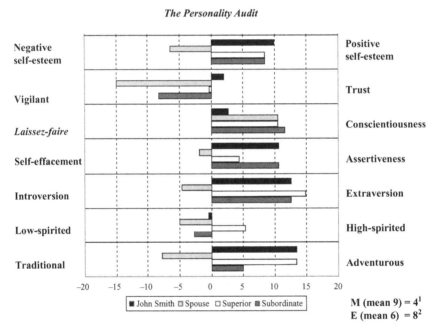

Figure A.2   Sample PA personal graph

[1] The "M" score indicates the number of times you scored in the middle position. An "M" score of more than 9 signifies that you have a tendency to take a middle-of-the-road position in life situations. This can indicate emotional indifference.

[2] The "E" score indicates the number of times you scored in the extreme position. An "E" score of more than 6 can signify a mercurial disposition—a tendency to approach the world in extreme ways and/or a lack of self-control, anxiety, and feelings of helplessness.

reflect on their own motivations, and the way they relate to others both inside and outside the work environment. It highlights the differences between the ways they behave in private and in public. As the feedback given is not anonymous, and is often given by family members (partner, parents, and children) and friends, the information received can be very powerful, in that it may create a tipping point for change.

The seven dimensions of the instrument—derived from basic aspects of personality—provide a glimpse of the executive's inner world and can help people understand the complexities of personality functioning. Each of the seven dimensions of personality assessed in the PA has two anchor points, for example, high self-esteem and low self-esteem.

- High—Low self-esteem
  High self-esteem: Feel attractive, liked, respected, valued in their activities, confident, self-assured; self-reliant and interested in presenting a positive image.
  Low self-esteem: Feel unattractive, disliked, disrespected; belittle themselves; feel criticized in their activities; doubt themselves; self-deprecating, self-abasing and not interested in presenting a positive image.
- Trustful—Vigilant
  Trustful: Warm, empathetic, caring, affectionate, kind, friendly, open, considerate, agreeable, naïve.
  Vigilant: Wary, watchful, bothered by feelings of misgiving and disbelief, skeptical, contrary, prudent, guarded, dissonant, argumentative.
- Conscientious—Laissez-faire
  Conscientious: Scrupulous, principled, earnest, exact, hardworking, detail-oriented, dedicated, reliable, dependable, thorough, orderly, meticulous, perfectionist.
  Laissez-faire: Laid-back, happy-go-lucky, casual, carefree, undirected, untroubled, unrestricted, unworried, easy going.

- Assertive—Self-effacing
Assertive: Controlling, competitive, ambitious, dominating, mastering the situation, overshadowing, commanding, overpowering, ruling, overseeing, dictating, supervising.
Self-effacing: Submissive, accommodating, yielding, agreeable, assenting, unassertive, compliant, deferential, unpretentious.
- Extroverted—Introverted
Extroverted: Outgoing, outwardly directed, sociable, congenial, amicable, people-oriented, approachable, gregarious, unreserved, easy going.
Introverted: Self-observing, self-scrutinizing, reserved, a loner, a brooder, shy, timid, quiet, unapproachable, remote, aloof, distant, unreachable, stand-offish, self-contained, self-reliant, private, withdrawn.
- High-spirited—Low-spirited
High-spirited: Optimistic, ebullient, exhilarated, vivacious, sparkling, excited, enthusiastic, lively, cheerful, bubbly, buoyant, lighthearted, animated; have élan, gaiety, and passion.
Low-spirited: Pessimistic, somber, unhappy, sad, melancholic, blue, heavy, disheartened, glum, cheerless, solemn, dejected, disconsolate, discouraged, depressed.
- Adventurous—Prudent
Adventurous: Inquisitive, searching, venturesome, curious, eager for knowledge, original, nonconformist, creative, exploratory, daring, incautious.
Prudent: Conventional, conformist, conservative, rigid, prosaic, methodical, habitual, careful, orthodox, pedestrian, cautious.

3. THE GLOBAL EXECUTIVE LEADERSHIP INVENTORY

The *Global Executive Leadership Inventory* (GELI) investigates what it means to be a world-class leader. Effective leaders have two roles—a charismatic one and an architectural one. In the charismatic role, leaders envision a better future, and empower and energize their subordinates. In the architectural role, leaders address issues related to organizational design and control and reward systems. What's more, these roles can be subdivided into different leadership styles, or archetypes.

Both the charismatic and architectural roles are necessary for effective leadership, but it is a rare leader who can fulfill both roles seamlessly. Usually, alignment is only achieved within a leadership role constellation when it is constructed of team members with complementary archetypal leadership styles. A group of carefully selected individuals can become a highly effective team that delivers much more than the sum of its parts.

The GELI looks at 12 dimensions of leadership behavior and encourages participants to examine their own effectiveness in critical areas, such as their visioning, empowering, and energizing functions as a leader, their emotional intelligence, their life balance, and their resilience to stress (see Figure A.3) [8, 9, 10]. It also provides feedback of their position vis-à-vis a control group of hard-driving, global executives (the normalization is based on large group of Advanced Management Program participants spanning the world).

The 12 dimensions covered by the GELI are:

- *Visioning:* articulating a compelling vision, mission, and strategy with a multi-country, multi-environment, multi-function, and multi-gender perspective that connects employees, shareholders, suppliers, and customers on a global scale.
- *Empowering:* giving workers at all levels a voice by empowering them through the sharing of information and the delegation of decisions to the people most competent to execute them.
- *Energizing:* motivating employees to actualize the organization's specific vision of the future.
- *Designing and aligning:* creating the proper organizational design and control systems to make the guiding vision a reality,

Global Executive Leadership Inventory
Programme Name
Personal Graph

Participant Name
Programme Duration

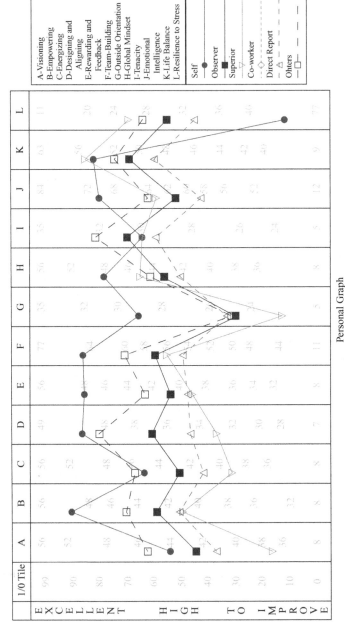

Personal Graph

** -In order to protect your observers' anonymity, scores from some categories have been mixed with "others"

Figure A.3   Sample GELI personal graph

and using those systems to align employees' behavior with the organization's values and goals.

- *Rewarding and giving feedback:* setting up the appropriate reward structures and giving constructive feedback to encourage the kind of behavior that is expected from employees.
- *Team building:* creating team players and focusing on team effectiveness by instilling a cooperative atmosphere, building collaborative interaction, and encouraging constructive conflict.
- *Outside stakeholder orientation:* making employees aware of their outside constituencies, emphasizing particularly the need to respond to the requirements of customers, suppliers, share-holders, and other interest groups, such as local communities affected by the organization.
- *Global mindset:* inculcating a global mentality in the ranks—that is, instilling values that act as a sort of glue between the regional and/or national cultures represented in the organization.
- *Tenacity:* encouraging tenacity and courage in employees by setting a personal example in following through on reasonable risks.
- *Emotional intelligence:* fostering trust in the organization by creating, primarily through example, an emotionally intelligent workforce whose members know themselves and know how to deal respectfully and understandingly with others.
- *Life balance:* articulating and modeling the importance of the need for life balance for the long-term welfare of employees.
- *Resilience to stress:* paying attention to work, career, life, and health stress issues, and balancing appropriately the various kinds of pressures that life brings.

These dimensions are graphically represented in a report by various groupings—superiors, subordinates, colleagues, and others. In addition, there will be a graph indicating "self," and a graph summarizing all "others." Although all scores are anonymous, if the subject has only one superior, he or she will not be anonymous. The scores for each dimension are represented and qualitative information about the subject listed. This 360-degree feedback survey is normalized with a group of high-achievement-oriented executives.

4. THE INNER THEATER INVENTORY

Through self-exploration and self-analysis we can create greater awareness of our values, beliefs, and attitudes. The *Inner Theater Inventory* (ITI) assesses the most important drivers in an individual's life [11, 12] and is designed to help executives and others in their personal growth and development—to navigate the journey of self-discovery (see Figures A.4 and A.5). The insights provided by the ITI help executives understand the drivers in their inner theater, the values, beliefs, and attitudes that guide their behavior.

Inner Theater Inventory
Test Inner Theater Inventory - IGLC   28 to 28 April 2009
Top Three Most Important Values

Figure A.4 Sample ITI feedback: overall view of most important values

Inner Theater Inventory
Test Inner Theater Inventory - IGLC   28 to 28 April 2009
Top Five Most Important Values - Self

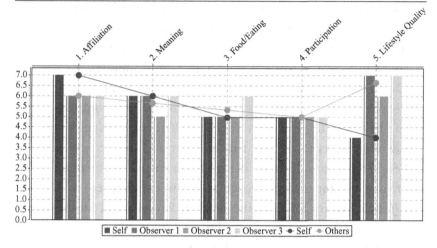

Figure A.5 Sample ITI feedback: top 5 most important values

Answers to these questions are not easily found, as our individual make-up is complex. And that complexity is increased by the fact that what we see is not necessarily what we get. To identify the drivers of our inner theater, it is not sufficient to look at manifest behavior; it is essential that our observations take into account underlying motivational forces.

The ITI consists of the following 22 key life anchors:

- **Aesthetics** refers to the appreciation of beauty. People for whom aesthetics are a main life anchor consider music, theater, art, or nature essential for their well-being.
- **Achievement** refers to the drive to be successful in whatever one does. People for whom achievement is a main life anchor are highly competitive and work extremely hard to attain the goals they have set for themselves.
- **Affiliation** refers to the high value given to close relationships. People for whom affiliation is important will have a strong

desire to be around others, and to be loved, liked, and accepted by them.

- *Autonomy* refers to the need to be self-reliant and independent. People for whom autonomy is a main life anchor have a strongly developed sense of self. They are not easily influenced by others and act according to their own reasons and motives.

- *Care* refers to the need to look out for and nurture others. People for whom care is a main life anchor are compassionate and have a genuine concern for the welfare/well-being of others.

- *Learning* refers to the need to discover and master new things. People for whom learning is a main life anchor are in an intense, lifelong pursuit for knowledge and new experiences.

- *Lifestyle quality* refers to the need to have a good life balance. People for whom lifestyle quality is a main life anchor seek a satisfactory balance between all the priorities in their lives, such as work, family, and friends.

- *Food/eating* refers to a preoccupation with food and the experience of eating in general. People for whom food is a key life anchor consider eating as an act of pleasure, and a sign of a zest for living.

- *Health* is a key life anchor for people who are interested in their physical well-being, and make a great effort to adopt a healthy lifestyle (e.g., regular exercise, weight control, sleeping well, eating well, etc.).

- *Inclusion* refers to the need to be involved in the decisions and events that affect our life. People for whom inclusion is a key life anchor want to be involved in the decision-making process, and have a sense of responsibility for the decisions made.

- *Integrity* refers to adherence to a set of moral and ethical principles. People for whom integrity is a key life anchor hold themselves to a code of honor and always strive to do what they believe is right.

- *Meaning* refers to the need to make a contribution to society, going beyond narrow personal interest. People for whom meaning is a key life anchor need to be connected to something larger than themselves, to believe that they are doing something of value, and that they are making a difference.

- **Money** refers to the preoccupation with the acquisition of money. People for whom money is a key life anchor often feel that they must strive to achieve financial security.
- **Order** refers to the need for things to be in their proper place. People for whom order is a key life anchor like to arrange and organize things. They are scrupulously precise and preoccupied with details, rules, lists, and organization.
- **Power** refers to the exercise of authority or influence. People for whom power is a key life anchor want to make decisions and control or command the behavior of others.
- **Pride** refers to the intrinsic feeling of pleasure or satisfaction in one's accomplishments or possessions. People for whom pride is a key life anchor have a very high opinion of their own dignity, importance, merit, or superiority, and reason that if they can't do something perfectly, they shouldn't do it at all.
- **Recognition** refers to the strong need for popular acclaim, public esteem, and social approval. People for whom recognition is a key life anchor strive to rise above the crowd and to earn public recognition for their contributions and efforts.
- **Security** refers to the need to protect oneself from danger or risks. People for whom security is a key life anchor like predictability and certainty. They strive for a comfortable, uneventful life and seek careers that offer a considerable dose of safety and security, and require steady, predictable performance.
- **Sensuality/sexuality** refers to the need for sensual and/or sexual gratification. People for whom sensuality/sexuality is a key life anchor derive pleasure from the senses of sight, touch, smell, and taste.
- **Spirituality** refers to the incorporeal, as opposed to the physical, part of human life. People for whom spirituality is a key life

anchor focus on the moral or religious purpose of life and believe that without spiritual faith, life has no direction, meaning, or justification.

- *Status/rank* refers to the position of an individual in relation to another or others, especially in regard to social or professional standing. People for whom status/rank is a key life anchor have a tendency to rank themselves and others according to criteria such as beauty, intellect, physique, wealth, and power.
- *Revenge* refers to retaliation for injuries or wrongs. People for whom revenge is a key life anchor have a strong desire to inflict punishment in return for injury or insult they have endured.

5. THE ORGANIZATIONAL CULTURE AUDIT

What an organization strives to be and what executives think they endorse may be different from the beliefs and values that are actually being played out within the organization. It is therefore critical to find out what those beliefs and values really are before deciding what they should be.

The *Organizational Culture Audit* (OCA) is designed to provide an orgnaization with a comprehensive diagnostic of its current organizational culture as well as a detailed understanding of the culture it is striving for, by examining employees' perceptions of the organization's current values and the values they consider important (see Figures A.6 and A.7). The OCA takes a more macro approach to organizational analysis, shifting the focus from the drivers of individual behavior to the drivers of the organization as a whole, and highlighting discrepancies in cultural values [13, 14].

Because it gathers perceptions from people within the organization and not those outside of it, "looking in," the OCA is not, strictly speaking, a 360-degree instrument. However, it is included

Organizational Culture Audit
Organizational Culture Audit for *Company Name*   1 to 30 June 2010
Overall Organizational View: Values vs Practice (N = 51)

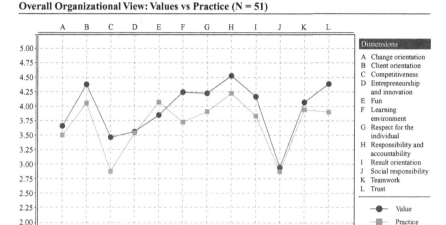

Figure A.6 Sample OCA graph: values vs actual practice

Organizational Culture Audit
Organizational Culture Audit for *Company Name*   1 to 30 June 2010
Overall Organizational View: Gap Analysis, in order of largest to smallest gap

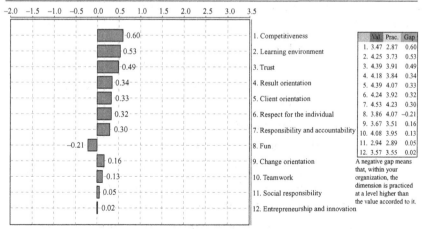

Figure A.7 Gap analysis of values vs actual practice

as a tool because a gap analysis is still possible: It compares the espoused values of the organization with employees' perceptions of how these values are being practiced in the organization. By doing so, it provides a useful complement to the tools that are focused solely on perceptions of the individual.

The OCA covers the following 12 dimensions of organizational culture that research and interviews with large numbers of senior executives have shown to be the most salient in high performing global organizations:

- *Change orientation:* How comfortable organizational members are with change and how well they manage both internal and external demands for change.
- *Client/stakeholder orientation:* Whether the organization develops a real understanding of client issues and is able to foresee and/or adapt to clients' needs.
- *Competitiveness:* The degree to which the organization strives to outperform its competitors and takes its competitors seriously.
- *Entrepreneurship:* Whether creativity and innovation are encouraged at all levels of the organization and resources are made available to promote entrepreneurial behavior.
- *Fun:* Whether the organization encourages people to be playful and to enjoy their work.
- *Learning environment:* The degree to which the organization encourages members to engage in ongoing learning, develop new knowledge and skill sets, and mentor and coach colleagues.
- *Respect for the individual:* The degree to which individual members of the organization have the right to express themselves freely, as long as they meet performance targets, and how flexible the organization is in accommodating individual needs.
- *Responsibility and accountability:* Whether the people in the organization act as owners who take responsibility for their own projects and remain accountable for their decisions and actions.

- ***Result orientation:*** Whether the organization places a high degree of importance on results, analyzes mistakes in order to learn from them, and has high performance expectations for all its members.
- ***Social responsibility:*** How much effort the organization makes to respond to the needs of its environment and act as a responsible social citizen.
- ***Teamwork:*** The degree to which the organization achieves individual and organizational success through teamwork and collaboration.
- ***Trust:*** How much attention the organization devotes to building trust by encouraging communication at all levels and creating an environment of openness, honesty, integrity, fairness, and mutual respect.

REFERENCES

1. Kets de Vries, M. F. R. (2006b). *Leadership Archetype Questionnaire: Participant Guide.* Fontainebleau, France: INSEAD Global Leadership Centre.
2. Kets de Vries, M. F. R. (2006c). *Leadership Archetype Questionnaire: Facilitator Guide.* Fontainebleau, France: INSEAD Global Leadership Centre.
3. Kets de Vries, M. F. R. (2007). "Decoding the Team Conundrum: The Eight Roles Executives Play." *Organizational Dynamics*, 36 (1), 28–44.
4. Kets De Vries, M. F. R., Vrignaud, P., Agrawal, A., and Florent-Treacy, E. (2010). "Development and Application of the Leadership Archetype Questionnaire." *International Journal of Human Resource Management*, 21 (15), 2848–2863.
5. Kets de Vries, M. F. R. (2005b). *Personality Audit: Participant Guide.* Fontainebleau, France: INSEAD Global Leadership Centre.
6. Kets de Vries, M. F. R. (2005c). *Personality Audit: Facilitator Guide.* Fontainebleau, France: INSEAD Global Leadership Centre.

7. Kets de Vries, M. F. R, Vrignaud, P., Korotov, K., and Florent-Treacy, E. (2006). "The Development of The Personality Audit: A Psychodynamic Multiple Feedback Assessment Instrument." *International Journal of Human Resource Management*, 17 (5), 898–917.
8. Kets de Vries, M. F. R. (2005d). *The Global Executive Leadership Inventory Questionnaire: Participant's Guide.* San Francisco, CA: Pfeiffer.
9. Kets de Vries, M. F. R. (2005e). *The Global Executive Leadership Inventory Questionnaire: Facilitator's Guide.* San Francisco, CA: Pfeiffer.
10. Kets de Vries, M. F. R., Vrignaud, P., and Florent-Treacy, E. (2004). "The Global Leadership Life Inventory: Development and Psychometric Properties of a 360° Instrument." *International Journal of Human Resource Management*, 15 (3), 475–492.
11. Kets de Vries, M. F. R. (2010b). *Inner Theatre Inventory: Participant Guide.* Fontainebleau, France: INSEAD.
12. Kets de Vries, M. F. R. (2010c). *Inner Theatre Inventory: Facilitator's Guide.* Fontainebleau, France: INSEAD.
13. Kets de Vries, M. F. R. (2010d). *The Organizational Culture Audit: Participant Guide.* Fontainebleau, France: INSEAD.
14. Kets de Vries, M. F. R. (2010e). *The Organizational Culture Audit: Facilitator's Guide.* Fontainebleau, France: INSEAD.

INDEX

Printed in the United States
By Bookmasters